Jean Racine

Jean Racine

FIVE PLAYS, TRANSLATED INTO ENGLISH
VERSE, AND WITH AN INTRODUCTION
BY

KENNETH MUIR

A MERMAID DRAMABOOK

 HILL AND WANG   —   NEW YORK

Kenneth Muir, King Alfred Professor of English Literature and Dean of the Faculty of Arts in the University of Liverpool, is best known for his books on Shakespeare and Milton, and for his editions of *Macbeth, King Lear,* and the poems of Sir Thomas Wyatt. He has also written a volume of verse and edited three anthologies and he is on the editorial boards of *Essays in Criticism* and *Shakespeare Survey.* He has been a Visiting Fellow at the Folger Shakespeare Library and a visiting lecturer at Wayne State University, Detroit. He has translated and directed a number of French plays. His version of *Athalie,* which appears in this volume, was written for a production by G. Wilson Knight at Leeds University, and it was successful enough in performance to encourage him to make versions of four more of Racine's plays.

FIRST DRAMABOOK PRINTING AUGUST 1960

Standard Book Number (clothbound edition) 8090-8030-3
Standard Book Number (paperback edition) 8090-0717-7

Library of Congress Catalog Card Number: 60-6182

Manufactured in the United States of America

101112131415

DEDICATION
TO G. WILSON KNIGHT

My dear Wilson,

Some ten years ago, after reading a scene which I had translated from *Athalie* for use with a recording made by the Comédie Française, you asked me to translate the whole play so that you could produce it. Your production of my version was so successful that I was encouraged from time to time to try my hand at four more of Racine's plays. Although I share the view that translations of his work are doomed to partial failure, I can claim that these versions have proved useful in extramural work where a knowledge of French could not be assumed.

Mr. Martin Turnell, in his valuable book *The Classical Moment*, expresses the view that Racine is one of the few great masters who is absolutely untranslatable:

When you know him, almost every line he wrote, however simple, however commonplace the vocabulary, has a charm and music of its own; but if you try to translate him, everything goes. Racine in English dress is practically indistinguishable from the authors of the minor tragedies of the Restoration period.

If this were entirely true, Racine would not be a major dramatist, but Mr. Turnell may have been thinking of Otway's free version of *Bérénice*, of which the following lines are a good specimen:

To your Barbarity there's nothing hard;
Go on, and Infamy be your Reward.
Long since my Fears your Falsehood had display'd;
Nor would I at your Suit have longer stay'd.
Would I the base Indignities have borne
Of a rude People, public Hate and Scorn?
No, to this Breach I would have spurr'd you on,

v

And I am pleased it is already done.
No longer shall the Fear of me prevail,
Alas! you must not think to hear me rail,
Or Heav'n invoke its Vengeance to prepare;
No, for if Heav'n vouchsafe to hear my Pray'r,
I beg no Memory may there remain,
Of either your Injustice, or my Pain.

This is reasonably close to the sense of the original, and the couplets are workmanlike. But it can hardly be doubted that their effect on a modern audience would be that of artificiality. Instead of a suffering woman pouring out her heart, we inevitably hear a well-trained elocutionist declaiming a set speech. And this, dramatically, is disastrous. As Giraudoux remarks:

Racine does not recite, does not even speak. All his lines are taken from a dictionary, not of beauties but of silences. . . . They are without false echoes, without even true echoes.

This is well said, and it emphasizes the necessity of choosing a medium which will not appear too artificial.

I therefore abandoned the idea of using rhymed couplets after some initial experiments. I had to dismiss Alexandrines as a possible medium because of the differences between French and English versification, and because they were liable to sound both flabby and foreign. I had to reject the forms of verse used by Mr. T. S. Eliot and Mr. Louis MacNeice because something more regular was obviously required. I was driven back on blank verse, the standard medium for tragic drama between 1587 and 1930, which enables a translator to keep close to the sense of the original, and to be natural without being prosaic—though Racine often skims the surface of prose.

I am only too well aware that the beauty of Racine's poetry, which depends hardly at all on the use of imagery, has largely evaporated in my translation. Giraudoux wittily observed:

All Racine's words seem to have retired from the world for twenty years in solitude and in a passionate chastity, and the most ordinary parts of speech come together like lovers on their wedding night.

It is hardly to be expected that any translation could give of such an impression.

Nevertheless, in spite of the difficulties, Racine's actual drama is, I am sure, robust enough to survive transplanting into a foreign soil. The grandeur of the conception, the perfect structure, the irony, the sheer excitement of the action in most of the plays, the extraordinary psychological penetration can all be carried over into English prose. And my verse is at least better than my prose would have been, and it makes better stage dialogue.

I would ask you, therefore, as the "only begetter of these ensuing" translations, inadequate as they are, to accept them as a small repayment of the debt that we all owe you, not only as an interpreter of Shakespeare, but as an inspiration to students of drama at Leeds and elsewhere, both as teacher and producer.

Yours sincerely,

KENNETH MUIR

Liverpool, 1959.

ACKNOWLEDGMENTS

The plays are translated from Raymond Picard's beautiful edition in the *Bibliothèque de la Pléiade,* and thanks are due to him and to his publishers for permission to quote (in translation) from his introduction to *Bérénice.* I am greatly indebted to my colleagues, Mr. Kenneth Allott, the late Mr. Arnold Davenport, Dr. G. K. Hunter, Professor F. T. H. Fletcher, and Dr. C. Chadwick for their advice. To Mr. R. Eyquem I owe a special debt of gratitude for criticizing my first drafts. Any inaccuracies which remain in my versions are not due to him. Mr. Eric Bentley offered some helpful criticisms. But in one or two cases I have clung to my own renderings. He would have preferred the banishment of " 'Tis" from the text. "It's" appeared to be too flat and prosaic; and "It is" in one or two instances would have made the line intolerably flabby. I have aimed at a neutral diction, neither obviously modern, nor obviously archaic; but it is possible that, as much of my work during the past twenty-five years has been concentrated on the sixteenth and early seventeenth centuries, words and phrases which seem natural to me may sound artificial to some of my readers. The footnotes are mine.

K.M.

CONTENTS

INTRODUCTION

I

Jean Racine was born at La Ferté-Milon on December 21, 1639, and educated at the Jansenist seminary at Port Royal. His teachers' rigid and puritanical views on the stage were a trouble to the poet in later years; and though he reacted against Jansenism for some years, he was reconciled to it in the end. At school Racine was introduced to Greek literature, and this was to be of great influence on his own plays. His first play was rejected, and his second, on Ovid's loves, was never finished. He then sought, with the aid of his uncle, to secure a benefice, and at one time he was even prepared to become ordained. Luckily for drama, the project fell through, and Racine returned to Paris. His third play, *La Thébaïde* (1664), written with Molière's encouragement and based, like several of his plays, on Euripides, was largely written in the manner of the other great tragic dramatist of the age, Pierre Corneille. This was followed by another experimental play, *Alexandre le Grand* (1665), but *Andromaque* (1667) was the first typical work of Racine's genius. His only comedy, *Les Plaideurs* (1668) was followed by two more masterpieces, *Britannicus* (1669) and *Bérénice* (1670)—written in rivalry with the veteran Corneille, who was writing a play on the same subject at the same time —and by three plays, *Bajazet* (1672) and *Mithridate* (1673), which are, perhaps, not quite on the level of the great masterpieces, and *Iphigénie en Aulide* (1674), which Voltaire regarded as his greatest. It is the one play which ought to be added to the five included in this volume in order to give a fully representative selection of Racine's work. Greatest of all, perhaps, is *Phèdre* (1677), which, owing to the machinations of Racine's enemies, was an initial failure, while Pradon's worthless play on the same theme was a success.

At the age of thirty-eight, but only partly on account of the reception given to his masterpiece, Racine was reconciled to Port Royal, retired from the stage, gave up his sexual adventures, married a simple, pious woman, took to writing indifferent religious verse, and was appointed, along with Boileau, Historiographer Royal, a post which the poet accepted on the understanding that he would sever his connection with the stage, and which he probably regarded as more respectable than his previous job as a dramatist. His conversion seems to have been sincere, even though its causes may have been mixed.

In 1689, however, a way was found to reconcile poetry and piety. He was asked by Madame de Maintenon to write the biblical play *Esther*, for performance by schoolgirls, his earlier plays being regarded as unsuitable for the purpose; and he seems to have obeyed with some reluctance. This play was followed in 1691 by *Athalie*, written this time at the King's own suggestion, although he would never allow it a proper stage performance. This was Racine's last play. In his final years he wrote a history of Port Royal, in spite of Louis XIV's hostility to the Jansenists, and he expressed a wish to be buried at the foot of Hamon, who had taught him Greek. He died on April 21, 1699, in his sixtieth year.

II

Racine was one of the greatest of dramatists, and this essay is not directly concerned with his life and character. He was less amiable, perhaps, than any other great poet or dramatist. He was something of a snob; he was ambitious for the kind of success which a poet should disdain; he was ungenerous in his attitude to women he had once loved [1]; in his last period he lapsed into the stern views of

[1] He wrote callously about La Champmeslé—the actress who played Phèdre—when she was on her deathbed. On the other hand, there is no reason to believe the accusation that he poisoned Marquise du Parc, the original Andromaque, out of jeal-

his early teachers; and some of his prefaces make us realize how lucky we are not to have Shakespeare's. But the conflicts in Racine's mind which were partly the cause of his less attractive traits were also the means of preventing these perfect classical plays from being academic exercises.

The five plays included in this volume represent all phases of his career—the first masterpiece, two plays of his middle period, the last great secular play, and the greater of the two biblical plays. Some years ago Giraudoux declared that "there is not a sentiment in Racine that is not a literary sentiment." In reaction against this view of the purely objective and disinterested artist, a number of recent critics in France and England have sought to show that Racine was profoundly involved in the themes of his plays, and others go further and seek to show that he was dramatizing his own inner conflicts and the events of his time. It is suggested, for example, that Nero represents both Louis XIV and Racine; that Agrippina represents Port Royal, Mlle. Champmeslé (from which and from whom Racine was trying to escape), and Anne of Austria, from whom Louis was trying to free himself; and that Junia represents both Marquise du Parc and Mlle. de La Vallière. There is more reason for believing that Titus and Bérénice reflected the thwarted love of Louis for Marie Mancini or Henriette d'Angleterre; and it is possible that *Athalie* was partly inspired by the English Revolution and that it was a secret and perhaps unconscious reaction against Louis' absolute monarchy. But, on the whole, although some topical allusions may be suspected in Racine's plays, and although they were not written in a void, it seems safer to suppose that they reflect more general conflicts in the mind of the dramatist; and in the following remarks the plays will be considered as dramatic masterpieces rather than as keys to the inner history of the reign of Louis XIV.

The English reader of Racine, accustomed to Shakespeare and the other Jacobean dramatists, is likely to find Racine's plays narrower in scope, more monotonous in theme, and lacking in variety and relief. Each hero is pro-

ousy. The accusation was made by the poisoner La Voisin eleven years after the actress' death.

vided with a confidant, each heroine with a confidante. The speeches are long, eloquent and rhetorical, and never colloquial, and Racine's vocabulary is limited and repetitive. The rhymed Alexandrines, wonderful as they sound on the lips of great actresses, continually remind us that we are listening to great poetry, when we would prefer to forget the poetry and give ourselves up to the illusion that we are listening to men and women. Nevertheless, Racine is much closer to Shakespeare than he is to the English classical dramatists, the droning authors of *Gorboduc*, the prim Daniel, Addison with his now unreadable *Cato*, or Congreve with his *Mourning Bride*. Even *All for Love*, the masterpiece of the Restoration theatre, is tame indeed compared with any of the greater plays of Racine.

To appreciate the greatness of Racine as a poet the reader must, of course, go to the originals. But even in translation, I believe, some of Racine's greatness as a dramatist should be apparent. The plays are wonderfully constructed so that the maximum of significance is extracted from the theme as a whole and from each individual situation; each play is complete and rounded so that the audience feels there is nothing more to say; and Racine's psychological penetration is unsurpassed by any dramatist, ancient or modern.

III

Andromache is based partly on twenty lines of Virgil and partly on the play of Euripides on the same subject, but it as little resembles the original as Anouilh's *Antigone* that of Sophocles. It is a play on the theme of frustrated passion. The heroine loves only the dead Hector; Pyrrhus loves Andromache; Hermione loves Pyrrhus; Orestes loves Hermione. Hermione, on hearing that Pyrrhus, to whom she is officially betrothed, is going to marry Andromache, incites Orestes to assassinate him and then commits suicide. Pyrrhus is prepared to plunge his country into war for the sake of Andromache, for not only is his jilting of Hermione an insult to Greece, but his protection of Astyanax, Andromache's son, is itself a cause of war since the Greeks wish to slay him. Hermione, for her part, is pre-

pared to kill the man she loves rather than see him marry
another woman, and she is ready to use the love of Orestes,
which she does not return, as an instrument of her vengeance. Orestes is prepared to murder a man he admires for
the sake of a woman who dislikes him; and since as an
envoy he is instructed to get hold of Astyanax and further
the marriage of Hermione and Pyrrhus, he is guilty also of
a double breach of faith. Nor is this the full extent of the
perfidy of the main characters. Even Andromache tricks
Pyrrhus into a marriage from which she intends to escape
by suicide. Pyrrhus blackmails her into marriage by threatening to hand over Astyanax to the Greeks. Hermione, in
a famous passage, after she has driven Orestes to assassinate Pyrrhus, asks him why he has done it: *"Qui te l'a dit?"*
("Who asked you to do it?")[2] Throughout the play her
ambivalent attitude to Pyrrhus—loving him when it seems
likely that he will after all marry her, hating him when he
seems likely to marry Andromache, loving him murdered,
and indeed, loving him passionately even when she hates
him most—is the motive force of the action. But Orestes
and Pyrrhus are equally enslaved by their passions. Honor,
reason, humanity itself are all overthrown by the blind
force of sex. The tragic conclusion exhibits the working
out of the fourfold frustration with which the play begins
—Pyrrhus assassinated, Hermione slain by her own hand,
Orestes pursued by furies. Only the innocent Andromache
is left.

In spite of the title, Andromache has a less important
role than the other main characters. She is placed in a
tragic situation where she has to choose between her loyalty to the memory of Hector and the safety of his son.
At the end of the play she has preserved both, and unex-
pectedly she herself does not have to die to accomplish
these ends. One of the most moving scenes in the play is
the one where she is confronted by her cruel dilemma;
but her character, noble and simple as it is, has not the
dramatic interest of the other three, all of whom are in
their different ways swept away by their uncontrollable

[2] Some critics, however, while admitting the theatrical effec-
tiveness of this question, have suggested that it is psychologi-
cally false.

sexual desires, though all of them struggle against the inevitable—Hermione assisted by pride, Pyrrhus by political duty, and Orestes by honor.[3]

IV

Although Britannicus is the nominal hero of the play which bears his name and although the action is concerned with his murder by his rival in love, this theme is subordinated to that of the relationship between Nero and his mother. Britannicus is young, noble, sincere, and impetuous. He might almost be described in Chapman's words:

> He would believe, since he would be believed:
> Your noblest natures are most credulous.

The man he trusts most, Narcissus, is a spy in the service of Nero; and we know from the moment when the double-dealing of Narcissus is revealed at the beginning of Act Two that the doom of Britannicus is certain, since at the same time we are informed of Nero's passion for Junia, Britannicus' lover.

The "budding monster" Nero is a more complex character. Racine presents him at the very beginning of his career of crime, before his natural proclivities have shown themselves. The early years of his reign have been exemplary: he has two high-principled advisers; he is popular with the people, and just and merciful in his dealings. But Racine makes it clear that Nero, though he has behaved virtuously, is vicious at heart; and the play deals with the crisis in his life when he throws over his advisers, exiles Pallas, kills his rival in love, and escapes from his mother's yoke. The real struggle, indeed, is between Nero and his mother. Agrippina by her plots and crimes had succeeded in making Nero Emperor, in spite of the superior claims of Britannicus; and she does this not because she loves him

---

[3] René Jasinski (*Vers le vrai Racine*, 1958, Vol. I, pp. 183 ff.) points out the resemblances between Andromache and Racine's mistress, Marquise du Parc—both were seductive young widows, devoted to their children—and he argues that Racine depicted himself as Pyrrhus. We know too little about Racine's relations with Marquise du Parc to tell if there is any truth in this theory.

but because she hopes to rule through him. The defeat of Agrippina, therefore, is a just retribution for her crimes, though Nero is wickeder than his mother, and uses his power for baser purposes.

The innocent lovers, Britannicus and Junia, are partly victims of the struggle between Nero and Agrippina. In a sense, as M. Raymond Picard suggests, Nero kills Britannicus in order to strike Agrippina; and the audience knows that he will eventually kill her also. Agrippina supports the marriage of Britannicus and Junia, not out of the kindness of her heart, but because she knows that if Nero divorces his first wife and marries the girl for whom he has conceived a passion, Agrippina's power over him will pass to the new Empress.

The great scene between Nero and Agrippina in the fourth act, carefully prepared for during the first three acts, apparently ends with the triumph of Agrippina, for Nero pretends to accede to all her demands. In the scene which follows he confesses to Burrhus that he is going to embrace his rival only to stifle him. (Perhaps Lenin remembered these words when he advised the communists to embrace social democrats in order to strangle them.) But Nero, who is not yet finally committed to evil, though he has shown his sadistic instincts in his treatment of Junia, is won over by Burrhus for a moment, and then won back by his secular Evil Angel, Narcissus, to embark on his career of crime. He is liberated equally from obedience to his mother and from the habit of virtuous behavior. He comes to illustrate Lord Acton's maxim that absolute power corrupts absolutely.

In most tragedies the hero, whatever crimes and sins he wittingly or unwittingly commits, never quite loses the sympathies of the audience. But in *Britannicus* the nominal hero is pushed to the background and our attention is concentrated on the political and personal struggle between two evil characters, a struggle the more terrible because it is one between mother and son. Perhaps Jonson's *Sejanus*, like Racine's play based on Tacitus, aims at something of the same effect. Both dramatists expose the corruption of absolutism in presenting a struggle for power, but Racine is more concentrated and more violent; and, despite the evil of his main characters, their conflict is more absorbing than Jonson's because it reflects in a monstrous form the universal ambivalence in the relationship between parents and children.[4]

V

In *Berenice* the Racinian drama is reduced to its simplest terms. There are only three real characters, Titus, Berenice, and Antiochus, though each is provided with a shadow confidant to dispense with the necessity of many soliloquies. Titus loves Berenice, and he renounces her when he becomes Emperor because of the Roman objection to marriage with queens and foreigners. Berenice loves Titus and, in the end, approves of the sacrifice he makes. Antiochus loves Berenice and admires Titus. At the end we are left with three broken hearts, but no one is killed. Berenice and Titus threaten suicide, but they both decide to go on living. Racine explains in his preface that Berenice was not obliged to commit suicide because she had not consummated her love. This may seem a peculiar rule, as though Racine were indulging in special pleading against those critics who assumed that a tragedy should end in at least one death. Although Berenice is a charming and sympathetic heroine, there are few members of an audience who would suspect from the play itself that she had not been Titus' mistress. But none of Racine's lovers consummate their passions—they are all, in their different ways, frustrated—and the conventions of the tragic drama were very different from those obtaining in France itself in the seventeenth century.

Berenice is a play on which the critics are greatly

[4] Jasinski (*op. cit.*, p. 304) thinks that the vices of which Nero is accused—ingratitude, the renunciation of sacred principles, pride, etc.—were the vices of which Racine had been accused by Port Royal; that Junia is an idealized portrait of Marquise du Parc; that Agrippina represents Port Royal; and that Britannicus represents the young Racine. Since Racine based his play on Tacitus one is bound to be skeptical of such interpretations, just as one is of the identification of Katherine the Shrew with Anne Shakespeare or of Cerimon (in *Pericles*) with Dr. John Hall.

divided. One of its earliest critics, Madame de Sévigné, dismissed it as *pièce folle*, and there have been many French critics who have regarded it as below the level of the great masterpieces. On the other hand, there are critics who think that it is the most perfect of his plays, the one in which is the quintessence of Racinian poetry. It was one of the first plays to be translated into English and its comparative popularity among English critics has been ascribed to its freedom from violent passions and to the fact that duty triumphs in the end. Two of the best recent critics of Racine take diametrically opposed positions. Francis Fergusson in *The Idea of the Theater* treats the play as the typical example of Racinian tragedy, while Martin Turnell in *The Classical Moment* complains of its sentimentality.[5] Mr. Turnell, indeed, suggests that the conflict in the play is not so much between love and duty as between love and reputation. Both Berenice and Titus are concerned with *gloire;* and Berenice at the end is too much concerned with the figures they will cut before the eyes of posterity:

> Let us all three
> Serve as example to the world of love,
> The tenderest and most unfortunate,
> Of which the sorrowful tale may be recorded.

Titus decides, since he must yield, to yield to glory rather than love. Perhaps Mr. Turnell does not make allowance for the convention, commonly used by Shakespeare, by which a character may be given lines to speak which are more a choric commentary on the action than a revelation of character. Perhaps, too, Mr. Turnell does not allow for the fact that in a historical tragedy the actors are performing not merely in the theatre but on the stage of the world, with posterity as audience.

Titus is concerned with *gloire,* like so many heroes and heroines of French classical tragedy; and in this respect we

---

[5] Turnell's view is shared by Geoffrey Brereton: "Through most of the five acts, he is writing a finger's breadth above the level of the sentimental novelette. . . . By an immense effort of virtuosity he succeeds in maintaining just the necessary height."

may sometimes feel out of sympathy with them. But there is the same difficulty in Shakespeare. Mowbray is more concerned with his reputation than with his actual guilt or innocence:

> The purest treasure mortal times afford
> Is spotless reputation; that away,
> Men are but gilded loam or painted clay.

In the dialogue between Ulysses and Achilles in *Troilus and Cressida* both characters are concerned with the question of reputation, not what Achilles essentially is, but what people think of him: and even Cassio speaks of reputation as the immortal part of himself.

But it would be unfair to pretend that Titus is concerned only with reputation. He is thinking of *gloire* as intrinsic virtue as well as the value that other people put upon it. Racine establishes the reality of his love for Berenice and shows how he can only marry her by defying Roman law and custom. That the law and custom are cruel is irrelevant to the issue. Titus and Berenice had both assumed that when he became Emperor he would be able to do what he wished. But in the days following his father's death he comes to realize that he can govern well only in accordance with the law; that though he could, like previous emperors, impose his arbitrary will on the Empire, this would be a disastrous start for a ruler who wished to govern constitutionally. Several times Titus' resolution is nearly overthrown, and at the end it is Berenice who takes the side of duty. At the climax of the struggle Titus expresses in soliloquy the significance of what he has to do:

> I come to pierce a heart which I adore,
> A heart that loves me. Why should I pierce it then?
> Who orders it? Myself.

M. Picard asks:

Why this sudden change? Why does Titus become his own executioner? It is because a grace has fallen on him, a secular grace, no doubt, but one which, sudden and gratuitous, has the same characteristics as the other. The accession to the imperial dignity has been a sort of baptism.[6]

---

[6] Racine, *Oeuvres Complètes*, p. 475.

In spite of the exiguous plot which is miraculously spun out to five acts, and in spite of the static situation, Racine plays so many variations on his theme that scenes which might be repetitive reveal new aspects of the basic theme. Antiochus, for example, has two interviews with Berenice. In the first one he believes that Titus is about to marry Berenice and that his own love is hopeless. In the second one he is charged by Titus to inform Berenice that she must leave Rome; and since he is given the task of escorting her his hopes are reawakened. But Berenice's anger is directed against Antiochus instead of against her faithless lover, and Antiochus believes that he is cured of love. In the same way Berenice and Titus have three scenes together. In the first Titus tries in vain to inform her of his intentions. In the great scene in the fourth act, following Titus' soliloquy, Berenice overwhelms him with reproaches. In the last act it is Titus who begs Berenice not to leave Rome, and Berenice who, hearing Antiochus' blessings on their love, makes the renunciation which concludes the play.[7]

It may be added that *Berenice* may be regarded as a deliberate contrast to *Britannicus*. The protagonist of each play is an emperor. One is governed by his passions; the other subordinates even his virtuous love to what he regards as his duty. The health of the Empire depends on the subordination of desire to law. The Rome of Nero is corrupt because he is unable to make the sacrifice which Titus exacts of himself. The two plays together provide what the Elizabethans called "a mirror for magistrates."

[7] As Jasinski shows (*op. cit.* pp. 407 ff.) there is some reason to believe that the separation of Titus and Berenice may reflect Louis XIV's separation from Marie Mancini in 1659 and his later love for Henriette d'Angleterre. When he parted from Marie, she said to him in a tone of sorrowful reproach: "Sire, you are king, you weep, and I depart." Compare the words of Berenice: "You are Emperor, my lord, And yet you weep!" . . . "You love me, you maintain; and yet I leave at your command!" It is less easy to see any real connection between Berenice and Marquise du Parc.

VI

About the greatness of *Phaedra* there is no dispute. It is based on the *Hippolytus* of Euripides, but Racine is careful to minimize the guilt of his heroine. She suppresses her guilty passion for her stepson, and she drives him away from her husband's court in order to free herself from temptation; on his return she determines to let herself die rather than tell her secret; and she finally tells Œnone only when she thinks she has not long to live. Then false news arrives that Theseus is dead. Œnone persuades her that she must go on living to insure the welfare of her son, and argues that her love, no longer adulterous, is now an ordinary passion which can be satisfied without guilt. Phaedra, although not deceived on this point, has her defenses weakened; and she is surprised into confessing her love to Hippolytus himself. Immediately afterwards Theseus returns home; and Phaedra, terrified of exposure, allows Œnone to tell him that Hippolytus had attempted to seduce her. In Euripides' play Phaedra herself accuses Hippolytus of having violated her. But although Euripides could introduce Aphrodite and Artemis into his play and thereby make his heroine the plaything of the gods, Racine could not go as far in minimizing her responsibility for her actions. The first reference to Phaedra in the play as *la fille de Minos et de Pasiphaé* reminds the audience of her heredity and of the way her mother was cursed with unnatural desires; and we hear later of the story of her sister, Ariadne. Yet Phaedra has free will, and she is fully aware of her own guilt which she seeks to expiate by suicide. Racine points out in his preface:

. . . the least faults are severely punished; the very thought of a crime is regarded with as much horror as the crime itself; the weaknesses of love are shown as true weaknesses; the passions are displayed only to show all the disorder of which they are the cause; and vice is everywhere depicted in colors which make the deformity recognized and hated. That is properly the end which every man who works for the public should propose to himself . . .

We may suspect that Racine is defending his play against
his critics, and particularly against his old teachers of Port
Royal who regarded the stage as a school of wickedness.
He was perfectly justified in believing that his play was
more moral in its intention and its effect than the rival
play by Pradon, in which there is neither adultery nor incest; but it is worth noting that Phaedra is the only one of
his lovers who knows that she is guilty of sin, the only one
who struggles with her passion, the only one who experi-
ences remorse and horror. The others are frustrated. She
realizes that she could find no happiness even if she were
to achieve her desires:

> Past reason hunted, and no sooner had
> Past reason hated, as a swallowed bait
> On purpose laid to make the taker mad;
> Mad in pursuit and in possession so.

From the beginning of the play to the end Phaedra is
tortured by the consciousness of her sinful desires. She
hopes to die; and would have died without a sinful act
but for the trap which fate springs on her—the rumor of
Theseus' death. When she has confessed her love to Hippolytus, she begs him to kill her. When she learns that
Hippolytus loves Aricia, the tortures of jealousy are added
to those of remorse. She imagines that her father, Minos,
will be horrified at her "crimes yet unknown in hell"; and
yet, in spite of her horror, she is racked by the sense of
frustration that

> never has my sad heart
> Once plucked the fruit of the atrocious crime
> Whose shame pursues me.

When Œnone tries to comfort her by minimizing her guilt
and justifying her "lawless fires" by the example of the
gods, she turns from her in horror. In the new moral tone
of *Phaedra* it is legitimate to see the first symptoms of the
conversion which led to Racine's retirement from the
professional stage.

Yet, as critics have pointed out, one of the greatest triumphs of the poet is that in the last scene, where Phaedra
makes her third and last confession—to Theseus—Racine

is able to arouse more pity for her than for her innocent victim, Hippolytus, who is destroyed by his father's rash curse, or than for her husband, whose life is in ruins.

The whole play is magnificently designed. If the scenes between Hippolytus and Aricia are not quite on the same poetical level as the Phaedra scenes, their innocence—for no one takes very seriously the "guilt" of Hippolytus in loving a girl of whose family Theseus disapproves—is a necessary contrast to the atmosphere of guilt in the Phaedra scenes. All these are dramatically perfect, though only one example of their perfection can be given here. In the speech in which Phaedra reveals her passion to Hippolytus, she begins with a pretense that she loves the supposedly dead Theseus. Then, by a series of calculated ambiguities, she speaks of Theseus when he was young at the time when her sister Ariadne fell in love with him, and wishes that Hippolytus had been old enough to come with him:

> For then you would have slain
> The Minotaur, despite the devious ways
> Of his vast lair: my sister, to redeem you
> From your confusion, with the fateful thread
> Would have armed your hand—but no, for I myself,
> Inspired by love, would have forestalled her plan.
> It would have been me, Prince; by timely aid
> I would have led you through the labyrinth.
> How many cares that charming head of yours
> Would then have cost me! I would not have trusted
> To that weak thread alone, but walked before you,
> Companion of the peril which you chose:
> And going down into the labyrinth,
> Phaedra would have returned with you, or else
> Been lost with you.

These lines not only express the way in which Phaedra's imagination is working, with the use of obvious sexual symbolism, but they recall for the audience another episode in the history of her unfortunate family. The legendary past is brought close to the violent present, so that we are prepared for the intervention of Neptune and the destruction of Hippolytus by the sea monster.

VII

After *Phaedra,* twelve years elapsed before Racine wrote another play. The last two plays, *Esther* and *Athaliah,* were written for performance by schoolgirls. He chose the biblical themes partly to suit the performers, but chiefly as a means of reconciling poetry and piety. The overthrowing of Queen Athaliah and the preservation and restoration of Joas seem at first sight to have little connection with Christianity; but although our sympathies are not wholly on the side of the High Priest, and although Athaliah is not wholly evil, the Queen's court is another example of the corruption of absolute power, and it is apparent that the religion of Mathan is false and the religion of Joad true. Racine was attracted to the theme because Joas was in the direct line of descent between David and Jesus, and his preservation illustrated the working of divine providence, and was a means of insuring the redemption of man.

It has been said that providence in the play is more pitiless than the fate of the ancients, and that *Athaliah* surpasses in ferocity the tragedies of passion. Certainly the tender Josabeth hails with delight the assassination of the old Queen; and if Athaliah is stained with numerous crimes, she has good reason to hate and fear the followers of Jehovah. In the course of the play we are reminded again and again of the murder of Jezebel, and one of the greatest speeches recounts the appearance of Jezebel to Athaliah in a dream:

> Her sorrows had not quenched her pride, but still
> Her face was decked and painted to repair
> The irreparable ravages of time.

She warns her daughter that the cruel God of the Jews would soon overcome her also.

> In uttering these frightful words,
> Her ghost, it seemed, bent down towards my bed;
> But when I stretched my hands out to embrace her,
> I found instead a horrible heap of bones,
> And mangled flesh, and tatters soaked in blood

Dragged through the mire, and limbs unspeakable
For which voracious dogs were wrangling there.

Not only was Athaliah's mother murdered but she had seen her father and brother killed and the butchering of eighty princes.

In her last speech Athaliah prophecies that the innocent child Joas will turn to evil and profane Jehovah's altar, thereby avenging Ahab, Jezebel, and Athaliah. We know from the Bible that the curse was fulfilled, and that even though David's line is preserved Athaliah will triumph after her death.

The irony here is unbearably poignant, for Athaliah is betrayed to her death not merely by her avarice and her desire to seize David's treasure but by the attraction she feels for the boy Joas, the love of a ravaged old woman for her lost innocence. Joas, who is the real "treasure" of David, displays in his interview with Athaliah the courage of innocence; and his unstained nature is hymned in some of the most beautiful lines of the chorus. But Joad realizes how easily virtue can be corrupted by power; and in lines which, on the eve of the French Revolution, were interrupted at almost every line by enthusiastic applause, and which had to be omitted during the rule of Napoleon, he warns Joas of the way flatterers will assure him that a king is not bound by the laws, and that the people must be oppressed, until he comes to hate the truth. It has been suggested that Louis XIV disliked the play he had asked Racine to write because of the attack on absolutism and because Racine could not conceal his Jansenist views.[8]

Racine constructed his play from a few verses in the Bible and his characters are created from the barest hints. Into Joad he was able to put the passion for righteousness which appears to have been the main result of his own conversion. There is no sign in Racine's last period of the love and forgiveness apparent in Shakespeare's. Voltaire thought that Joad was fanatical and superstitious. He is not that: but he has the sternness and single-mindedness which his

[8] Several contemporary writers thought that Joad was in some sense a portrait of Arnauld, the head of Port Royal.

historical position requires and which were necessary in Jehovah's champion at that time.

But the play is not confined within the limits of a violent episode of Old Testament history. It embraces both the past and the future. There are many references in the dialogue to previous episodes in the history of the Jews and their conflict with paganism; in the choruses Racine provides the religious justification of the action; and in the prophecy of Joad we are given a glimpse of the Christianity which sprang from Judaism.

The play is superbly constructed. Each scene follows without a break the one preceding it,[9] so that the action exactly corresponds to the time taken in performance. As the scene is laid in the Temple, the use of the chorus appears perfectly natural. The necessary information about past events is provided in conversations between Joad and Abner, Joad and Josabeth, Athaliah and Mathan. Racine employs only a single confidant, who has none of the artificiality sometimes apparent in those of previous plays. The action is exciting throughout, with revelation following revelation, and suspense being maintained to the very end when Athaliah, by threatening to destroy the Temple if she is refused the boy Eliacin and the treasure of David, is delivered into Joad's hands, David's treasure being the boy who is to be her successor.

VIII

André Gide, after admitting that Lytton Strachey's essay on Racine was remarkable for an Englishman, went on to complain that although Strachey admired Racine very much, he did

not perhaps admire him just as one should. Seen through him, Racine appears, despite him, gray, timid, cramped. The quotations he makes could be better chosen, more typical. If one does not bring out Racine's perfection, the smallness of his orchestra, just like Mozart's, might seem poverty.[10]

[9] Racine, when he had mapped out the scenes of a play, used to say, "My tragedy is finished," though he had not written a line of the actual dialogue.

[10] *The Journals of André Gide,* ed. Justin O'Brien, 1956, Vol. 1, p. 327.

An English critic of Racine runs the same risks as a French critic of Shakespeare, and however much one admires, one is liable to admire in the wrong way. The conventions of the Racinian theatre are apt to be as much of a stumbling block to English readers as the Shakespearian conventions are to a French reader. But at least we can now see that the classical form does not make *Phaedra* or *Athaliah* cold or statuesque. They both have the intensity which Keats regarded as the chief excellence of every art, "capable of making the disagreeables evaporate." Several modern French critics have rightly protested against the attempt to see nothing in his work but eloquence, order, moralizing, and pure poetry. He is, in fact, one of the most terrifying of dramatists. The characters, in spite of the propriety of their diction, are often frenzied characters plotting violent crimes, and their violence is often more horrifying than that of the jungle. The plays often end in the quiet of exhaustion rather than in the restoration of order. We seem to be not far from the subhuman world expressed by the animal imagery in *King Lear*. Racine would never have made such a comment as Albany's, but the reader may be inclined to echo it after reading some of the scenes in his plays:

> If that the heavens do not their visible spirits
> Send quickly down to tame these vile offences,
> It will come,
> Humanity must perforce prey on itself,
> Like monsters of the deep.

The characteristics which modern critics have found in Racine's work—brutality, ferocity, frenzy, murderous rage, religious exaltation—coexist with the perfection of the classical form. But the form does not have the effect of damping down the emotional content: it merely concentrates it.

ANDROMACHE

FIRST PREFACE

. . .[1] My characters are so famous in antiquity that
even those who know little of it will see plainly that I have
represented them just as the ancient poets have given
them: and I did not think I was allowed to alter their
manners. All the liberty I have taken is to soften a little
the ferocity of Pyrrhus, which Seneca in the *Troades,* and
Virgil, in the second book of the *Æneid* have carried further than I thought I ought to do. Yet people have been
found to complain that he inveighed against Andromache,
and that he wished to wed a captive at any price; and I
admit that he is not resigned enough to the will of his
mistress, and that Celadon understood perfect love better
than he. But what could I do? Pyrrhus had not read our
romances; he was naturally violent, and all heroes are not
made to be Celadons.

However that may be, the public has been too kind to
me for me to be embarrassed by the particular annoyance
of two or three people who would like us to reform all the
heroes of antiquity to make them into perfect heroes. I find
their desire that we should represent on the stage only im-
peccable men quite admirable; but I beg them to remember that it is not my place to alter the rules of the drama.
Horace recommends us to paint Achilles wild, inexorable,
violent, just as he was, and just as his son is depicted;
Aristotle, far from asking of us perfect heroes, wants, on
the contrary, that tragic characters, that is to say those
whose misfortune makes the catastrophe of the tragedy,
should be neither entirely good, nor entirely wicked. He
does not wish them to be extremely good, because the

[1] A passage from Virgil and the paragraph which follows are
omitted here because Racine repeated them in the Second
Preface.

punishment of a virtuous man excites more indignation than pity in the spectator; nor that they should be excessively wicked, because one has no pity for a scoundrel. It is therefore necessary for them to have a moderate goodness, that is to say a virtue capable of weakness, and that they should fall into misfortune by some fault which makes them pitied without making them detested.

SECOND PREFACE [2]

Virgil in the third book of the *Æneid*—it is Æneas who speaks:[3]

> The sight of high Phaeacia soon we lost,
> And skimm'd along Epirus' rocky coast.
> Then to Chaonia's port our course we bend,
> And, landed, to Buthrotus' heights ascend.
>
> . . . .
>
> By chance, the mournful queen, before the gate,
> Then solemniz'd her former husband's fate.
> Green altars, rais'd of turf, with gifts she crown'd:
> And sacred priests in order stand around,
> And thrice the name of hapless Hector sound.
>
> . . . .
>
> With eyes dejected, in a lowly tone,
> After a modest pause, she thus begun:
> 'Oh, only happy maid of Priam's race,
> Whom death deliver'd from the foe's embrace!
> Commanded on Achilles' tomb to die,
> Not forc'd, like us, to hard captivity,
> Or in a haughty master's arms to lie.
> In Grecian ships, unhappy we were borne,
> Endur'd the victor's lust, sustain'd the scorn!
> Thus I submitted to the lawless pride
> Of Pyrrhus, more a handmaid than a bride.
> Cloy'd with possession, he forsook my bed,
> And Helen's lovely daughter sought to wed;
>
> . . . .
>
> Till young Orestes, pierc'd with deep despair,
> And longing to redeem the promis'd fair,
> Before Apollo's altar slew the ravisher.'

[2] This preface replaced the first in 1676.
[3] Dryden's translation, instead of the original Latin.

There, in a few verses, is the whole subject of this tragedy; there is the place where the scene is laid, the action which passes, the four principal actors, and even their characters, except that of Hermione whose jealousy and rage are evident enough in the *Andromache* of Euripides.

This is almost the only thing I have borrowed here from that author. For although my tragedy carries the same title as his, the subject of it is yet very different. Andromache, in Euripides, fears for the life of Molossus, who is a son she has had by Pyrrhus and whom Hermione wishes to have killed with his mother. But here there is no question of Molossus: Andromache knows no other husband than Hector, nor any other son than Astyanax. I thought in this to keep to the idea which we have now of this princess. Most of those who have heard speak of Andromache scarcely know her except as the widow of Hector and as the mother of Astyanax. They do not believe that she should love another husband, or another son; and I doubt whether the tears of Andromache would have made the same impression on the minds of the spectators if they had flowed for a son other than the one she bore to Hector.

It is true that I have been obliged to make Astyanax live a little longer than he did; but I write in a country where this liberty could not be badly received. For, without speaking of Ronsard, who chose this same Astyanax for the hero of his *Franciade,* who does not know that our ancient kings have been made to descend from this son of Hector, and that our old chronicles save the life of this young prince, after the desolation of his country, to make him the founder of our monarchy?

How much bolder was Euripides in his tragedy of *Helena:* he openly shocked the common belief of all Greece; he supposed that Helen had never set foot in Troy, and that after the burning of that town, Menelaus found his wife in Egypt, which she never had left; all this founded on an opinion which was only accepted among the Egyptians, as one can see in Herodotus.

I do not believe that I needed this example of Euripides to justify the small liberty which I have taken. For there is a great difference between destroying the chief foundation of a fable and altering some incidents which change considerably in all the hands which deal with them. So Achilles, according to most poets, could only be wounded in the heel, although Homer makes him wounded in the arm, and does not think him invulnerable in any part of his body. So Sophocles makes Jocasta die soon after the recognition of Œdipus, unlike Euripides who makes her live until the fight and death of her two sons. And it is concerning some contrarieties of this nature that an ancient commentator of Sophocles remarks very well "that it is unnecessary to amuse oneself with cavilling at the poets for some changes which they may have made in the fable; but one should strive to consider the excellent use which they have made of these alterations, and the ingenious manner with which they have known how to accommodate the fable to their theme."

DRAMATIS PERSONÆ

ANDROMACHE, *widow of Hector, captive of Pyrrhus*
PYRRHUS, *son of Achilles, King of Epirus*
ORESTES, *son of Agamemnon, in love with Hermione*
HERMIONE, *daughter of Helen, engaged to Pyrrhus*
PYLADES, *friend of Orestes*
CLEONE, *confidante of Hermione*
CEPHISE, *confidante of Andromache*
PHOENIX, *tutor of Achilles, and later of Pyrrhus*
SOLDIERS

SCENE—BUTHROT, a town of EPIRUS, in a room in the palace of Pyrrhus

ANDROMACHE

ACT ONE

ORESTES *and* PYLADES.

ORESTES. Since I have found my faithful friend again,
My Fortune now assumes a different face;
Since by her aid we have been reunited,
Her wrath seems to be calmed. Who would have said
That this same shore, so fatal to my vows,
Would give me sight of Pylades; that you
After six months would be restored to me
At the court of Pyrrhus?
    Pylades.   I render thanks
To heaven which ceaselessly prevented me
And stopped my road to Greece, since that dread day
When the waves' fury overwhelmed my vessels
Within sight of this shore. How many fears
Have come to me in exile! How I have wept
For your misfortunes, dreading every day
Some peril for you which I could not share!
I dreaded above all that melancholy
Deep-rooted in your soul: I feared lest heaven
By cruel aid should offer you the death
You always sought. But now, my lord, I see you:
And, if I dare to say it, a happier fate
Now brings you to Epirus: the lordly train
Which follows in your steps does not denote
A wretch who seeks for death.
    Orestes.   Alas! who knows
The fate which brings me now? Love makes me seek
A cruel woman here; but who knows what
My fate ordains, and if I come to seek
Life or death?
    Pylades.   What! your soul enslaved

7

To Love, entrusts to him your life's direction?
By what enchantment, forgetting all the torments
Which you have suffered, can you consent to don
His chains again? Do you think Hermione,
Inexorable in Sparta, prepares for you
A fate more favorable in Epirus?
Ashamed of having uttered in the past
So many useless vows, you would abhor her.
But this you do not mention any more.
You deceived me, my lord.

    Orestes.   I have deceived myself!
Friend, do not overwhelm a wretch who loves you.
For did I ever hide from you my heart
Or my desires? You saw the birth of love
And my first sighs: and then when Menelaus
Disposed his daughter's hand in gratitude
To the avenger of his family, Pyrrhus,
You saw my deep despair; and since that time
You've seen me drag my weary chain of griefs
From sea to sea. I saw you, with regret,
In my sad state, ready to follow me,
Checking my fury's course and every day
Saving me from myself. But when I knew
In the midst of all this that Hermione
Was then exerting all her charms on Pyrrhus,
You know how I was wroth, and that I wished,
Forgetting her, to punish all her scorn.
So I supposed, and thought my victory certain.
I thought my violence was the effect of hate;
Detesting her cruelty and making light
Of all her charms, I then defied her eyes
Ever to trouble me again. I thought
I thus had stifled love. I came to Greece
In this delusive calm and found her princes
Gathered together in a common peril.
I hastened there, and thought that war and glory
Would fill my mind with more important cares,
That my senses would regain their primal vigor,
And love, at last, would be driven from my heart.
But wonder with me at the fate which makes me
Run ever to the snare I shun. I hear

The threat to Pyrrhus; and the whole of Greece
Resounds with murmurings confused, complaining
That he, forgetful of his blood and promise,
Has raised within his court the enemy
Of Greece, the young unfortunate son of Hector,
Astyanax, relic of many kings
Now buried under Troy. Andromache,
To save her child from death, deceived Ulysses—
Another infant from her arms was torn,
And murdered in his place. It is said my rival,
Insensible to Hermione's charms, elsewhere
Carries his heart and crown; and Menelaus,
Though not believing, seems afflicted by it,
Complaining of a wedding that has been
So long neglected. But what displeases him
Fills me with secret joy. I triumph; and yet
I flattered me at first that only vengeance
Aroused this transport. But the ungrateful one
Resumed possession of my heart. I knew
The embers of my love were not extinguished;
I felt my hate had run its course, or rather
I felt I loved her still. And so I canvassed
The voice of all the Greeks, and I was chosen
To go to Pyrrhus. I undertook this voyage.
I came to see whether this child whose life
Makes many states afraid can from his arms
Be torn; but in my passion I'd be happy
If I could seize in place of Astyanax
My princess from him! Think not the greatest peril
Can check the flames of my redoubled passion.
Since, after all my efforts, it is vain
Further to struggle, blindly I submit
To the passion that possesses me. I love.
I come to seek Hermione in this place
And either make her yield, and come with me,
Or die before her eyes. You who know Pyrrhus,
What do you think he'll do? Tell me what's happening
Here in his court, and in his heart. Does he
Regard himself as bound to my Hermione?
Do you imagine he'll restore to me
The treasure he has seized?

Pylades.   I would abuse you
If I should dare to promise that he wished
To place her in your hands. Not that he seems
Pleased by his conquest; for he is in love
With Hector's widow; but till now inflexible,
She has repaid her lover but with hatred.
And yet each day he's seen to try all means
To make his captive bend, or frighten her;
He utters menaces against her son
Whom he hides from her; sheds tears which soon he stays.
Hermione herself a hundred times
Has seen him come beneath her yoke again,
And bringing her the homage of his vows
Sigh at her feet with rage rather than love.
Therefore expect me not to answer now
For a heart so little master of itself.
He can, my lord, in this extreme disorder
Wed whom he hates, and punish the one he loves.

Orestes. But tell me how Hermione beholds
Her wedding day deferred, her powerless charms.

Pylades. Hermione, my lord, as it appears,
Disdains her lover's long inconstancy,
Believing that, delighted in his conquest,
He'll beg her to accept his heart again.
She let me see her tears. She weeps in secret
The scorning of her charms. She is always ready
To leave Epirus, but she always stays.
Sometimes she calls Orestes to her aid.

Orestes. If I believed that I would go at once
And throw myself . . .

Pylades.   Perform your embassage,
My lord. You now await the King. Speak to him
And show him how the Greeks have sworn together
Against the son of Hector. Far from delivering
His mistress' son to them, their hate will only
Excite his love. The more they wish to part them,
The more they will unite them. Ply him hard.
Ask everything in order to obtain
Nothing. He's coming.

Orestes.   Go, prepare the cruel one
To see a lover who only comes for her.   [*Exit* PYLADES.

Enter PYRRHUS *and* PHOENIX.   (I.2)

Orestes. Before all Greece speaks to you by my voice
Allow me first to say how pleased I am
To have been chosen for this task, my lord,
And let me show some joy that I behold
Achilles' son, the conqueror of Troy.
Yes, we admire your deeds as much as his.
Great Hector fell beneath him: Troy expired
Beneath you; and you showed by happy courage
That Achilles' son alone could fill his place.
But Greece with sorrow sees you, unlike him,
Relieve the luckless blood of Troy and, touched
With fatal pity, care for the survivor
Of that long war. Do you no more remember
What Hector was, my lord? Our weakened peoples
Remember still. His name alone can make
Our widows and our daughters quake with fear,
And in all Greece there's not a family
Which does not ask of this unfortunate son
To render an account of a dear father
Or of a husband snatched from them by Hector.
And who knows what this son, when grown to manhood,
Can undertake? Perhaps we shall behold him
Descend upon our ports, as once his father
Set fire to our ships, and torch in hand
Follow them on the waters. Shall I dare,
To tell you what I think? You yourself, my lord,
Fear now the recompense of all your kindness,
And that this serpent nurtured in your breast
Will punish you one day for having saved it.
Comply, then, with the wish of all the Greeks,
Assure their vengeance, and assure your life:
Destroy a foe, so much the more a peril,
Since he will first try out his strength on you.

Pyrrhus. Greece is too much concerned for me. I thought
That greater cares were vexing her, my lord,
That her ambassador had greater projects.
Who would believe that such an enterprise
Deserved the choice of Agamemnon's son
To undertake it? That the people of Greece,

So many times triumphant, should have stooped
To plot the death of a child? To what indeed
Should he be sacrificed? Has Greece some right
Over his life? And am I not allowed—
Alone of all the Greeks—to have full power
Over a captive fate has given me?
Yes, my lord, when beneath the smoking walls
Of Troy, the bloodstained victors shared their prey,
Chance, whose decisions then were always followed,
Assigned Andromache and her son to me.
Hecuba found her ultimate misery
With Ulysses; Cassandra went to Argos
With your great father. Have I claimed any rights
Over them or their captives? Or have I disposed
The reward of their exploits? But it is feared
That Troy will be reborn; that Hector's son
May rob me of the light I let him keep.
My lord, excessive prudence must involve
Too much of care. I can't anticipate
Such distant ills. I think of what that town
Was once—so proud its walls, so rich in heroes,
Mistress of Asia; then I think of the fate
And destiny of Troy. I see its towers
Covered with ashes; a river red with blood;
The devastated fields; a child in chains;
And I cannot suppose that in this state
Troy hopes to be avenged. If the destruction
Of Hector's son was sworn, why for a year
Have we postponed it? Could we not have slain him
On Priam's breast? Beneath so many dead,
And under Troy itself he should have died.
All then was just. Old age and infancy
Relied in vain upon their feebleness.
Darkness and Victory, more cruel than us,
Excited us to murder, and our blows
Were struck at random. My wrath to the vanquished
Was but too harsh. But should my cruelty
Survive my anger? And despite the pity
With which I am possessed, should I at leisure
Bathe now in this child's blood? No, no, my lord.
Let the Greeks now seek out some other prey,

Let them pursue elsewhere what's left of Troy.
My enmities have run their course. Epirus
Will save what Troy has saved.

Orestes.   You know too well
How cunningly a false Astyanax
Was led to execution. It is not
The Trojans, it is Hector who is pursued.
Yes, it is true, the Greeks are persecuting
The father in the son. With too much blood
He bought their anger, and only his can quench it.
And since it can draw them to Epirus now,
Prevent them.

Pyrrhus.   No. I consent to it with joy
That they should seek to make the city here
A second Troy; that they should be confused
In hatred, and not be able to distinguish
The blood that made them conquer and the blood
Of the conquered. It is not the first injustice
With which the Greeks have paid Achilles' service.
Hector once profited by it, my lord;
And one day in his turn Astyanax
May likewise profit from it.

Orestes.   And so in you
Greece finds a rebellious child?

Pyrrhus.   And have I then
Conquered but to depend on her?

Orestes.   My lord,
Hermione will stay your blows: her eyes
Will plead between you and her father.

Pyrrhus.   Hermione,
My lord, may be forever dear to me,
But I can love her without being the slave
Of Menelaus; and I will know some day
The way to reconcile the needs of greatness
With those of love. But you can see the daughter
Of Helen: I know close ties of blood unite you.
And after that, my lord, I won't detain you;
You can inform the Greeks of my refusal.   [*Exit* ORESTES.

(I.3)

Phoenix. And so you send him to his mistress' feet!

Pyrrhus. He long has loved the Princess, it is said.

Phoenix. But if his passion should be lit again,
My lord, if he should offer her his heart
And make himself beloved?

Pyrrhus.   Ah! let them love,
Phoenix; I give consent. Let her depart;
Let them, in mutual love, return to Sparta.
Our ports are open for them. Let her spare me
Vexation and constraint.

Phoenix.   My lord . . .

Pyrrhus.   Another time
I will disclose the secrets of my soul.
Andromache is here.

Enter ANDROMACHE and CEPHISE.   (I.4)

Pyrrhus.   Were you seeking me,
Princess? May such a sweet hope be allowed me?

Andromache. I was going to the quarters where my son
     is guarded.
Since you permit me once a day to see
All that remains to me of Troy and Hector,
I was going, my lord, to weep a moment with him;
I have not kissed him yet today.

Pyrrhus.   Ah! madam!
The Greeks, if I can credit their alarms,
Will give you soon another cause to weep.

Andromache. What is the fear, my lord, which strikes
     their hearts?
Some Trojan has escaped them?

Pyrrhus.   Their hate of Hector
Is not extinguished yet. They fear his son.

Andromache. A worthy object of their fear! A poor child
Who does not know yet Pyrrhus is his master
Or that he's Hector's son.

Pyrrhus.   But all the Greeks
Demand that he should die. Agamemnon's son
Has come to speed his execution.

Andromache. And will you then pronounce so cruel a
     sentence?
And does my interest make him criminal?
They do not fear he will avenge his father

But that he'll wipe his mother's tears. He would
Have taken the place of father and of husband;
But I must lose all, and always by your blows.

   Pyrrhus. No, madam, my refusals have forestalled
Your tears; and all the Greeks have threatened me
With force of arms. But should they come again
With a thousand vessels to demand your son,
Although it cost the blood that Helen spilt,
And after ten years I must see my palace
A blackened ruin, I should not hesitate,
But fly to aid you. I would defend his life
At the cost of my own. But yet amidst these perils
To which I run to please you, will you refuse me
A softer look? Hated by all the Greeks,
And pressed on every side, should I encounter
Your cruelties still? I offer you my arm.
Can I yet hope you will accept a heart
That loves you? May I now, in fighting for you,
Not reckon you among my enemies?

   Andromache. What are you doing, my lord? What will
     Greece say?
And should so great a heart display such weakness?
Do you want so fine and generous a scheme
To seem a lover's rapture? Can you wish
That Andromache, a captive, always sad,
Self-vexed, should love you? And what charms, my lord,
Can these unhappy eyes, condemned by you
To everlasting tears, now hold for you?
No, no, respect the misery of a foe;
Save the unfortunate; restore a son
Unto his mother; combat the cruelty
Of a hundred peoples for him, without demanding
That for his safety I should give my heart.
In spite of me, if need be, give him asylum:
Such are the deeds, my lord, which would be worthy
Of the son of great Achilles.

   Pyrrhus.   What! has your anger
Not run its course? Will your hate never die?
And will you always punish me? No doubt
I have made many miserable, and Phrygia
A hundred times has seen my hand besmeared

With blood of yours. But how your eyes have turned
Upon me in reproach! and I have paid
Dearly for all your tears! Of what remorse
Have I been made the prey! I suffer all
The harms I did at Troy—myself am conquered,
Laden with chains, and with regrets devoured,
Burned with more fires than I myself have kindled,
As many cares, and tears, and unquiet passions . . .
Alas! was I ever as cruel as you are now?
There's been enough of mutual punishment;
Our common enemies should now unite us.
Madam, if you would tell me but to hope,
I'd give you back your son, and be his father;
I will instruct him to avenge the Trojans,
And I will go to punish all the Greeks
For the wrongs we both have suffered. Fired by one glance
I can do all. Your Ilion can yet
Rise from its ashes. In a shorter time
Than the Greeks took to conquer it, I can
Rebuild its walls, and crown your son in them.

    Andromache. My lord, such greatness now can scarcely
       touch us:
Thus would I promise while his father lived.
No, sacred walls, which could not save my Hector,
You will not hope to see us any more.
The unfortunate pretend to lesser favors,
My lord; it is an exile that my tears
Demand of you. Far from the Greeks and far
Even from you, let me go hide my son
And mourn my husband. Since your love has kindled
Too much of hate against us, return, return
To Helen's daughter.

    Pyrrhus.   And can I, madam? Ah!
How you torment me! How can I give to her
A heart that you possess? I know she was promised
The sovereignty of my desires; I know
She came to reign here in Epirus. Fate
Was pleased to bring you both—you bearing chains,
And her to give them. But have I taken care
To please her? Would it not be said indeed,
Your charms all-powerful and her charms disdained,

That she is captive here, and that you reign?
One sigh my heart has sent you, had it but
Escaped for her, would have brought joy.
 Andromache.   And why
Should she repulse your sighs? Has she forgotten
Your former services? Would Troy and Hector
Revolt her soul against you? Does she owe
Love to a husband's ashes? And what a husband!
Ah! cruel remembrance! His death alone
Has given your father an immortal name;
To Hector's blood he owes his whole renown,
And you are both known only by my tears.
 Pyrrhus. Well, madam, you must be obeyed. I must
Forget you, hate you rather. Yes, my desires
Have gone too far, have been too violent,
To stop in calm indifference. So think well.
Henceforth my heart, its boundless love refused,
Will hate with fury. I will nothing spare
In my just anger. The son will answer me
For the mother's scorn. Greece asks for him; no longer
Do I intend to stake my reputation
To save a thankless woman.
 Andromache.   Then he will die.
He has for his defense his mother's tears,
His innocence, no more. And after all,
Perhaps, in my sad state, his death will bring
The end of my griefs sooner. I would prolong
For him my life and misery, but yet
Following his footsteps I will see again
His father. So, my lord, all three will be
By your care reunited. . . .
 Pyrrhus.   Go, madam:
Go see your son. Perhaps, in seeing him,
Your love, more fearful, will not thenceforth take
Your anger for a guide. To know our fate
I'll come to find you. In embracing him,
Madam, remember how to save his life.

ACT TWO

HERMIONE *and* CLEONE.

HERMIONE. I do what you wish, consent that I should see
　　him.
I'm willing still to grant that joy to him.
Pylades will soon conduct him here
But yet, to tell the truth, I would not see him.
　　Cleone. Why should the sight of him be dreadful,
　　madam?
Is he not still the Orestes whose return
You have wished a hundred times, whose constancy
And love you have regretted?
　　Hermione.　　　　　　　　It is this love,
Paid with ingratitude, which makes his presence
Unpleasant to me. What a shame for me,
What a triumph for him, to see my state
Equal to his distress. "Is this," he'll say,
The proud Hermione? She scorned me once:
Another jilts her now. The ungrateful one,
Who set so high a price upon her heart,
Now learns to suffer scorn?" Ah! Gods!
　　Cleone.　　　　　　　　　　　Dispel
These needless fears. For he has felt too well
The power of your charms. Do you suppose
A lover comes to insult you? He brings a heart
He could not take away. But you don't tell me
Your father's orders.
　　Hermione.　　　　If Pyrrhus perseveres
In his delays, if he will not consent
To the Trojan's death, my father orders me
To leave with the Greeks.
　　Cleone.　　　　　　　　Then, madam, listen to Orestes.
Pyrrhus has now begun: do you the rest.
To do things well you must forestall his act.
Have you not said you hate him?
　　Hermione.　　　　　　　　I do, Cleone
My honor is at stake. He has forgotten

My kindness to him. So dear he was,
But he betrayed me! I have loved too well
Not to detest him now.
    Cleone.   Then fly from him.
And since another loves you . . .
    Hermione.   Ah! leave my rage
Still time to grow. Let me confirm myself
Against my enemy. I wish to leave him
With horror, Cleone. He will work for that
Only too well, the traitor!
    Cleone.   What! you'll await
Fresh injury from him? To love a captive,
And love her in your sight, is't not enough
To make him hateful to you? And after this
What more can you expect? He would have now
Displeased you, if he ever could displease you.
    Hermione. Why, cruel, do you wish to excite my griefs?
In my present state I fear to know myself.
Try and believe nothing of what you see.
Believe that I do not love him any more,
Boast of my victory; believe my heart
Is hardened in his scorn; if possible,
Alas! make me believe it too. You wish
That I should flee? Well, nothing stops me. Come,
Let's grudge no longer his unworthy conquest;
And let his captive extend her power on him;
Let's fly. . . . But if the ingrate should return
To duty; if fidelity should find
Some place within his heart; if he should come
To ask for pardon at my feet; if, Love,
You could enlist him underneath my laws;
And if he would . . . But he wants but to insult me.
Let us remain a while to vex their fortune,
Taking some pleasure in importuning them,
Or forcing him to break a solemn tie,
Make him a criminal in the eyes of Greece.
I have already drawn their direst wrath
Upon the son: I wish that they would come
To demand of him the mother. Let us give her
The torments she has made me suffer. Let her
Lose him, or rather let him make her perish.

Cleone. Do you think that eyes forever shedding tears
Would wish to challenge the power of your beauty,
And that a heart that's overwhelmed with sorrows
Solicited her persecutor's sighs?
Look if her sorrow now seems comforted:
Why then the grief in which her soul is plunged?
Why so much pride against a welcome lover?

Hermione. Alas! to my misfortune I have listened
Too much to him: and I have not affected
The mystery of silence. I supposed
That, without danger, I could be sincere;
And not for a moment did I arm my eyes
With coldness; I've only spoken from my heart.
Why should I not have done, when he had sworn
His love for me? Did he behold me then
With the same eyes as now? You will remember
How all conspired for him: my family
Avenged, the Greeks in triumph, our vessels filled
With the spoils of Troy, the exploits of his father
Effaced by his, his love which I believed
More vehement than mine, and you, my heart,
So dazzled by his fame that, ere he betrayed me,
You had betrayed me quite. But, Cleone,
It is too much. Whatever Pyrrhus is,
Hermione is sensitive to love,
Orestes has virtues. He can love at least,
Even without return, and he may find
The way to make me love him. So let him come.

Cleone. Madam, he's here.

Hermione.   Ah! I did not suppose
He was so near.

Enter ORESTES.   (II.2)

Hermione.   May I believe, my lord,
That some remains of tenderness have made you
Seek out a sad princess? Or should I ascribe
To duty only the happy haste which brings you
To see me.

Orestes. Such is my love's fatal blindness,
You know it, madam. Orestes' destiny
Is to come ceaselessly to adore your charms,

And to swear always that he will not come.
I know your looks will make my wounds reopen,
That every step towards you is a perjury;
I know it, and I blush that it is so.
But I attest the gods, the witnesses
Of my rage when last we parted, that I've run
To any place where certain death would free me
From all my vows, and end at last my torment.
I've begged for death amidst a cruel people
Who appeased their gods only with human blood.
They barred their temple against me, and became
Miserly with the blood I threw away.
At last I come to you, and see myself
Reduced to seek within your eyes a death
That has eluded me. For my despair
Only expects now their indifference:
They need but to forbid the hope that's left;
They need, to hasten on the death I seek,
But tell me once what they have always told me.
That, for a year, has been the only thing
To animate me. Madam, it is for you
To take a victim that the Scythians
Had stolen from your blows, if I had found them
As cruel as you.

    Hermione. Leave, my lord, such dismal talk.
You are employed now in more pressing tasks.
Why do you speak of Scythia and my cruelties?
Remember all those kings you represent.
Should their revenge depend on amorous passion?
Is it Orestes' blood that's asked of you?
Discharge your duties.

    Orestes.   Pyrrhus' refusal
Discharges me of them. He has dismissed me.
Some other power makes him embrace the defense
Of Hector's son.

    Hermione.   Faithless!

    Orestes.   And, therefore, ready
To leave, I come to consult you on my fate.
But even already I think I know the answer
Your hate, in secret, utters.

    Hermione.   What! still unjust

In your sad speeches? Will you yet complain
Of my hostility? What is this harshness
Alleged so often? I came into Epirus,
Where I was banished, by my father's orders.
But who knows if since then I have not shared
Your griefs in secret? Do you think you alone
Have felt alarms, Epirus never seen
My flowing tears? And who has told you, my lord,
That I, despite my duty, have not wished
Sometimes to see you?

    Orestes.   Wished to see me! Ah!
Divine Princess . . . but is it indeed to me
To whom you speak? Open your eyes. Remember
Orestes is before you, Orestes, for so long
The object of their anger.

    Hermione.   Yes, it is you,
Whose love, born of their charms, first made them know
Their conquering might. You whom a thousand virtues
Compel me to esteem; you whom I pity,
Whom I would love.

    Orestes.   I see. Such is my lot.
Your heart is Pyrrhus's, your vows for me.

    Hermione. Ah! do not wish the destiny of Pyrrhus—
I'd hate you too much.

    Orestes.   You'd love me more for it.
Ah! how contrarily you'd look at me!
You want to love me, and yet I cannot please you.
And, love alone being master, you would love me
In wishing to hate me. O Gods! So much respect,
Such tender friendship . . . What reasons in my favor,
If you could listen to me! You alone
Argue today for Pyrrhus, despite yourself
Perhaps, and doubtless in despite of him.
For now he hates you; his soul, elsewhere attracted,
No longer . . .

    Hermione.   Who has told you that he scorns me,
My lord? Or have his looks, his speech informed you?
Do you judge that my appearance earns his scorn,
And kindles in a heart such transient fires?
Other men's eyes, perhaps, are kinder to me.

    Orestes. Go on. It is in vain you thus insult me.

Cruel, so it is I who scorn you now?
Have not your eyes long proved my constancy?
I am a witness of their lack of power?
I have scorned them! How they would wish to see
My rival scorn their power as I have done!

Hermione. What matters, my lord, his hatred or his love!
Go, arm all Greece against a rebel. Bring him
The price of his rebellion, that Epirus
May be a second Troy. Go. After that,
Will you say that I love you?

Orestes. Madam, do more, and come away yourself.
Would you remain a hostage in this place?
Come, make your eyes to speak in every heart;
Unite us in a common hatred.

Hermione.   Meanwhile,
My lord, if he weds Andromache?

Orestes.   Eh, madam!

Hermione. Think what a shame for us if he became
The husband of a Phrygian!

Orestes.   And you hate him?
Confess it, madam, love is not a fire
That can be locked in a soul; for all betrays us,
Voice, silence, eyes; and fires half hidden blaze
Only the better.

Hermione.   My lord, I see too well
Your soul, forewarned, spreads on my speech the venom
That kills it; searches for some hidden meaning
In all my reasons, and believes that hatred
In me is an effect of love. Therefore
I must explain myself—then you can act.
My duty keeps me here; I cannot leave
Unless my father or Pyrrhus makes me go.
Go, tell him from my father, that the foe
Of Greece can never wed his daughter. Make him
Decide between me and the Trojan. Let him think
Which of us two he will give up or keep;
Then let him send me back, or else deliver
Astyanax to you. Farewell. If he
Consents to it, I'm ready to follow you.

                    [*Exeunt* HERMIONE *and* CLEONE.

(II.3)

Orestes. Yes, you will follow me. Doubt it not. Already
I can answer for his consent. I do not fear
That Pyrrhus will keep her, for he has no eyes
Save for his darling Trojan. All other objects
Offend him; and perhaps today he awaits
Only a pretext for his separation.
We have only to speak: and that is all. What joy
To carry from Epirus such a prey!
Save what remains of Troy and Hector; keep
His son, his widow, and a thousand others,
Epirus! It is enough that Hermione
Will never see thy shores and prince again.
But a happy fate now brings him to this place.
Let me speak with him. To her attractions, Love,
Shut fast his eyes.

Enter PYRRHUS and PHOENIX.   (II.4)

Pyrrhus.   I was seeking you, my lord.
A little of violence has made me fight
The power of your reasons—I confess it;
And since I left you I have felt their force,
And seen their equity. I have realized,
As you, that I had become opposed to Greece,
To my father, and in a word even to myself;
That I was restoring Troy and undermining
All that Achilles did, all I have done.
No more do I condemn a lawful anger;
My lord, your victim will be handed over.

Orestes. My lord, by this decision, stern and prudent,
You purchase peace with the unfortunate's blood.

Pyrrhus. Yes; but I wish, my lord, to assure it more:
Hermione is pledge of lasting peace,
And I will wed her. So sweet a spectacle
Awaited but a witness like yourself.
You represent her father and the Greeks
Since Menelaus sees his brother live
Again in you. See her then. Go, tell her
That I await, tomorrow, at your hands,
Her heart, and with it, peace.

Orestes [aside]. O Gods!   [*Exit* ORESTES.

(II.5)

Pyrrhus.   Well, Phoenix,
Is Love the master? Do your eyes refuse
To know me yet?
    Phoenix.   I recognize you now:
Your righteous wrath restores you to yourself
As well as to the Greeks. You are no longer
The plaything of a servile love, but Pyrrhus,
The son and rival of Achilles, brought
Beneath the laws of glory in the end,
Who triumphs over Troy a second time.
    Pyrrhus. Say rather that my victory begins
Only today. For the first time I rejoice
In my reputation, and my heart as proud
As once it was submissive, in love has conquered
A thousand enemies. Consider, Phoenix,
The troubles I avoid, what crowd of evils
Love draws in its train. How many friends
And duties I was going to sacrifice!
What perils . . . I was forgetting everything
For a woman's glance. The Greeks were sworn together
To crush a rebel; and I took some pleasure
In ruining myself for her.
    Phoenix.   I bless,
My lord, the happy cruelty which makes you . . .
    Pyrrhus. You have seen how she has treated me. I
        thought,
In seeing her fearful love, her son would drive her
Into my arms. I went to see the result
Of her embraces, and I found but tears
Mingled with passion. Her misery made her bitter;
And, wilder still, a hundred times she uttered
The name of Hector. Vainly I relied
Upon her son. " 'Tis Hector!" she exclaimed,
Embracing him again. "These are his eyes,
His mouth, and his audacity already.
'Tis he. 'Tis you, dear husband, I embrace."
What does she think? Does she expect today
That I shall leave a son to feed her love?

Phoenix. Doubtless that is the price which she exacts,
But leave her, my lord.
    Pyrrhus.   I see what flatters her.
Her beauty reassures her, and despite
My anger, she expects me at her feet.
I shall see her at mine, Phoenix, with tranquil eye.
She is Hector's widow: I'm Achilles' son.
Too much of hatred separates Andromache
And Pyrrhus.
    Phoenix.   Then begin, and speak no more.
Go to Hermione and, content to please her,
Forget your anger at her feet. You should
Yourself dispose her hand, and not rely
Upon a rival. He loves her but too much.
    Pyrrhus. Do you suppose, if I marry her, that Androm-
       ache
Will not be jealous in her heart?
    Phoenix.   My lord!
Does Andromache still possess your mind?
What does her joy or rancor matter to you?
What charm, despite yourself, still draws you to her?
    Pyrrhus. No Phoenix, I have not yet fully said
All that I ought to say to her. My anger
Has only partly shown itself to her.
She does not know how far I am her foe.
Let us return. I wish to face her now
And give my hatred rein. Let us see, Phoenix.
All her attractions quite humiliated.
Come.
    Phoenix. Go, my lord. Throw yourself at her feet:
Go, swear you adore her; and encourage her
To offer scorn afresh.
    Pyrrhus.   I see too well
You think that, ready to excuse, my heart
Runs after her and seeks to be appeased.
    Phoenix. You love. That is enough.
    Pyrrhus.   I love? An ingrate
Who hates me more than my love flatters her?
Without friends or relations, without hope
Except in me? I can destroy her son,
Perhaps I should. A foreigner! . . . Nay, a slave

In my Epirus, I give her son to her,
My soul, my empire; and I can only gain
In her perfidious heart the name of persecutor!
No, I have sworn it. My vengeance is resolved.
For once her hatred must be justified.
I cast away her son. What tears will flow!
By what name will her grief entitle me!
And what a spectacle for her today
Will be displayed! Phoenix, she'll die of it,
And I shall be the cause. 'Tis I myself
Who puts a dagger in her breast.
    Phoenix.   Why then
Announce your plan? Why do you test so soon
The extent of your weakness?
    Pyrrhus.   I hear you. But excuse
A remnant of my love. Do you fear my wrath
Will fight so feebly? It is the final flash
Of a love which is extinct. I now surrender
To your advice. Must I give up her son?
Must I see Hermione?
    Phoenix.   See her, my lord.
Protest to her by your submitted vows,
That you . . .
    Pyrrhus.   Let us do all that I have promised.

ACT THREE

ORESTES *and* PYLADES.

PYLADES. Moderate then, my lord, your boundless rage
I do not know you; you are not yourself.
Suffer . . .
    Orestes. No, your advice is not in season,
Pylades: I am tired of sober reason
Which lengthens out my life and punishment:
Either I take her with me, or I perish.
That is my plan—I wish to carry it out.
I will do so.
    Pylades. Well, you must take her then.
I agree. But remember where you are.

What would be thought of you, if it were known?
Conceal your purpose, calm your excited state,
Order your eyes to keep the secret. These guards,
This court, the air which surrounds you, all
Depend on Pyrrhus, and still more on her.
Conceal your anger from her eyes. O Gods!
Why do you seek her in this state?

    Orestes.   I know not.
Was I the master of myself? My rage
Transported me, and I came perhaps to threaten
The ingrate and her lover.

    Pylades.   What result
Should issue from your rage?

    Orestes.   Tell me what soul
Would not be amazed by such a blow as this
Which overthrew my reason? He informed me
That he would wed Hermione tomorrow;
To honor me, he wants to take her hand
From mine. Ah! rather in his barbarous blood
Let my hand be . . .

    Pylades.   You accuse him, my lord,
Of this strange destiny. But he, tormented
By his own plans, perhaps is to be pitied
As much as I do you.

    Orestes.   No, no, I know him.
He's flattered by my despair. Without my love
He would disdain her. Till now all her charms
Were powerless to touch him. Now he takes her
Only to snatch her from me. Ah, Gods!
It was all settled. Hermione was won,
And would have vanished from his sight forever;
Her heart, confused 'twixt love and hate, awaited
But a refusal to give itself to me.
Her eyes were opened, Pylades; she listened
To me, spoke to me, pitied me. A word
Would have done the rest.

    Pylades.   You think so!

    Orestes.   Yes, her anger
Inflamed against a faithless . . .

    Pylades.   He was never
More loved. Do you think when he granted her to you,

There was no pretext ready to detain her?
Take my advice; tired of her treacherous charms,
Instead of seizing her, flee her forever.
Your love will else be burdened with a fury
Who will detest you, who throughout your life,
Regretting a marriage which was nearly settled,
Would . . .

   Orestes. That is why I wish to bear her off.
All would smile on her—and for my share
Should I then be content with useless rage,
And far away seek vainly to forget her?
No, no, I want my torments to be shared by her.
It is too much to groan in isolation.
I'm tired of being pitied. I am resolved
The heartless one shall fear me in her turn
And that her cruel eyes, condemned to weep,
Shall render me the names I've given her.

   Pylades. So that will be the outcome of your mission—
Orestes turned into a ravisher!

   Orestes. What matter, Pylades? When our States,
      avenged,
Rejoice at the success of my endeavors,
Will she rejoice the less to see my tears?
What use for Greece to admire me, when I'll be
The fable of Epirus? But, to hide nothing,
My innocence begins to be a burden.
I know not what unrighteous power there is
Which, leaving crime in peace, dogs innocence.
And when I turn my eyes upon myself,
I everywhere behold misfortunes only
To which the gods have doomed me. Let me deserve
Their wrath, and justify their hate, enjoy
The fruits of crime before its punishment.
Why do you wish upon yourself to turn
The wrath that's meant for me? Too long indeed
My friendship has afflicted you. Avoid
A wretched man, flee from my guilt. Dear Pylades,
You are seduced by pity. Leave me in perils
The fruits of which I wait. Bear to the Greeks
This child that Pyrrhus has abandoned to me.
Go.

Pylades. Come, my lord, let us seize Hermione
And sail away with her. In the midst of perils
Courage rejoices. What cannot friendship do
When led by love? Encourage now the spirits
Of all your Greeks. Our ships are ready to sail.
The wind is favorable. I know the palace
With all its hidden ways. You see the waves
Beat on the walls; and without difficulty
Tonight by a secret passage we'll conduct
Your prey to your vessel.
    Orestes.   I abuse, dear friend,
Your too great friendship. But by the ills
Which you alone have pitied, forgive me now.
Excuse a wretch who loses all he loves,
Hated by all, and even by himself.
Perhaps, one day, in happier . . .
    Pylades.   Dissimulate, my lord.
That's all I wish. Take care not to reveal
Your scheme before you act. Forget your love.
Forget Hermione's ingratitude.
She's coming now. I see her.
    Orestes.   Answer for her.
I'll answer for myself.   [*Exit* PYLADES.

Enter HERMIONE *and* CLEONE.   (III.2)

    Orestes.   I have succeeded
In rendering you your conquest. I have seen
Pyrrhus, madam, and the preparations
For your marriage are in hand.
    Hermione.   So it is said.
And I have further been informed, you seek me
To make me ready for it.
    Orestes.   And will you not
Rebel against these bonds?
    Hermione.   Who would have thought
That Pyrrhus was not faithless? That his passion
Would be so tardy? That he would return
To me, when I was leaving him? I suppose
With you that he's afraid of Greece—he follows
His interest, not his love—that my eyes wielded
Over your soul more absolute power.

Orestes.   No, madam.
I do not doubt he loves you. Cannot your eyes
Do all they wish to do? And you, no doubt,
Had no wish to displease him.
   Hermione.   But, my lord,
What can I do? My faith is promised him.
Shall I snatch from him a gift I never gave?
Love does not rule the fate of a princess.
The glory of obedience is all
They leave to us. Yet I was about to go;
You could have seen how I relaxed my duty
Only for you.
   Orestes.   How well you know. . . . But, madam,
Each one can, at his choice, dispose his soul.
Yours was your own to give. I therefore hoped:
But you could not have given it, unless
I had committed theft. I accuse you less
Than fortune. But why should I weary you
With my complainings? Such is your duty, madam:
That I confess, and mine is but to spare you
An unhappy interview.   [*Exit* ORESTES.

(III.3)

   Hermione.   Did you expect
So mild an anger, Cleone?
   Cleone.   A speechless grief
Is but more fatal: and I pity him more
That he's the author of his grief—the blow
Which has destroyed him came from him alone.
Reckon how long your marriage was arranged.
He spoke, madam, and Pyrrhus at once decides.
   Hermione. Think you that Pyrrhus feared? That he fears
    still?
People who fled for ten years before Hector,
Who, oft affrighted in Achilles' absence,
Sought for asylum in their burning ships;
And who'd be seen, without his son's support,
Still asking Helen from the unpunished Trojans?
No, Cleone, he is not his own foe.
He wills his deeds; and if he marries me,
He loves me. Let Orestes, if he likes,

Impute to me his griefs: what have we had
Except his tears in all our intercourse?
Pyrrhus returns to us! Well, dear Cleone,
Do you conceive Hermione's joy? Do you know
What Pyrrhus is? Have you yet reckoned up
The number of his deeds? But who can count them?
Intrepid, he is followed everywhere
By victory, charming, and now faithful. Nothing
Is lacking in his glory. Think . . .

    Cleone.   Dissimulate.
Your weeping rival brings her sorrows to you. . . .

    Hermione. O Gods! Can I not give up my soul to joy?
Let us go. What would I say to her?

Enter ANDROMACHE *and* CEPHISE.   (III.4)

    Andromache.   Whither
Do you fly, madam? Is not the spectacle
Of Hector's widow weeping at your feet
Sweet enough to your eyes? I've not come here,
With jealous tears, to envy you a heart
Which has surrendered to your charms. I've seen
The only one on whom I looked with love
Pierced by a cruel hand. My flame once kindled
By Hector is shut within his tomb. A son
Is all that I have left. You'll know some day
How much we can love a son. But you'll not know
(At least I hope not) in what mortal pain
Our love can throw us, when of many comforts
He only is left, and they wish to take him from us.
Alas! when tired of ten years' misery
The wrathful Trojans threatened your mother, Helen,
I would persuade my Hector to support her:
You can move Pyrrhus, as I once could him.
Why do they fear a child who has survived
The loss of all he had? Let me conceal him
On a desert island. I'll look after him,
And he will only learn to weep with me.

    Hermione. I appreciate your griefs; but a strict duty,
When my father has spoken, bids me hold my peace.
He has aroused the wrath of Pyrrhus. Who
Better than you, can persuade Pyrrhus? Your eyes

Have for a long time ruled his soul. So now
Get his consent. I will subscribe to it, madam.
                    [*Exeunt* HERMIONE *and* CLEONE.

                                                (III.5)

   Andromache. How scornfully the cruel one refused me.
   Cephise. I know her counsels and will go to Pyrrhus.
One look will yet confound Hermione
And Greece. But here he comes to seek for you.

              Enter PYRRHUS *and* PHOENIX.   (III.6)

   Pyrrhus [*to* PHOENIX]. Where, then, is the Princess? Did
      you not tell me
That she was here?
   Phoenix.   I thought so.
   Andromache [*to* CEPHISE].   Now you see
The power of my eyes!
   Pyrrhus.   What does she say,
Phoenix?
   Andromache. Alas! now all is failing me!
   Phoenix. Come, my lord, let's follow Hermione.
   Cephise. Why do you wait? Break now your obstinate
      silence.
   Andromache. He's promised my son.
   Cephise.   He has not given him up.
   Andromache. No, no, my tears are vain. His death's
      resolved.
   Pyrrhus. Will she not even look on us? What pride!
   Andromache. I shall but irritate him more. Let's go.
   Pyrrhus. Deliver the son of Hector to the Greeks!
   Andromache [*throwing herself at his feet*]. Ah, my lord!
      Stay! What do you mean to do?
If you give up the son, give up the mother!
Your recent vows have sworn me so much friendship!
Could I not touch your pity now at least?
Have you condemned me without hope of pardon?
   Pyrrhus. Phoenix will tell you. My word is given.
   Andromache.   You,
Who risked for me so many diverse perils!
   Pyrrhus. I was blind then. My eyes are opened now.

I could have been compliant to your wishes.
You would not even ask. Now it's too late.

   Andromache. Ah! my lord! You might have understood
My sighs which feared to be repulsed. Forgive
My once illustrious fortune this residue
Of pride which fears to be importunate.
You know too well that Andromache, but for you
Would never have clasped a master's knees.

   Pyrrhus.   No, no,
You hate me, and at the bottom of your heart
You fear to owe the least thing to my love.
Even your son, the object of your cares,
If I had saved him, you'd have loved him less.
Hatred and scorn against me are arrayed.
You hate me more than all the Greeks together.
Enjoy your noble anger at your leisure.
Come, Phoenix.

   Andromache. Let us rejoin my husband.
   Cephise.   Madam . . .
   Andromache [*to* Cephise]. What more should I say to
     him? He is the author
Of all my woes—do you think he does not know them?

                           [*To* Pyrrhus.
My lord, you see to what you have reduced me.
I've seen my father dead, our walls destroyed;
I've seen the days of all my family
Cut short, my bleeding husband dragged through the dust,
His son, alone with me, reserved for chains.
But what can't a son do? I breathe, I serve.
I have done more; I am sometimes consoled
That fate has exiled me here, not elsewhere;
That, happy in his misfortune, this son of kings,
Since he must serve, was fallen beneath your laws.
I've thought his prison would become a refuge.
Priam when he submitted was respected
' By great Achilles. And from his son I hoped
Still greater bounty. Forgive me now, dear Hector,
For my credulity! I could not have suspected
Your enemy of a crime. In spite of himself
I have believed him still magnanimous.
Ah! were he generous enough to leave us

The tomb that holds your ashes, and that there
Ending his hatred and our miseries,
He would not separate our precious dust!
    Pyrrhus. Await me, Phoenix.   [*Exit* PHOENIX.

(III.7)

    Pyrrhus.   Madam, remain. The son
You mourn can be restored to you. I feel
With some regret that causing you to weep
I've only given you arms to use against me.
I thought that I should bring more hatred here.
But, madam, at least, towards me turn your eyes:
See if my looks are those of a stern judge,
If of an enemy, who seeks to hurt you.
Why do you force me to betray you thus?
Now in your son's name let us cease our hatred.
Save him at last— It is I who beg you now.
Must my sighs beg his life of you? Must I
Embrace your knees for him? For the last time,
Save him, and save ourselves. I know what oaths
I break for you; what hates will burst on me.
I will send back Hermione, and set
Upon her brow, instead of a royal crown
An everlasting insult. I will lead you
To the temple where her marriage is prepared:
And deck you with her crown. It is no more
An offer to be scorned. I tell you plainly
You must either die or reign. My heart is desperate
With a year's ingratitude and can no longer
Suffer my fate's uncertainty. It is to fear,
To threaten, and to groan too long. I die
If I lose you; but if I wait, I die. Think on it.
I leave you; and I will come to lead you soon
To the temple where I'll have your son await me,
And there you'll see me, obedient or enraged,
Crown you, madam, or kill him in your sight.
                              [*Exit* PYRRHUS.

(III.8)

    Cephise. As I foretold, and in despite of Greece,
You'll yet be mistress of your fate.

Andromache.   Alas!
Where do your speeches tend? There but remains
For me to condemn my son.
    Cephise.   That is to be
Too faithful to your husband. Too much of virtue
Could make you criminal; and he himself
Would bring your soul to mildness.
    Andromache.   What! I would give him
Pyrrhus as his successor?
    Cephise.   Yes, for your son's sake,
Whom the Greeks snatch from you. Do you imagine
His ghost would blush at it? That he would scorn
A royal victor who would put you back
In the rank of your ancestors, who tramples for you
Upon your wrathful conquerors, who remembers
No longer that Achilles was his father,
Disowning his deeds and rendering them superfluous?
    Andromache. Should I forget, though he remembers not?
Should I forget that Hector was denied
His funeral rites, and dragged around our walls?
Should I forget his father lying dead,
Bleeding upon the altar which he clasped?
Think, Cephise, of that cruel night which proved
For our whole nation an eternal night.
Then picture Pyrrhus, with his flashing eyes,
Using for light our burning palaces,
Making a passage o'er my slaughtered brothers,
And, covered all with blood, arousing carnage.
Think of the victors' shouts; think of the cries
Of dying men, fallen beneath the sword,
Or choked by the flames. Think of Andromache
Dismayed amidst those horrors. That was how Pyrrhus
Appeared to me; those are the glorious deeds
For which he once was crowned; this is the husband
You wish to give me. No, I will never be
Accomplice in his crimes; but let him seize us
For his last victims, if he wills it so.
All my resentments will submit to him.
    Cephise. Let us go then to watch your son expire.
They wait for you alone. You tremble, madam.

Andromache. With what remembrance do you strike my
    soul,
Cephise! Shall I go to watch him die,
My son, my only joy, and Hector's image?
The son he left me as his pledge of love?
Alas! I remember now, the day his courage
Made him Achilles seek, or rather death,
He asked for his son and took him in his arms.
"Dear wife," said he, in wiping off my tears,
"I know not what result fate holds in store
For these my arms. I leave my son to you
As pledge of my true love. If he should lose me,
In you, I know, he'll find me once again.
And if the memory of a happy marriage
Is dear to you, then show the son how much
You would the father cherish." And can I see
A blood so precious shed? Can I allow
With him his ancestors to perish too?
Barbarous king, must he be doomed for me?
And if I hate you, is he guilty of it?
Has he reproached you for his kinsman's death?
Does he complain of ills he does not feel?
But yet, my son, you die, if I arrest not
The sword that is uplifted o'er your head.
I could avert it, and I'll let it fall?
No, son, you shall not die. I can't endure it.
Let us find Pyrrhus. But no, dear Cephise, go
And find him for me.
    Cephise.   What should I say to him?
    Andromache. Tell him my love for my son is strong
        enough. . . .
Think you that in his heart he's sworn his death?
Can love drive men to such barbarity?
    Cephise. Madam, he will return in fury soon.
    Andromache. Go and assure him.
    Cephise.   Of what? Of your consent?
    Andromache. Alas! and is the promise mine to give?
O ashes of a husband! Trojans! Father!
O son! How costly are your days to me!
Let's go.

Cephise. Where, madam? What have you resolved?

Andromache. Let's go to consult my husband on his
tomb.

ACT FOUR

ANDROMACHE *and* CEPHISE.

CEPHISE. I do not doubt it, madam; it is your husband,
'Tis Hector who has worked this miracle
Within your soul! He wants Troy to arise
With this happy son he's made you to preserve.
Pyrrhus has vowed it: you have heard him, madam.
He waited but a word to give him up.
Trust to his joyful raptures: father, sceptre,
Allies, he puts them at your feet, contented
But with your heart. Over himself and kingdom
He makes you sovereign. Is this conqueror
Worthy of so much hate? Already filled
With noble wrath against the Greeks, the care
Of your son is his concern as much as yours.
He anticipates their rage; leaves him his guard,
Not to expose him, hazards his own life.
But at the temple all now is prepared;
And you have promised. . . .

 Andromache.   Yes, I shall be there.
But let us see my son.

 Cephise.   What is the hurry?
His sight no longer is forbidden you.
Soon you can lavish all your bounties on him.
And your embraces will no more be numbered.
What joy to raise a child whom one sees grow,
No more a slave that's brought up for his master,
But to see in him so many kings reborn!

 Andromache. Cephise, let's see him now for the last
  time.

 Cephise. What do you say? O Gods!

 Andromache.   O dear Cephise,
My heart does not disguise itself with you—
Your loyalty has been too well displayed

In my misfortunes. But I thought indeed
You would have known me better. Have you supposed
That Andromache, unfaithful, could betray
A husband who thought he lived again in her?
And that, reviving the grief of many dead,
The care of my repose would trouble theirs?
Is that the love I promised to his ashes?
But his son would die, and he must be protected.
In wedding me, Pyrrhus declares himself
The boy's defender. That's enough. I trust him.
I know what Pyrrhus is: violent indeed,
But yet sincere, Cephise, and he will do
More than he promises. I rely too
Upon the anger of the Greeks: their hatred
Will give a father to the son of Hector.
Therefore, since I must sacrifice myself,
I'll pledge to Pyrrhus my remains of life;
I go, accepting his faith upon the altars,
To bind him to my son eternally.
But then my hand, fatal to me alone,
Will cut the remainder of a faithless life.
Saving my virtue, I'll render what I owe
To Pyrrhus, to Hector, to my son, and me.
That is my innocent stratagem of love:
My husband has ordained it. I'll go alone
To rejoin Hector and my ancestors.
Cephise, it is for you to close my eyes.

    Cephise. Ah! do not think I can survive . . .
    Andromache.   No, no,
You must not follow me. I confide to you
My only treasure. If you lived for me,
Live now for Hector's son. The sole depositary
Of the hope of the Trojans, think you have become
Needful to many kings. Watch beside Pyrrhus.
Make him keep faith. If it is necessary
You may speak of me to him, and make him value
This marriage to which I now submit myself;
Say that before my death I was pledged to him,
That his resentments ought to be effaced;
In leaving my son to him, I value him
At his true worth. Let my son hear of all

The heroes of his race; and, if you can,
Guide him to follow them. Tell him the deeds
For which their names are famous—what they did
Rather than what they were. Speak every day
Of his father's virtues, and sometimes speak of me.
But let him no more think of avenging us:
We leave a master to him he should respect.
Let him, with modesty, recall his forbears.
He is of Hector's blood, all that remains,
And for that in a day I've sacrificed
My blood, my hatred, and my love.

    Cephise.   Alas!

    Andromache. If your heart, fearful of what must be,
Foresees that it could not restrain its tears,
Follow me not. Someone is coming. Hide
Your tears, Cephise; and remember that the fate
Of Andromache is confided to your care.
It is Hermione. Come. Flee her violence.

                  [*Exeunt* ANDROMACHE *and* CEPHISE.

        Enter HERMIONE *and* CLEONE.   (IV.2)

    Cleone. I wonder at your silence. You say nothing.
This cruel scorn of his has not disturbed
Your spirits at all: and you sustain in peace
So rough an onslaught—you, who used to tremble
To hear the very name Andromache!
You who, without despair, could not endure
That Pyrrhus with one glance should honor her!
And now he marries her. He gives to her
Both crown and faith that you had just received:
And yet your mouth, dumb underneath the blow,
Has not yet deigned to open to complain!
I fear such fatal calm. It would be better . . .

    Hermione. Have you sent for Orestes?

    Cleone.   He is coming, madam.
He is coming; and you can be assured that soon
He will be at your feet, ready to serve you
Without hope of reward. Your eyes are certain
To please him now as always. But he enters.

Enter ORESTES. (IV.3)

Orestes. Ah! madam! Is it true for once that I,
In seeking you, obey you? Am I not flattered
By a false hope? Have you indeed desired
My presence? Shall I believe your eyes, disarmed
At last, wish that . . .
    Hermione.   I want to know, my lord,
Whether you love me?
    Orestes.   Whether I love you! Gods!
My oaths, my perjuries, my flight from you
And my return, my injuries, my pleas,
My eyes that always drown with bitter tears,
And my despair; what witnesses will you credit,
If you won't credit them?
    Hermione.   If you avenge me,
I will believe them all.
    Orestes.   Then, madam, come.
Let us, once more, set all the Greeks ablaze;
In making my prowess and your name renowned,
You shall be Helen and I Agamemnon.
Let us revive the miseries of Troy
Here in Epirus. Let men speak of us
As of our fathers. Let us go. I'm ready.
    Hermione. No, my lord. Let us stay. I do not wish
To carry such affronts to these extremes!
Crowning the insolence of my enemies,
I should await a tardy vengeance on them!
I should resign myself to the chance of battle,
Which, in the end, perhaps, would not avenge me!
I wish, when I depart, that all Epirus
Should mourn. And therefore if you would avenge me
Avenge me in an hour. All your delays
Count as refusals to me. Run to the temple.
He must be slain.
    Orestes.   Who?
    Hermione.   Pyrrhus.
    Orestes.   Pyrrhus, madam!
    Hermione. What! does your hatred waver? Run and fear
Lest I should call you back. Do not allege

Rights that I would forget. 'Tis not for you
To justify him.
   Orestes.   I excuse him? Madam,
Your bounties have engraved his crimes too deeply
Upon my soul. Let us avenge ourselves—
I do consent to it—but by other ways.
Let's be his foes, but not his murderers;
Let's make a righteous conquest of his ruin.
For answer to the Greeks shall I bring home
The head of Pyrrhus? And have I assumed
The welfare of the State, only to quit me
By an assassination? In the name of the gods,
Allow Greece to decide, and let him die
Charged with the public hatred. Do not forget
He reigns, and that a king . . .
   Hermione.   Is it not enough
That I have condemned him; that my wounded honor
Demands a victim that is mine alone;
That Hermione's the prize for a dead tyrant;
That I hate him, my lord; and that I loved him?
I will hide nothing: the traitor knew the art
Of pleasing me; it does not matter now
Whether my love, or my father, ordered it.
But guide yourself by this. Despite my vows,
Deceived most shamefully, my lord, despite
The righteous horror that his crime arouses,
So long as he lives, fear lest I pardon him.
Until his death, distrust my uncertain anger!
I tell you if he does not die today,
I can love him tomorrow.
   Orestes.   So I must kill him,
And thus forestall his pardon. I must. . . . But yet
What must I do? How can I serve your anger
So soon? In what way can I strike him down?
I've only just arrived, you wish my hands
To overthrow an empire; you wish a king
To die; and for his punishment you give me
Only a day, an hour, only a moment!
In the sight of all his people I must slay him.
Let me conduct my victim to the altar.

I don't resist; I only wish to survey
The place where I should kill him. This night I'll serve you:
This night I will attack him.
    Hermione.   But yet this day
He weds Andromache. The throne is raised
Already in the temple; my shame's confirmed,
His crime completed. Why are you waiting then?
He offers you his head. Without his guards,
Without defense, he goes to the ceremony:
Around the son of Hector he has ranged them,
And to an avenging arm he is abandoned.
Will you, in spite of him, preserve his life?
Arm, with the Greeks, all those who follow me.
Raise up your friends. All mine are yours, my lord.
He betrays me, tricks you, and scorns us all.
Already, indeed, their hatred equals mine,
And spares a Trojan's husband with reluctance.
Speak. My foe cannot escape you; or rather
You need but let them strike. Lead them or follow
So fine a rage. Return to me at once
Steeped in his faithless blood; and in that state
You may be sure of my heart.
    Orestes.   But, madam, think . . .
    Hermione. This is too much, my lord. So many excuses
Excite my anger. I have wished to give you
A means of pleasing me, contenting you.
But now I see too well that you prefer
Still to complain, and nothing to deserve.
Go. Boast elsewhere of your constancy and leave me
The task of vengeance. With my cowardly kindness
My heart's confused; and I have met too many
Refusals in one day. I'm going alone
To the temple where you dare not go, to earn
My conquest. There I will approach my foe
And pierce the heart I could not touch with love.
And my red hands, then turned upon myself,
In spite of him will soon unite our fates;
And, ungrateful as he is, it will be sweeter
To me to die with him than live with you.
    Orestes. I will deprive you of that dismal pleasure.

He shall die only at Orestes' hands.
Your foes are going to be destroyed by me,
And you may thank me for my pains.
   Hermione.   Go then.
Leave me the conduct of your fate, my lord:
And let our ships be ready for our flight.   [*Exit* ORESTES.

(IV.4)

   Cleone. You are destroying yourself, and you should
      think . . .
   Hermione. Even if I'm destroyed, I mean to avenge me.
I do not know, whatever he has promised,
Whether I should have left the task to others
Or taken it on myself. In his eyes, Pyrrhus
Is not so guilty as in mine, and I
Would strike more surely. What pleasure to avenge
My injury for myself, pull back my arm
Red with the perjurer's blood; and to make both
His punishment and my own pleasure greater
To hide my rival from his dying eyes!
Ah! if Orestes, in punishing his crime,
At least makes clear to him he dies my victim!
Go and find him. Tell him to make the traitor
Know that he's sacrificed unto my hatred,
Not to the State. Cleone, run. My vengeance
Is lost if he is ignorant as he dies
That it is I who killed him.
   Cleone.   I will obey
But what do I see? O Gods! Who would have thought it?
It is the King.
   Hermione.   Run after Orestes. Tell him,
Cleone, not to undertake the deed
Without first seeing me again.   [*Exit* CLEONE.

Enter PYRRHUS *and* PHOENIX.   (IV.5)

   Pyrrhus.   Madam,
You weren't expecting me, and it is plain
That my arrival interrupts your talk.
I do not come, armed with unworthy cunning,
To veil injustice with a show of law.
Let it suffice now that my guilty heart

Condemns me secretly; and I'd ill maintain
What I do not believe. I wed a Trojan.
Yes, madam; and I confess I vowed to you
The faith I vow to her. Another man
Might say that on the Trojan fields our fathers
Fashioned these bonds without us; and that we,
Regardless of our wishes, without love,
Were plighted to each other. But enough
That I submitted. My heart was promised you
By my envoys; far from revoking them,
I wished to subscribe. I saw you arrive with them,
And though the brightness of another eye
Already had forestalled the power of yours,
I did not bar myself from this new love.
I wished to continue faithful to you; I received you
As queen; and till today I thought my vows
Would take the place of love. But love has conquered;
And by a fatal stroke, Andromache
Has snatched from me a heart which she detests.
Dragged by each other, we hasten to the altar
To swear, despite ourselves, eternal love.
After that, madam, rage against a traitor,
Who's one with sorrow, and yet desires to be it.
Far from constraining such a righteous anger,
It might relieve my heart as much as yours.
Call me the names reserved for perjurers:
I fear your silence, rather than your insults;
And, raising a host of secret witnesses,
My heart will reproach me more the less you say.
    Hermione. My lord, in this confession, stripped of art,
I'm glad to see at least that to yourself
You render justice, and that, in severing
A solemn tie, you give yourself indeed
A criminal to crime. Is it right, after all,
That a conqueror should stoop his neck beneath
The servile law of promise-keeping? No,
No, perfidy has something tempting to you;
And you have sought me but to boast of it.
No oath or duty restrains you. To seek a Greek,
And love a Trojan! To leave me, take me back,
And then return from Helen's daughter to

The widow of Hector! To crown in turn the princess
And then the slave, sacrifice Troy to the Greeks,
Then Greece to the son of Hector! All that comes
From a heart that's always master of itself,
From a hero who is not the slave of his word.
To please your wife perhaps you had to lavish
The charming names of perjurer and traitor.
You came to see the pallor of my brow,
To go, within her arms, to mock my grief.
You'd have them see me weep after her chariot,
But that, in one day, would be too much of joy;
And without searching far for borrowed titles,
Will those you have already not suffice you?
The beaten valor of Hector's father, Priam,
At the feet of his family, dying in your sight,
While buried in his breast your sword is seeking
For his remaining blood that age has frozen;
Troy, burning Troy, immersed in streams of blood;
Polyxena, in the sight of all the Greeks,
Slain by your hand. O what can be refused
To strokes so generous!
    Pyrrhus.   Madam, I know too well
To what excess of rage I was transported,
Avenging Helen. I can complain to you
Of all the blood I've shed. But now at last
I can forget. I render thanks to heaven
That your indifference has taught me now
The innocence of my happy sighs. My heart,
Too prompt to worry, ought to have known you better,
And analyzed itself. For my remorse
Does you a mortal injury. One must think
Oneself beloved, to think that one is faithless.
You don't aspire to keep me in your chains.
I feared to betray you, but perhaps I serve you.
Our hearts were not dependent on each other;
I followed duty and you acquiesced;
You were not pledged to give your love indeed.
    Hermione. I have not loved you? What then have I
        done?
I have disdained for you our princes' vows,

Myself sought for you in your own domains;
I am still here despite your faithlessness,
Despite my Greeks, ashamed of my kindness to you.
I ordered them to hide my injury:
I waited for a perjurer's return;
I thought that, soon or late, restored to duty
You'd bring me back a heart that was my due.
I loved you faithless: what would I have done
Had you been faithful? And even at this moment,
When your cruel lips come calmly to announce
My death, ungrateful man, I'm still in doubt
Whether I do not love you. But, my lord,
If this must be, and if the heavens reserve
To other eyes the fame of pleasing you,
Conclude this marriage. I consent to it.
But do not force my eyes to witness it.
For the last time I speak to you, perhaps.
Postpone it for a day. You will be master
Tomorrow. . . . You do not answer? Traitor, I understand.
You count the moments that you lose with me.
Your heart, impatient to behold again
Your Trojan, but reluctantly endures
To hold speech with another. In your heart
You commune with her, seek her with your eyes.
I won't detain you longer. Leave this place.
Go swear the faith that you have sworn to me;
Profane the sacred majesty of the gods;
Those gods, those righteous gods, will not forget
That the same oaths have bound you unto me.
Take to the altar that heart which casts me off;
Go, run; but fear to find Hermione there.

[*Exit* HERMIONE.

(IV.6)

Phoenix. You hear, my lord; beware of taking lightly
A furious lover seeking her revenge.
Here in Epirus she has strong support:
The quarrel of the Greeks is tied to hers.
Orestes loves her still; and at that price . . .
    Pyrrhus. Andromache awaits me. Guard her son.

ACT FIVE

HERMIONE *alone.*

HERMIONE. Where am I? What have I done? What should
   I do?
What transport seizes me? What grief devours me?
Wandering aimless, I've run into the palace.
Can I not know whether I love or hate him?
With what a cruel eye did he dismiss me—
With neither grief nor pity, even feigned.
Did I behold him troubled? Did he give me
One moment's pity? Could I draw one groan?
Deaf to my sighs, and calm amidst my fears,
Did he, indeed, take notice of my weeping?
And still I pity him! And to top all
My base heart pleads for him. I tremble now
Only to think of the blow which threatens him!
Ready for vengeance, I yet grant him pardon!
No! Let's not revoke the sentence of my wrath:
Let him perish! He lives no more for me!
The traitor triumphs, laughing at my anger;
He thinks to see this storm disperse in tears;
He thinks that, ever weak and wavering,
I'll parry with one arm the blows of the other.
He judges me by my past kindness still.
But no, the traitor now has other thoughts.
Triumphant in the temple, he does not care
Whether elsewhere his life or death's desired.
He leaves me, the traitor, this terrible dilemma.
No, let Orestes act; let Pyrrhus die,
Because he should have known what would ensue,
Because he's forced me in the end to wish it.
To wish it? What? Is it I who order it?
And will his death spring from Hermione's love?
This prince, whose deeds my heart took so much pleasure
To hear recounted; to whom, in secret even,
I once was destined before this fatal marriage
Had been arranged; I have not therefore crossed

So many seas, so many distant lands,
But to prepare his death? Assassinate him,
Destroy him? Ah! before he dies . . .

Enter CLEONE.   (V.2)

Hermione.   Cleone,
What have I done? What have you come to tell me?
And what is Pyrrhus doing?
       Cleone.   He's at the top
Of expectation; proudest of mortal men
And the most loving, I have seen him go
Towards the temple, leading triumphantly
His latest conquest, and with an eye that shines
With joy and hope, drunk as he goes with pleasure
At seeing her. Andromache proceeds
Through shouts of joy to the altars, and carries there
The memory of Troy; incapable
Of loving or of hating, without joy
And without murmuring, she seems to obey.
       Hermione. And the traitor? Has he to the bitter end
Carried the outrage? Did you scrutinize
His face, Cleone? Does he taste his pleasure
In calm perfection? Did he never turn
His eyes towards the palace? Tell me. Did he
Catch sight of you? And did he blush to see you?
Did his uneasiness avow his guilt?
Has he maintained his pride unto the end?
       Cleone. He nothing sees: his safety and his glory
Seem to have vanished from his memory
With you. Unconscious of those who follow him,
Subjects or enemies, he just pursues
His amorous projects. He has ranged his guard
Around the son of Hector, in the belief
That peril threatens him alone. Phoenix
Is answerable for him: he has with speed
Taken him to a fort, that's far removed
From both the temple and the palace. That,
Among his joys, remains his sole concern.
       Hermione. The traitor! He shall die. What of Orestes?
What did he say to you?

Cleone.   Orestes entered
The temple with his Greeks.
    Hermione.   Well! is he not
Prepared to avenge me?
    Cleone.   I do not know.
    Hermione. You do not know? What then? Orestes too,
Orestes betrays me?
    Cleone.   He adores you, madam.
But yet his mind, attacked by many scruples,
Sometimes believes his love, sometimes his virtue.
He respects in Pyrrhus the honor of his crown;
He respects Achilles in him, and respects
Pyrrhus himself; he fears the Greeks; he fears
The world in anger; but, above all, he says,
He fears himself. He would in triumph bring you
The head of Pyrrhus, but the name of murderer
Arrests his frightened hand. So he has entered,
Not knowing in his heart if he'll come forth
A criminal, or spectator.
    Hermione.   No, he'll see them
Triumph without a check. He will keep himself
From interfering with the spectacle.
I know with what remorse his heart's affected:
The coward is afraid of death—that's all
He fears. My mother, without a single prayer,
Armed Greece to fight for her; her eyes beheld
In ten long years of battles twenty kings
Perish, who did not know her; while I who wish
Only a perjurer's death, and charge a lover
To recompense my wrong, with me as prize,
Without a risk, I who surrender myself,
Cannot avenge me? Come! it is for me
Alone to render justice to myself.
Let cries of sorrow echo in the temple,
Prevent the sealing of their fatal marriage,
And let them be united, if at all,
Only a moment. In this confusion
I shall not pick and choose. All will be Pyrrhus
To me, even Orestes. I shall die,
But at least my death will avenge me. I shall not die

Alone—someone will follow me.

Enter ORESTES.   (V.3)

Orestes.   Madam,
The deed is done, and you are served;
Pyrrhus at the altar renders up his life.
    Hermione. He is dead!
    Oretes.   He is dying; and our angry Greeks
Have washed his infidelities with blood.
I promised this to you, and though my courage
Called up a deadly image of this plot,
I ran towards the temple where the Greeks
Had slipped among the crowd, close to the altar.
Pyrrhus caught sight of me, but did not blench;
It seemed to excite his boldness to behold me;
That all the Greeks, in their ambassador
Defied, would lend an added luster to his marriage.
So, with delight, he took his diadem
And placed it on Andromache. "I give you,"
He said, "My crown and faith. Andromache,
Reign over Epirus and over me. I swear
A father's friendship to your son. I attest the gods.
I swear it to his mother: his foes are mine;
I recognize him as the Trojan king."
These words, which drew the approval of the people,
Were greeted by our Greeks with cries of rage;
The faithless King was everywhere hemed in;
I could have found no room to strike at him;
Each vied for the glory of his overthrow;
I saw him struggling for a while, all bloody,
Trying to escape their blows; but in the end
He fell before the altar. I pushed my way
Through the frightened crowd, to get back to the palace
And take my princess to the port, where soon
Our friends will come, all covered with the blood
Which I have promised you.
    Hermione.   What have they done?
    Orestes. Forgive their impatience. They have, I see it
        well,
Betrayed your vengeance. You wished my hand to bear

The first blows, so that he would feel in dying
That he was dying because of you. But yet
It was my zeal which served them for example;
For you alone I brought them to the temple,
Madam; and you can justly claim a death
Their arms have merely executed.

Hermione.   Traitor,
Be silent, and impute to yourself alone
Your cowardly parricide. Go make the Greeks
Admire your fury. Go. I disavow it;
You horrify me. Savage, what have you done?
With what vile rage have you cut short the course
Of such a splendid life? How could you slay him
Without your very blood arising for him!
But speak: who made you his fate's arbiter?
Wherefore assassinate him? What had he done?
By what right? Who set you on?

Orestes.   O Gods!
What? did you not yourself, this very hour,
Here in this place, demand his death?

Hermione.   Must you
Believe a maddened lover? Should you not
Read my unspoken thought? Did you not see
That in my rage my heart denied my lips?
Need you agree to my wishes, and not ask me
A hundred times to repeat them? Before the deed
Come to consult me, return again, or rather
Shun my presence? Why not leave to me
The task of vengeance? Who brought you to this place
To which I fled your presence? This is the fruit
Of your detested love. You brought me, cruel man,
The ill which follows you. Your embassy,
Fatal to both, made him, to his misfortune,
Incline towards my rival. I would have seen him
Share all his cares with me. He would, perhaps,
Have loved me; or pretended to, at least.
Farewell. You can depart. I shall remain here.
I renounce Greece and Sparta and its rule,
And all my family: it's enough for me,
That it produced a monster such as you.

                    [*Exeunt* HERMIONE *and* CLEONE.

(V.4)

Orestes. What do I see? Is this Hermione?
And what have I just heard? For whom did flow
The blood which I have shed? If I'm to believe her,
I am a traitor and a murderer.
Did Pyrrhus die? And am I still Orestes?
O Gods! I stifle reason in my heart,
Which was a lantern to my feet; I slay
A king whom I revere; I violate,
In a single day, the rights of sovereigns,
Those of ambassadors, and those of man,
And those of the altars where I butchered him;
I become murderer and sacrilegious.
For whom? For an ingrate whom I promised it,
Who, if he had not died, would have refused
Ever to see me, whose rage I have espoused.
And when I have served her, she asks me to restore
His blood and life! She loves him! And I am
A raging monster! I see her separated
Forever from my sight! And fleeing from me
The ingrate leaves me for my salary
The odious names that I have earned to please her.

Enter PYLADES *and* SOLDIERS. (V.5)

Pylades. We must depart, my lord. Either leave this
    palace,
Or else resolve never to leave. Our Greeks
Defend the doorway only for a moment;
The assembled people fiercely hem us in.
All submit to Andromache: they treat her
As Queen, and us as foes. Andromache,
To Pyrrhus once rebellious, renders him
The duties of a faithful widow: orders
That he should be avenged—perhaps on us
Would avenge Troy and her first husband. Come!
Our Greeks will join us. While Hermione
Holds yet the people round her at a standstill,
Our road is clear, and we can leave in safety.
    Orestes. No, no, it is Hermione, my friends,
I wish to follow. I cannot any longer

Survive her sentence. Leave. I did the deed,
And I am going to expiate it.
    Pylades.   Hermione,
My lord? You must forget her. Must you still,
The instrument and object of her rage,
Seek now among the dead some fresh disaster?
And must you die because she now is dying?
    Orestes. Dying! O Gods! What do I hear?
    Pylades.   Do you not know?
Returning hither, we encountered her,
Running towards the temple, all distraught.
She found King Pyrrhus carried by his soldiers
Stirred by his blood to vengeance. At this sight,
Doubtless, her rage was stirred. But from the gateway
We saw her with a dagger in her hand
Bend over Pyrrhus, lift her eyes to heaven,
Then stab herself, and fall.
    Orestes.   Thanks to the gods!
For my calamity exceeds my hope.
Yes, heaven, I praise thee for thy perseverance.
By dint of unremitting punishment,
Thou hast brought me to the very height of sorrow.
Thy hate has taken pleasure to conceive
This misery of mine. I was born to serve
As example of thy wrath, a finished model
Of absolute misfortune. I die content,
My fate accomplished. Where are these two lovers?
To crown my joy, in their blood and in mine
I must be drowned. I wish to look on them
Even as I die. Let us reunite three hearts
Which could not be agreed. . . . But what thick night
Surrounds me suddenly? Whence does it come?
Why do I shiver? What horror seizes me?
Thanks to heaven, I glimpse . . . O Gods!
What streams of blood flow round me!
    Pylades.   Ah! my lord!
    Orestes. What! Pyrrhus, do I still encounter you?
Shall I find everywhere a hated rival?
Pierced with so many blows, how were you saved?
Hold, hold, there's the blow I kept for you!
But what do I behold? Hermione

Before my eyes embraces him. She comes
To snatch him from the threatening blow! O Gods!
What terrible looks she casts on me! What demons,
What hideous serpents follow in her train!
Daughters of hell, are your hands ready? For whom
Those serpents which are hissing on your heads?
For whom the dread array which follows you?
Ah! have you come to carry me away
Into eternal night? Come, to your furies
I now surrender me. But no, avaunt,
And leave Hermione: she better knows
The way to torture me, and I will bring her
My heart for her to devour.

Pylades.   He has lost his senses.
My friends, the time is short. Use well the moments
This fit provides us with. Come, let us save him.
Our efforts will be useless, if with his senses
His rage returns as well.

BRITANNICUS

FIRST PREFACE

Of all the works which I have given to the public there is none which has drawn upon me more plaudits or more censurers than this. Whatever care I have taken to fashion this tragedy, it seems that as much as I have striven to make it good, so much have certain people striven to decry it. There is no cabal they have not formed, no criticism they have not thought of. Some have even taken Nero's side against me: they have said that I have made him too cruel. As for me, I thought that the very name of Nero suggested something worse than cruel. But perhaps they refine on his history, and wish to say that he was a decent man in his early years: it is only necessary to read Tacitus to know that, although he was for some time a good emperor, he had always been a wicked man. My tragedy is not concerned with external matters: Nero is depicted here as a private individual and in his family; and they will please excuse me from recounting all the passages which could easily prove to them that I have no reparation to make.

Others, on the contrary, have said that I have made him too good. I confess that I have never formed the idea of a good man in the person of Nero: I have always regarded him as a monster. But he is here a budding monster. He has not yet set fire to Rome; he has not yet killed his mother, his wife, his tutors; except for that it seems to me that he lets slip enough cruelties to prevent anyone from misunderstanding him.

Some have taken the side of Narcissus and complained that I have made him a very wicked man and the confidant of Nero. One passage will suffice as a reply to them. "Nero," says Tacitus, "bore impatiently the death of Narcissus, because that freedman had a marvelous conformity with the vices of the prince, which were still hidden": *cujus abditis adhuc vitiis mire congruebat.*

Others were scandalized that I had chosen a man as young as Britannicus for the hero of a tragedy. I had quoted for them, in the preface to *Andromache*, Aristotle's opinion on the hero of a tragedy, that far from being perfect, he must always have some flaw. But I will tell them here that a young prince of seventeen years who has much courage, much love, much sincerity, and much credulity, ordinary qualities in a young man, seems to me very capable of exciting compassion. I do not ask for more.

"But," they say, "this prince was only entering into his fifteenth year when he died. You have made him live, he and Narcissus, two years longer than they did." I would not have mentioned this objection if it had not been raised with some heat by a man[1] who took the liberty of making an emperor reign for twenty years who only reigned for eight, although this change in chronology is a much more serious one since one reckons time by the years of the emperors.

Junia, too, did not lack critics. They say that of an old coquette, named Junia Silana, I have made a well-behaved maiden. What would they answer if I told them that this Junia is an invented character, like the Emilie of *Cinna*,[2] like the Sabine of *Horace*?[2] But I have to say to them that, if they were well read in history, they would have found a Junia Calvina, of the family of Augustus, sister of Silanus, to whom Claudius had promised Octavia. This Junia was young, beautiful, and according to Seneca, *festivissima omnium puellarum.* She loved her brother tenderly; and their enemies, says Tacitus, accused them both of incest, although they were guilty only of a slight indiscretion. If I present her as more discreet than she was, I have not heard that one is forbidden to rectify a character's manners, especially when he is unknown.

It is regarded as strange that she appears on the stage after the death of Britannicus.[3] Certainly the delicacy is

[1] A reference to Corneille who in *Heraclius* had made Phocas reign for twenty years.
[2] Plays by Corneille.
[3] In spite of this defense, Racine afterwards cut out Junia's reappearance on the stage.

great that wishes her not to say, in four touching lines,
that she is going to Octavia's house. "But," they say, "it is
not worth the trouble of making her return, another could
have reported her." They do not know that one of the rules
of the theatre is to put in the form of a report only things
that cannot be represented in action, and that all the ancients often made actors come on the stage, who have nothing else to say than that they have come from one place,
or that they are going to another.

"All this is useless," say my critics: "the play is finished
at the announcement of the death of Britannicus, and
one should not listen to the rest." Yet one does listen, and
even with as much attention as at the end of any tragedy.
As for me, I always understood that tragedy was the imita-
tion of a complete action in which several characters are
involved, and that this action was finished only when one
knows in what situation it leaves the same characters. It is
so that Sophocles uses it almost everywhere; it is so that
in the *Antigone* he employs almost as many lines to represent the madness of Haemon and the punishment of Creon
after the death of the Princess, as I have employed in the
imprecations of Agrippina, in the departure of Junia, in
the punishment of Narcissus, and in the despair of Nero,
after the death of Britannicus.

What would one have to do to content judges so difficult? The thing would be easy if only one were willing to
defy common sense. It is only necessary to avoid the natural to plunge into the extraordinary. In place of a simple
action, filled with little matter, such a one which ought to
be an action which takes a single day, and which, ad-
vancing by degrees towards the end, is maintained only by
the interests, the sentiments, and the passions of the characters, it would be necessary to fill this same action with a
quantity of incidents which could take place only in a
month, with a great number of theatrical tricks the more
surprising as they are less credible, with an infinity of
declamations in which one would make the actors say
quite the contrary of what they should say. It would be
necessary, for example, to represent some drunken hero,
who would have his mistress hate him out of gaiety of
heart, a Spartan braggart, a conqueror who would utter

nothing but maxims of love, a woman who would give lessons of pride to conquerors[4]: that is doubtless what would make all these gentlemen cry out with admiration. But what then would the small number of wise people say whom I endeavor to please? How should I dare to show myself to the eyes of the great men of antiquity whom I have chosen for models? For, to borrow the thought of an ancient, those are the veritable spectators whom we ought to propose for ourselves; and we should continually ask: What would Homer and Virgil say if they read these lines? What would Sophocles say if he witnessed this scene? However that may be, I have not sought to prevent them from speaking against my works; I should have sought in vain: *Quid de te alii loquantur ipsi videant,* said Cicero; *sed loquentur tamen.*

I merely beg the reader to pardon me this little preface, which I have written to justify my tragedy. There is nothing more natural than to defend oneself when one believes oneself to be unjustly attacked. I see that Terence himself seems to have written prologues only to justify himself against the criticisms of an old ill-intentioned poet, *malevoli veteris poetae,* who intrigued against him until the time when his comedies were performed.

> *Occepta est agi:*
> *Exclamat, etc.*

They could have made a difficulty for me which no one has done. But what has escaped the notice of the audience may be remarked by the readers. It is that I have made Junia become a Vestal Virgin, when, according to Aulus Gellius, no person was received who was less than six or more than ten. But the people here take Junia under their protection; and I thought that in consideration of her birth, her virtue, and her misfortune, they could dispense with the age prescribed by the laws, as they dispensed with the age for the consulship with so many great men who had deserved the privilege.

Lastly, I am very sure that many other criticisms could have been made with which I could have done nothing but profit from them in the future. But I greatly pity the mis-

[4] References to plays by Corneille.

fortune of a man who works for the public. Those who see our faults most clearly are those who dissimulate most willingly: they forgive us the parts they deplore, in favor of those which have given them pleasure. There is nothing, on the other hand, more unjust than an ignoramus: he always believes that admiration is the lot of people who know nothing; he condemns a whole play for a scene of which he disapproves; he attacks even the most brilliant passages, to show that he has wit; and if we make any resistance to his views, he treats us as presumptuous people who will not believe anyone, and does not dream that he sometimes exhibits more vanity than a very bad critic who thinks we have written a tolerable play.

Homine imperito nunquam quidquam injustius.[5]

SECOND PREFACE [6]

This of all my tragedies is the one on which I can say I have spent the greatest pains. Yet I confess that its success did not at first correspond with my hopes; scarcely had it appeared on the stage than it raised up a quantity of criticisms which seemed bound to destroy it. I myself supposed that its future fate would be less happy than that of my other tragedies. But in the end there happened to this play what always happens to works of some quality: the criticisms have vanished, the play remains. It is now the one of mine that the court and the public see again most willingly. And if I have made anything solid and praiseworthy most connoisseurs agree that it is this same *Britannicus.*

To tell the truth I had worked by models which had fully upheld me in the picture which I wished to make of

[5] Terence: "There is none so unjust as the ignoramus."
[6] This second preface, which first appeared in 1676, includes some of the substance of the first preface, but it omits the attack on Corneille and Racine's replies to the more ephemeral criticisms of the play.

the court of Agrippina and Nero. I had copied my characters from the greatest painter of antiquity, I mean Tacitus, and I was then so filled with the reading of that excellent historian that there is hardly a brilliant stroke in my tragedy of which he did not give me the idea. I had intended to put in this collection an extract from the finest places which I had tried to imitate; but I found that this extract would take almost as much space as the tragedy itself. So the reader will be pleased that I send him back to that author, who is in any case on everybody's shelves; and I will content myself to mention here some of his passages on each of the characters which I have brought on the stage.

To begin with Nero, it is necessary to remember that he is here in the first years of his reign, which were happy, as is known. So I was not allowed to represent him as wicked as he afterwards became. I do not of course represent him as a virtuous man, for he was never that. He had not yet killed his mother, his wife, his tutors, but he has in him the seeds of all those crimes; he is beginning to wish to shake off the yoke: he hates everybody; he hides from them his hatred under false caresses, *factus natura velare odium fallacibus blanditiis.* In a word, he is here a budding monster, but one who does not dare yet to declare himself, and who seeks to color his wicked actions: *Hactanus Nero flagitiis et sceleribus velamenta quaesivit.* He could not suffer Octavia, a princess of an exemplary virtue and goodness, *fato quodam, an quia praevalent illicita; metuebaturque ne in stupra feminarum illustrium prorumperet.*

I give him Narcissus for confidant. I have followed Tacitus in this, who says that Nero bore impatiently the death of Narcissus because that freedman had a marvelous conformity with the yet concealed vices of the prince: *Cujus abditiis adhuc vitiis mire congruebat.* This passage proves two things: It proves both that Nero was already vicious, but that he dissimulated his vices, and that Narcissus encouraged him in his evil inclinations.

I have chosen Burrhus to oppose an honest man to that plague of the court; and I have chosen him rather than Seneca. This is the reason for it: they were both the tutors

of Nero's youth, one for arms, and the other for letters;
and they were famous, Burrhus for his experience in war
and for the severity of his manners, *militaribus curis et
severitate morum,* Seneca for his eloquence and his agreeable turn of mind, *Seneca praeceptis eloquentiae et con-
flate honesta.* Burrhus, after his death, was extremely
regretted on account of his virtue: *Civitati grande deside-
rium ejus mansit per memoriam virtutis.*

All their care was to resist the pride and ferocity of
Agrippina, *quae cunctis malae dominationis cupidinibus
flagrans, habebat in partibus Pallantem.* This is all I am
saying about Agrippina, for there would be too many
things to say of her. It is her above all that I am forced
to make the most of, and my tragedy is not less the disgrace
of Agrippina than the death of Britannicus. That death was
a thunderbolt for her; and it appeared, says Tacitus, by her
terror and consternation that she was as innocent of this
death as Octavia. Agrippina lost in him her last hope, and
the crime made her fear a greater: *Sibi supremum auxilium
ereptum, et parricidii exemplum intelligebat.*

The age of Britannicus was so well known that I could
not otherwise represent him than as a young prince who
had much courage, much love, and much sincerity, ordinary qualities of a young man. He was fifteen years of age,
and it is said that he was very intelligent, whether truly,
or because his misfortunes had made people believe that
of him, without his being able to show signs of it: *Neque
segnem ei fuisse indolem ferunt; sive verum, seu periculis
commendatus, retinuit famam sine experimento.*

There is no need to be surprised that he had near him
only as wicked a man as Narcissus; since for a long time
orders had been given that the people around him should
have neither faith nor honor: *Nam, ut proximus quisque
Britannico, neque fas neque fidem, pensi haberet, olim
provisum erat.*

There remains to speak of Junia. She should not be confused with an old coquette who was called Junia Silana.
This is another Junia, whom Tacitus calls Junia Calvina, of
the family of Augustus, sister of Silanus, to whom Claudius
had promised Octavia. This Junia was young, beautiful,
and as Seneca says, *festivissima omnium puellarum.* She

and her brother loved each other tenderly; and their enemies, says Tacitus, accused them of incest, although they were guilty merely of no more than a slight indiscretion. She lived until the reign of Vespasian.

I make her become a Vestal Virgin, although, according to Aulus Gellius, they never received anyone less than six years of age or more than ten. But the people here take Junia under their protection; and I thought that in consideration of her birth, her virtue, and her misfortune, they could dispense with the age prescribed by the laws, as they dispensed with the age for the consulship with so many great men who had deserved the privilege.

DRAMATIS PERSONÆ

NERO, *Emperor, son of Agrippina*
BRITANNICUS, *son of the Emperor Claudius and Messalina*
AGRIPPINA, *widow of Domitius Ænobarbus, father of Nero,*
    and by her second marriage of the Emperor Claudius
JUNIA, *lover of Britannicus*
BURRHUS, *Nero's tutor*
NARCISSUS, *Britannicus' tutor*
ALBINE, *confidante of Agrippina*
GUARDS

SCENE—ROME, in a room in Nero's palace

BRITANNICUS

ACT ONE

AGRIPPINA *and* ALBINE.

ALBINE. Must you while Nero is given up to sleep
Come and wait for his awakening?
Must Caesar's mother, wandering in the palace
With no guards or attendants, thus keep watch
Alone before his door? Return, madam,
To your apartments.

    Agrippina.   I must not leave yet.
I wish to await him here: all the vexations
He causes me will accupy my time
While he reposes. All that I foretold
Is but too certain. Nero has come out
Against Britannicus. Impatient Nero
Constrains himself no longer; he is tired
Of making people love him, and he wishes
To make them fear him. Now Britannicus
Grates on his nerves, Albine; and every day
I feel that in my turn I am becoming
Importunate.

    Albine.   What? You to whom he owes
The day he breathes, who called him from so far
To rule the Empire; you who, disinheriting
The son of Claudius, have named as Caesar
The fortunate Domitius. Everything
Speaks to him on Agrippina's behalf:
He owes you love.

    Agrippina.   He owes it me, Albine.
All, if he's generous, prescribes that rule;
But all, if he's ungrateful, speaks against me.

    Albine. If he's ungrateful, madam? All his conduct
Shows him well versed in duty. For three whole years
What has he said or done that does not promise
To Rome a perfect emperor? Rome, for three years

Ruled carefully by him, believes herself
Back in the Consuls' time. He governs her
Even as a father; and Nero in his youth
Has all the virtues that Augustus had
In his old age.

   Agrippina.   No, no, my interest
Renders me not unjust: and it is true
That he begins where great Augustus ended;
But yet beware lest, what's to come destroying
What has been, he should end as Augustus started.
He masks himself in vain. Upon his face
I read the sad, wild humor of Domitius.
He mingles with the pride that he received
Through his father's blood, the arrogance of Neros
Drawn from my side. It is said that tyranny
Has ever-pleasant first fruits. For a time
Gaius was Rome's delight; but, his false kindness
Turning to fury, the delight of Rome
Became its horror. What does it, after all,
Matter to me that Nero is more faithful
And leaves an example of continued virtue
For future times? Have I put into his hands
The tiller of the State to lead him on
To the gratitude of the people and the Senate?
Ah! let him be the father of his country
If he remembers too a little more
That Agrippina is his mother. Yet
By what name can we call the violent outrage
This day has just revealed to us. He knows
(For now their love can scarcely be ignored)
That Junia by Britannicus is worshipped,
And this same Nero, who is led by virtue,
Has Junia seized in the middle of the night.
What does he wish? Is it hate, or is it love
Inspires him? Does he only seek the pleasure
Of blackening them: or rather is it merely
That his malignity on them would punish
The support I've lent them?

   Albine.   You, their support, madam?

   Agrippina. Stop, dear Albine. I know that I alone

Furthered their ruin; and that from the throne
To which his blood entitled him to mount
Britannicus by me was thrown; by me
Alone, the brother of Junia, when prevented
From wedding Octavia, resigned his life—
Silanus, on whom Claudius had cast
A favorable eye, who had Augustus
Among his ancestors. Nero took all:
And I to compensate must hold the balance
Between them: that Britannicus one day
By the same law may hold the balance even
Between my son and me.

Albine.   What a plan!

Agrippina. I thus assure myself a port in the tempest,
For Nero will escape me, unless this bridle
Prevents him.

Albine.   But to take against a son
Such needless precautions . . .

Agrippina.   I would fear him sooner
If he no more feared me.

Albine.   Perhaps your fears
May be unfounded. But if he is no more
What he should be for you, at least the change
Is not to us apparent, and these are secrets
Confined to you and Caesar. Whatever titles
Rome may bestow on him, Nero receives
None he gives not to you. His prodigal love
Keeps nothing for himself. Your name in Rome
Is holy as his own. The sad Octavia
Is scarcely mentioned. Your ancestor, Augustus,
Gave Livia less honor. Nero allowed you
To be the first one to have borne before her
The fasces crowned with laurel. What more fruits
Do you wish from his gratitude?

Agrippina.   A little less
Of his respect, and more of trust. His presents
Albine, arouse my wrath. I see my honors
Grow, and my credit fall. No, no, the time
Is now no more, when Nero, youthful still,
Passed on to me the offerings of a court

Which then adored him; when he and all the State
Reposed on me; when it was my command
Summoned the Senate to the palace; and,
Behind a veil, invisible and present,
I was the omnipotent soul of that great body.
Nero then ill-assured of Rome's desires
Was not yet drunk with grandeur. But that day,
That fatal day, still strikes my memory
When Nero was bedazzled by his glory,
When the ambassadors of so many kings
Came from the ends of the earth to offer homage.
I went to take my place upon the throne
Beside him; I do not know if my disgrace
Was prearranged. But Nero, it was clear,
Seeing me from afar, allowed his rancor
To gleam upon his face. My very heart
Felt it an evil augury. The ingrate,
Coloring his insult with a false respect,
Rose in advance; and, running to embrace me,
He kept me from the throne I was about
To occupy. And since that fatal blow
The power of Agrippina day by day
Has moved with rapid strides towards its fall.
I am left with but its shadow: they beseech only
The name of Seneca and the aid of Burrhus.

   Albine. Ah! if your soul is warned by this suspicion
Why nourish in your breast the fatal venom?
Go and discover how you stand with Caesar.

   Agrippina. Caesar no longer sees me without witness,
Albine. In public, at my appointed hour,
I am given audience. His reply's dictated
And even his silence. I behold one of two
Overseers, his masters and mine, preside
At all our conversations. But I'll pursue him
As much as he avoids me. I must profit,
Albine, from his confusion. I hear a noise.
The door is opening. Let us go forthwith
And ask the reason of this kidnapping.
Let us surprise, if it is possible,
The secrets of his soul. But stay! Already
Burrhus comes forth from him.

Enter BURRHUS.   (I.2)

Burrhus.   In the Emperor's name,
Madam, I come to inform you of an order
Which might first have alarmed you; but which is
The effect of a wise decision Caesar wishes
You should be informed of.

Agrippina.   Since he wishes it,
Let us go in. He will inform me better.

Burrhus. Caesar for some time is withdrawn from us.
Already by a door less known to the public
Both consuls have forestalled you; but allow me,
Madam, to return expressly . . .

Agrippina.   No, I don't disturb
His august secrets. Yet, do you not wish
That we with less constraint should talk together
For once without deception?

Burrhus.   Burrhus ever
Detested falsehood.

Agrippina.   How long do you mean to hide
The Emperor from me? Shall I see him only
In the guise of a suitor? Have I raised so high
Your fortune to erect a barrier
Between my son and me? Do you not dare
To trust him for a moment? Do you dispute
With Seneca the glory who shall soonest
Make him forget me? Have I entrusted him
To you to teach him but ingratitude,
That you should be the masters of the State
Beneath his name? The more I think of it,
The less I imagine you would dare to count me
Your creature—you whose ambition I could have left
To age in the humble honors of some legion;
And I, who on the royal throne have followed
My ancestors, I, daughter, wife, sister,
And mother of your masters! What therefore
Do you intend? Do you suppose my voice
Has made an emperor to saddle me
With three of them? Nero is no more a child:
Is it not time for him to reign? How long
Would you have the Emperor fear you? Must he see

Nothing except with eyes borrowed from you?
Has he not ancestors to guide his conduct?
Let him choose then from Augustus or Tiberius,
Or try to copy Germanicus, my father.
I dare not put myself among these heroes:
But there are virtues I can trace for him:
At least I can instruct him how his trust
Between a subject and himself should keep
Some distance.

   Burrhus.   I was but charged on this occasion
To excuse Caesar for a single action;
But, without wishing to justify him, since
You make me answerable for his life,
I will answer, madam, with a soldier's freedom
Who little knows how to dress up the truth.
You have entrusted me with Caesar's youth—
That I confess: and I ought continally
To remember it. But have I sworn to you
To betray him, to make of him an emperor
Who knows but to obey? No. It is no longer
To you that I should answer. He is no more
Your son, he is the master of the world.
I owe a reckoning to the Roman Empire,
Which thinks it sees his safety or his ruin
Within my hands. Ah! if he should have been
Tutored in ignorance, were there only I
And Seneca to seduce him? Why banish
Flatterers from his side? What need to seek
In exile for corrupters? The court of Claudius—
Fertile in slaves, for every two one looked for
A thousand would have eagerly come forward
To seek the honor of debauching him—
In a long childhood made him to grow old.
Of what do you complain? You are revered:
As well as by Caesar, people swear by his mother.
The Emperor, it is true, no longer comes
Each day to place the Empire at your feet
And to enlarge your train. But should he do it,
Madam? And can his gratitude shine forth
Only in his dependence? Should he be still
The humble, timid Nero, who dared to be

Augustus Caesar only in the name?
What more shall I say to you. Rome justifies him.
Rome to three freedmen so long enslaved,
Scarcely breathing under the yoke she bore,
Reckons her liberty from the reign of Nero.
What do I say? Virtue seems even reborn.
The Empire is no more a master's spoil,
The people on the field of Mars now choose
Their magistrates. Now Caesar, on the advice
Of the soldiers, names their leaders. Thraseus
In the Senate, Corbulon in the army,
Are innocent still, in spite of their renown.
The deserts, peopled once with senators,
Are now inhabited but with their denouncers.
What matter Caesar still believes in us
If our advice tends only to his glory,
If in a prosperous reign Rome still is free
And Caesar still all-powerful? But, madam,
Nero is able to conduct himself.
I obey, without pretending to the honor
Of teaching him what to do, for he has only
To model himself upon his ancestors.
Nero, to do well, has but to be himself;
And if his virtues linked together still
Bring back his earliest years throughout his life
I shall be happy.
    Agrippina.   So of the future,
Not daring to be confident, you think
That Nero without you would go astray.
But you who up till now are satisfied
With what you've done and come to testify
About his virtues, will you explain to us
Why Nero, become ravisher, has seized
The sister of Silanus? Does he intend
Only to mark with ignominy the blood
Of my own ancestors which shines in Junia?
Of what does he accuse her? By what deed
Has she become a criminal of state—
She who, till now brought up in humbleness,
Would never have seen Nero had he not
Abducted her; who would indeed have placed

Among his kindnesses the happy freedom
Of never seeing him?
    Burrhus.   I do not know
Of any crime of which she is suspected.
But Caesar has not yet condemned her, madam.
No object wounds her eyes here: she is in
A palace filled with ancestors of hers.
You know the rights she bears can make her husband
Into a princely rebel; that the blood
Of Caesar should be allied to those alone
Whom Caesar wants to trust; and you will admit
It would not be right without him to dispose
The niece of Augustus.
    Agrippina.   I understand. By your voice
Nero informs me that Britannicus
Assures himself in vain of my support.
In vain, to turn his eyes from his distress,
I've flattered his love with the marriage he desires:
To my confusion, Nero wishes it seen
That Agrippina promises beyond
Her power of granting. Rome's too much concerned
To gain my favor. He wishes by this insult
To undeceive her, that the world should learn
With terror no more to confound my son
And the Emperor. He can do so. But yet
I dare to tell him that this blow must weaken
His Empire, and that in reducing me
To the necessity of trying out
My weak authority, he exposes his;
And that my name when put into the balance
Will have more weight perhaps than he believes.
    Burrhus. What, madam! Still suspect his loyal regard!
Can he not make a step without suspicion?
Does he believe you are of Junia's party?
Does he believe you have been reconciled
With Britannicus? Have you become the prop
Even of your foes so as to find a pretext
To make complaint of him? On a casual speech
Passed on to you, will you be always ready
To share out the Empire? Will you be afraid
Without a stop? And will your embraces turn

Only to explanations? Leave, I beg you,
A critic's woeful diligence, and assume
The indulgence of an unexacting mother.
Allow some coldness without making scenes,
And by them do not warn the court to leave you.
    Agrippina. Who would be honored by my aid when
      Nero
Himself proclaims my ruin; when he seems
To banish me his presence; and when Burrhus
Dares to withhold me from his door?
    Burrhus.   Madam,
I see indeed that it is time for me
To hold my tongue, and that my freedom now
Begins to displease you. Sorrow is unjust
And all the reasons that do not flatter her
Aggravate her suspicions. Here's Britannicus.
I yield my place to him. I leave you to hear
And pity his disgrace, and perhaps, madam,
Blame those the Emperor consulted least. [*Exit* BURRHUS.

Enter BRITANNICUS *and* NARCISSUS.   (I.3)

    Agrippina. Where are you hurrying, Prince? What rest-
      less zeal
Casts you so blindly now among your foes?
What do you seek?
    Britannicus.   What do I seek? O Gods!
All that I've lost here, madam. Junia was seen
Surrounded by a thousand dreadful soldiers
And taken infamously to this palace.
Alas! with what horror would her timid spirits
By this new spectacle have been surprised?
So she is taken from me. A law too harsh
Divides two hearts their wretchedness unites.
Doubtless they wish us only, mingling our griefs,
To help each other to endure them.
    Agrippina.   Enough.
As you, I resent your injuries; my complaints
Already have forestalled your murmurings.
But yet I don't intend by impotent anger
To be released from the promise which I gave you.

I don't explain. If you wish to understand me,
Follow me to the house of Pallas, where
I will await you.   [*Exit* AGRIPPINA.

(I.4)

Britannicus.   Shall I believe her,
Narcissus? And should I, on her word,
Take her for judge between her son and me?
What do you say? Was it not the same
Agrippina who once wed my father
To bring about his ruin, and who hastened,
If I can believe you—the approach
Of his last days—too slow for her designs?
Narcissus. It is no matter. She feels herself outraged,
Like you; she is engaged to give you Junia.
Unite your grievances, your interests bind.
This palace resounds in vain with your regrets:
While you are seen here with a suppliant voice
Sowing complaint, not fear, and while in words
You dissipate your anger, there's no doubt
That you'll complain forever.
Britannicus.   Ah, Narcissus!
You know if I intend to make a habit
Of servitude; you know if I renounce
Forever, astonished by my fall, the throne
To which I was destined. But I'm still alone.
My father's friends are unknown quantities,
Paralyzed by my plight; and my very youth
Divides me from all those who in their hearts
Reserve for me their faith. And as for me,
To whom a year's experience has given
Sad knowledge of my fate, what do I see
Around me, save a troop of venal friends,
Who spy assiduously on all my steps,
Who, picked by Nero for this infamous trade,
Traffic with him the secrets of my soul?
Each day, Narcissus, I am sold by them.
He foresees my designs; he hears my speeches;
Like you, he knows what passes in my heart.
What does it seem to you, Narcissus?
Narcissus.   Ah!

What soul is vile enough. . . . It is up to you
To choose men of discretion and not lavish
Your secrets on all ears.

    Britannicus.   You tell me true,
Narcissus; but mistrust is the last knowledge
Which noble minds acquire. They are deceived
For a long time. But I believe you now;
Or rather swear to believe no one but you.
My father, I remember, gave me assurance
Of your great zeal; alone among his freedmen
You have been always loyal to me. Your eyes,
Continuously looking on my conduct,
Have saved me from a thousand hidden rocks.
Go, therefore; see if the news of this new storm
Will rouse the courage of our friends. Examine
Their eyes, observe their speech; see if I can
Expect loyal help from them; and above all
Note with what care Nero has set a guard
On the Princess; find if her lovely eyes
Are filled with peril, and if I'm still allowed
To speak with her. Meanwhile I'll go to find
The mother of Nero at the house of Pallas,
Like you my father's freedman. I go to see her,
Exasperate her, follow her, and, if I can,
Pledge myself further underneath her name
Than she desires.

ACT TWO

NERO, BURRHUS, NARCISSUS, *and* GUARDS.

NERO. Be sure, Burrhus; in spite of her injustice
She is my mother; and I fain would ignore
All her caprices; but I don't intend
Any longer to ignore or suffer
The insolent minister who dares nourish them—
Pallas with his advice poisons her mind
And every day corrupts Britannicus.
They listen to him alone. If they were followed
They would perhaps be found assembled now

At the house of Pallas. It has gone too far.
He must be separated from them both.
For the last time I wish, I order, him
To leave at once, and not to be found by nightfall
In Rome or in my court. Go. This command
Concerns the safety of the Empire. You,
Narcissus, approach. [*To the* GUARDS.] And you leave us
    alone.   [*Exeunt* BURRHUS *and* GUARDS.

                                    (II.2)

  Narcissus. Thanks to the gods, my lord; that you have
    Junia
Today within your hands assures you too
The rest of Rome. Your enemies, deprived
Of their vain hope, are gone to Pallas' house
To weep their impotence. But what do I see?
For you appear both troubled and astonished
And more dismayed than Britannicus himself.
What does this sadness signify and these looks
Turning this way and that? All is auspicious:
Fortune obeys your wishes.
  Nero.   I'm caught, Narcissus.
I am in love.
  Narcissus. You?
  Nero.   Since a little while,
But for my lifetime. I love—what do I say?
Love? I worship Junia.
  Narcissus.   You love her?
  Nero.   Stirred
By curiosity, this night I beheld her
Arrive at the palace, sad, lifting to the heavens
Her tear-bemoistened eyes, which shone between
The torches and the weapons, beautiful
Without adornment, in the simple dress
Of a beauty who had just been torn from sleep.
What then? I know not if this negligence,
The shadows cast by the torches, the cries and silence,
And the fierce aspect of her ravishers
Enhanced the timid sweetness of her eyes.
Whatever it was, transported by the sight,

I wished to speak to her, but lost my voice.
Motionless, seized for a long time with amazement,
I let her pass to her room. I went to mine.
There, solitary, I wished in vain to distract
My thoughts from her image. Still present to my eyes
I thought I spoke with her. I loved the tears
Which I had made her shed. Sometimes—too late—
I asked her pardon; I made use of sighs
And even threats. That's how, preoccupied
With my new love, my eyes without once closing
Have waited for the dawn. But I perhaps
Have formed too beautiful an image of her;
She appears to me more lovely than she is.
What do you say, Narcissus?

    Narcissus.   Who would have thought
She could so long have hidden herself from Nero?

    Nero. You know quite well, Narcissus, whether her anger
Blamed me for the fate that robbed her of her brother,
Or that her heart, filled with unbending pride,
Grudged to our eyes her budding loveliness,
Faithful to grief, and shut in obscurity,
She even shunned renown: and 'tis this virtue,
So novel in the court, whose constancy
Now stirs my love. Although there is in Rome
No woman who's not honored by my love,
Who's not made vainer by it, who does not come,
As soon as she dares to rely upon her looks,
To try them on the heart of Caesar: alone
The modest Junia in her palace thinks
Their honors are but ignominy; flees
And does not deign, maybe, to be informed
If Caesar is lovable, or even knows
The way to love. Tell me, Narcissus. Does
Britannicus love her?

    Narcissus.   Love her,
My lord?

    Nero. So young yet, does he know himself?
Or know the poison of enchanting looks?

    Narcissus. Love never waits on reason, Sire. Be sure
He loves her. Taught by such charms, his eyes
Already are inured to tears. He knows

How to comply with every whim of hers,
And he perhaps already has acquired
The art of persuasion.
    Nero.   What do you say? Has he
Some sway over her heart?
    Narcissus.   I do not know,
My lord; but I will tell you all I can.
I've sometimes seen him leave the palace here,
His heart full of a wrath he hides from you,
Weeping for the ingratitude of a court
Which shuns him now. Tired of your pomp and power,
And of his servitude, wavering between
Fear and impatience, he goes to Junia
And comes back happy.
    Nero.   All the more unlucky,
That he has learnt to please her: he should rather
Wish for her anger. Nero will not be
Jealous without revenge.
    Narcissus.   With what, my lord,
Are you disturbed? Junia could have pitied him
And shared his griefs. She'd seen no other tears
Than his; but now, my lord, her opened eyes
Will see at closer view your glory's blaze,
And kings around you without diadem
Unknown among the crowd, and even her lover,
Fastened upon your eyes, and highly flattered
By a stray glance of yours: when she shall see you
So glorious come to her with sighs, to avow
Her conquest, do not doubt you will be master
Of a heart already tamed. Then give command
That she should love you, and you will be loved.
    Nero. How many griefs and importunities
Must I expect to face!
    Narcissus.   Why? Who impedes you?
    Nero. All—Octavia, Agrippina, Burrhus,
Seneca, Rome, and three long years of virtue.
Not that one vestige of affection now
Still binds me to Octavia, or preserves
Some pity for her youth. For long my eyes,
Tired of her worries, have rarely deigned to be
Witnesses of her tears. I would be joyful

If soon a blessed divorce would ease a yoke
Imposed on me by force. The heavens themselves
Appear, in secret, to condemn her, since
Her prayers for four years have importuned them
In vain. The gods have given no sign at all
Her virtue touches them. They do not honor
Her couch with any pledge. The Empire vainly
Demands an heir.

Narcissus.   Why do you then delay
To cast her off, my lord? Your heart, the Empire,
All condemn Octavia. When Augustus,
Your ancestor, with Livia fell in love,
By a twofold divorce they were united:
And to that happy divorce you owe the Empire.
Tiberius, whom marriage brought within
The imperial family, dared to renounce
His daughter; and you only, contrary
To your desires, dare not assure your pleasures
By a divorce.

Nero.   And are you not acquainted
With the implacable Agrippina? Already
My anxious love imagines how she'll bring me
Octavia, and with flashing eyes attest
The sacred rights of a knot which she has tied,
And injuring my heart with harsher blows
Recite at length all my ingratitude.
How shall I bear this troublesome encounter?

Narcissus. Are you not, Sire, your own master and hers?
Shall we behold you cowering forever
Under her tutelage? Live, reign for yourself:
It is too much that you should reign for her.
Are you afraid? But, Sire, you do not fear her.
You have just banished haughty Pallas—Pallas
Whose boldness, as you know, she has abetted.

Nero. Far from her sight, I threaten and command,
Listen to your advice and dare to approve it;
I rouse myself against her, and defy her.
But I expose to you my naked soul.
As soon as I unhappily am brought
Again into her sight, I dare no more
Deny the power of eyes in which I've read

My duty for so long; or else, my memory,
Faithful to many benefits received,
In secret yields her all I hold from her,
So that my efforts are of no avail.
My genius, baffled, trembles before hers.
It is to free myself from this dependence
That I avoid her everywhere, insult her,
And sometimes even stir up her resentment,
To make her flee from me as I from her.
Too long I have detained you. Return, Narcissus,
Or else Britannicus may well accuse you
Of double-dealing.
   Narcissus.   No. Britannicus
Is certain of my loyalty. He believes
I see you by his orders, that I'll learn here
All that concerns him, wishing to be informed
By me of all your secrets—above all,
Impatient to behold his love, he waits for
My trusty aid in that.
   Nero.   I do consent.
Bear him those pleasant tidings. He shall see her.
   Narcissus. Banish him far from her, my lord.
   Nero.   Narcissus,
I have my reasons; and you can conceive
That I will dearly sell to him the pleasure
Of seeing her. But let him plume himself
On your happy stratagem. Tell him that I
Am duped on his behalf; and that he sees her
Without my orders. The door is opening.
It is she. Go, find your master—bring him here.

                        [*Exit* NARCISSUS.

Enter JUNIA.   (II.3)

   Nero. You're troubled, madam, and change countenance.
Do you read some sad presages in my eyes?
   Junia. My lord, I can't conceal my error from you.
I came to see Octavia, not the Emperor.
   Nero. I know that, madam; and I could not learn
Without some envy your kindness to Octavia.
   Junia. You, my lord?

Nero.   Do you think that in these precincts
Octavia alone has eyes to know you?
    Junia. What other, Sire, do you wish me to implore?
To whom shall I inquire about a crime
Of which I'm ignorant? You who punish it
Know what it is, my lord. Pray you, inform me
How I have trespassed.
    Nero.   Is it a light offense
So long to hide your presence from me, madam?
Have you received these treasures which heaven has
        pleased
To adorn you with, only to bury them?
And will Britannicus see without alarm
His prosperous love and your attractions grow
Far from our eyes? Why have you, without pity,
Banished me from your sight in my own court,
Excluded from this glory till today?
And they say more—that without being offended,
You let him dare to tell you all his thoughts.
For I will not believe that you, so strict,
Encourage him without consulting me,
Nor that you would consent to love, or even
Accept his love, without my knowing it
Save by report.
    Junia.   I'll not deny, my lord,
His sighs have sometimes told me his desires.
He has not turned his glances from a maid
Who is sole remnant of a ruined house,
Remembering, perhaps, in happier days
His father named me as his destined bride.
He loves me: he obeys the Emperor
His father; and, I dare to add, obeys
You and your mother. Your desires are always
Comformable with hers.
    Nero.   My mother, madam,
Has her own plans, I mine. Let's speak no more
Of Claudius and Agrippina here;
It is not by their choice that I decide.
It is for me alone to answer for you,
And I myself would choose for you a husband.

Junia. Do you recall that all alliance else,
My lord, would shame my ancestors, the Caesars?

Nero. No, madam; the husband I provide for you
Can join your ancestors and his together
Without reproach. You can without a blush
Accept his love.

Junia.   Who is this husband, Sire?

Nero. Madam, 'tis I.

Junia.   You!

Nero.   I would name you, madam,
Another name if I knew one above
Nero himself. To make for you a choice
To which you could subscribe, I have surveyed
The court, Rome, and the Empire. The more I've searched,
The more I still search, madam, in what hands
I should confide this treasure, the more I see
That Caesar, worthy alone of pleasing you,
Should be its fortunate depositary,
And that I can entrust you worthily
Only to hands to which Rome has entrusted
The rule of all mankind. Refer yourself
To your earliest years: Claudius had destined them
To his own son; but it was at a time
When he believed that he would one day name him
Heir to the Empire. The gods have spoken. Far
From contradicting them, it is for you
To pass with the Empire. They have honored me
In vain with this present if your heart should be
Divided from it, if so many cares
Should not be sweetened by your charms, if, while
I give the days to vigils and alarms,
Pitied and envied always, I could not have
Some respite at your feet. Let not Octavia
In your eyes seem an obstacle, for Rome
Is on your side, as well as I, renounces
Octavia, and makes me end a marriage
That heaven will not acknowledge. Think of it,
Weigh this careful choice, one that is worthy
Of a prince who loves you, worthy your lovely eyes,
Captive too long, worthy the world itself
To which you owe a duty.

Junia.   Not without cause,
My lord, I am astonished. I see myself
In the course of a single day as a criminal
Brought to this place; and when terror-struck
I appear before your eyes and scarcely trust
In my own innocence, then all at once
You offer me Octavia's place. And yet
I dare to say that I have merited
Neither this honor, nor this indignity.
And can you wish, my lord, a maid who saw
In infancy her family extinguished,
Who, in obscurity, fostering her sorrow,
Has shaped a virtue fitted to her fate,
Should pass on a sudden from this darkest night
To a rank which would expose her to the eyes
Of everyone, whose brightness, from afar,
I could not stand, and, finally, of which
Another fills the dignity?
Nero.   I have
Already told you I repudiate her:
Have less of fear, or less of modesty.
Do not accuse my choice of blindness. I
Answer for you. Only consent. Recall
The memory of the blood from which you spring,
And to the solid glory of the honors
Caesar would deck you with, do not prefer
The glory of refusal which one day
You may repent.
Junia.   The heavens know, my lord,
The bottom of my heart. I do not pride myself
On a mad glory. I know how to measure
The greatness of your presents; but the more
This rank shed splendor on me, the more it would shame
    me,
And bring to light the crime of having spoiled
The heiress of it.
Nero.   This is to take much care
Of her interests, madam. Friendship cannot go further.
But let us not delude ourselves, and leave
Concealment. The sister touches you much less
That the brother, and for Britannicus . . .

Junia.   My lord,
He has known how to touch my heart. I have not meant
To keep it secret. This sincerity
Is doubtless indiscreet; but my mouth always
Acts as my heart's interpreter, my lord.
I had not thought, being absent from the court,
That I should have to exercise the art
Of a dissembler. I love Britannicus.
I was his destined bride when it was thought
His marriage would be followed by the Empire;
But those misfortunes which have robbed him of it—
His honors lost, his palace now deserted,
The flight of courtiers whom his fall has banished—
Are bonds which keep me loyal. All you behold
Conspire to gratify you. Your halcyon days
Glide by in pleasures. The Empire is for you
Their inexhaustible source; or if some sorrow
Should stop their course, the world, solicitous
Your pleasures to maintain, hurries to wipe them
From your remembrance. Britannicus,
On the other hand, is alone. If some vexation
Presses upon him, he sees—such is his lot—
No one, save only me, concerned at it.
And his sole pleasure, Sire, is when some tears
Sometimes allow him to forget his griefs.

Nero. These are the pleasures and the tears I envy,
That all, but he, would pay for with their lives.
But for this prince I keep a kinder treatment:
Madam, he will appear before you soon.

Junia. My lord! Your virtues have ever reassured me.

Nero. I could forbid his entrance to the palace;
But I am willing to avert the danger
Which his resentment may involve him in.
I do not wish to destroy him: it is better
For him to hear his sentence from the lips
Of her he loves. If his days are precious to you,
Dismiss him from you, and do not give him cause
To think me jealous. Take upon yourself
The offense of his banishment; and make him know,
Whether by speech or silence, or at least

By coldness towards him, that he must take elsewhere
His hopes and vows.
    Junia.   I! I pronounce to him
So stern a sentence! My lips a thousand times
Have sworn the contrary. And even if I could
Betray myself so far, my eyes themselves
Would still refuse to obey me.
    Nero.   Hidden close by
I shall see you, madam. Lock up your love again
At the bottom of your soul: you will not have
Secrets from me. I'll understand the looks
Which you think mute; and his destruction
Will be the infallible wages of a gesture
Or of a sigh, escaped from you to please him.
    Junia. Alas! if I dare yet express a wish,
My lord, allow me nevermore to see him.

Enter NARCISSUS.   (II.4)

    Narcissus. Britannicus is asking for the Princess,
My lord. He approaches.
    Nero.   Let him come.
    Junia.   Ah! my lord!
    Nero. I'll leave you, madam. His fate depends on you
More than on me. In seeing him, remember
That I am watching you.   [*Exit* NERO.

(II.5)

    Junia.   Ah, dear Narcissus,
Run towards your master: tell him— I am lost!
I see him coming.

Enter BRITANNICUS.   (II.6)

    Britannicus.   Madam, what happy fate
Enables me to see you? Can I indeed
Rejoice in such sweet converse? But a grief
Is mingled with the pleasure. Can I hope
To see you yet again? Must I in future
Steal with a thousand shifts the happiness
Your eyes would once accord me every day?
What a night was this! What an awakening!

Your tears, your presence were powerless to disarm
Their cruel insolence! What did I do?
What envious demon took from me the honor
Of dying in your sight? When struck with fear,
Did you address in secret an appeal
For my assistance? Princess, did you deign
To wish for me? And did you think at all
Of the sorrows you would cost me? You say nothing.
What a cold welcome! Is it thus your eyes
Console me for disgrace? Speak! We're alone.
While I talk with you, our enemy, deceived,
Is occupied elsewhere. Let us employ
The moments of his lucky absence.
    Junia.   My lord,
This place is full of his power. These very walls
Have eyes; and from this place the Emperor
Is never absent.
    Britannicus.   And since when have you
Been so afraid? What! is your love already
Become a prisoner? What is become
Of the heart that always swore to make even Nero
Envy our love? But banish a vain fear;
The faith in every heart is not yet dead,
And everyone appears to approve my wrath;
The mother of Nero has declared for us;
And Rome herself offended by his conduct . . .
    Junia. Ah! my lord! You speak against your thought.
For you confessed to me a thousand times
That Rome has praised him with a single voice;
You always rendered homage to his virtue.
Doubtless it is your grief dictates this language.
    Britannicus. This talk surprises me, I must confess.
I did not seek for you to hear him praised.
To confide in you the grief which overwhelms me,
With much ado I snatch a lucky moment
And now this precious moment is consumed
Praising the foe by whom I am oppressed!
Who in a day has made you contrary
To what you were? Even your looks have learnt
How to say nothing? What do I see? You fear
To meet my eyes! Can Nero please you now?

Can I be hateful to you? If I believed that! . . .
In the name of the gods, throw light on the confusion
In which you cast my soul. Speak. Am I no more
In your remembrance?

Junia. Retire, my lord. The Emperor
Is coming.

Britannicus. After this blow, Narcissus, whom
Am I to trust? [*Exit* BRITANNICUS.

Enter NERO. (II.7)

Nero. Madam . . .
Junia. No, my lord,
I can hear nothing. You have been obeyed.
At least let some tears flow of which your eyes
Are not the witnesses. [*Exit* JUNIA.

(II.8)

Nero. Well, you can see
The violence of their love. It has appeared
Even in her silence! Junia loves my rival—
I can't ignore it—but it shall be my joy
To drive him to despair. I make myself
A pretty image of his misery;
And I have seen him doubt his lover's heart.
I'll follow her. My rival now awaits you
To break out. Go, hasten to torture him
With new suspicions; and while before my eyes
She weeps for him and loves him, make him pay dearly
For a happiness of which he is ignorant. [*Exit* NERO.

(II.9)

Narcissus. Fortune calls you once again, Narcissus.
Would you resist her voice? No, let us follow
Her favorable orders to the end;
To make us happy, let's destroy the wretched.

ACT THREE

NERO and BURRHUS.

BURRHUS. Sire, Pallas will obey.
    Nero.   How has my mother
Beheld his pride confounded?
    Burrhus.   Be sure, my lord,
This blow has struck her; already in reproaches
Her grief is given vent; her rage forthwith
Begun to burst out; may it waste itself
In useless cries!
    Nero.   Do you think her capable
Of hatching some design?
    Burrhus.   Agrippina, my lord,
Is always dangerous. Rome and all your troops
Revere her ancestors. Above all, her father,
Germanicus, is present to their eyes.
She knows her power. You know her courage; and
What makes me fear her more is you yourself
Support her wrath and give her arms against you.
    Nero. I, Burrhus?
    Burrhus.   This love which possesses you, my lord.
    Nero. I understand you, Burrhus; but the disease
Is without remedy. My heart has told me
More than you'll say: yet I must go on loving.
    Burrhus. You imagine it, my lord; and satisfied
With some resistance, you dread a disease
Weak at its birth. But if your heart, made strong
In duty, refused to parley with its foe,
If you thought of the glory of your early years,
If you deigned to recall the memory, my lord,
Of Octavia's virtues which do not deserve
Such a reward, and of her virtuous love,
The conqueror of your scorn; and if, above all,
You avoided Junia's presence and condemned
Your eyes to some days absence—believe me,
However love may seem to charm you now,

One does not love, my lord, unless one wishes
To love.

    Nero. I will believe you when in battle
We must uphold the glory of our arms;
Or when, more tranquil, seated in the Senate,
We must decide the destiny of State;
I would rely on your experience;
But, believe me, love is a different kind
Of knowledge, and it would be difficult
To make you humble your austerity
As far as that. Farewell. I suffer much
Away from Junia.   [*Exit* NERO.

                                   (III.2)

    Burrhus.   So at last, Burrhus,
Nero reveals his nature; this savagery,
You thought you could control, from your weak bonds
Is ready to escape. In what excesses
Will it indulge! O Gods! In this misfortune
What counsel should I take? For Seneca,
Who might relieve my mind, is busied now
Away from Rome, and ignorant of this danger.
But if I could arouse maternal love
In Agrippina— Here she is. My luck
Brings her to me.

        Enter AGRIPPINA *and* ALBINE.   (III.3)

    Agrippina.   Well, Burrhus, I was wrong
In my suspicions! You signalize yourself
By notable lessons. Pallas is exiled,
His crime, perhaps, that he has raised your master
To the imperial power. You know too well:
Never would Claudius, whom he controlled,
Without his counsel have adopted Nero.
What do I say? His wife is given a rival:
Nero is freed from his vows—a worthy task
Of a minister who is the enemy
Of flatterers, who was chosen to put a bridle
On youthful passions, to flatter them himself,
And nourish in his soul scorn for his mother,
And forgetfulness of his wife!

Burrhus.   It is too soon,
Madam, to accuse me thus. The Emperor
Has yet done nothing that cannot be excused.
For Pallas' exile, it was necessary;
For long his pride has asked for such reward,
And the Emperor has only with reluctance
Done what the whole court secretly demanded.
The rest's an evil not without resource:
The spring of Octavia's tears can be dried up.
But calm your anger: by a softer road
You could reclaim her wayward husband sooner,
While threats and cries will make him wilder still.

  Agrippina. Ah! vainly do you strive to shut my mouth.
I see my silence but arouses scorn,
And that it's too much for you to respect
The work of my hands. Pallas has not removed
All my support: heaven has left me enough
To avenge my ruin. The son of Claudius
Begins to feel the crimes for which I now
Have only the remorse. Be well assured
That I will go to show him to the army;
To pity his downtrodden infancy
Before the soldiers; to make them expiate
Their error by my example. On one side
The son of an emperor will be seen demanding
Again the loyalty that once was sworn
Unto his family; and they will hear
The daughter of Germanicus. On the other
The son of Ænobarbus will be seen
Backed but by Seneca and the tribune, Burrhus,
Who both recalled from exile by myself,
Share the supreme authority in my sight.
I wish that all should know our common crimes;
And they shall know the ways by which I've led him
To make his power, and yours, so odious.
I will admit the most injurious stories;
I'll confess all—exiles, assassinations,
Yes, even poison. . . .

  Burrhus.   Madam, they'll not believe you.
They will reject the unjust stratagem
Of an angry witness who is self-accused.

I, who was first to second your designs,
Who made the army swear allegiance to him,
Do not repent at all my honest zeal.
Madam, it was a son who thus succeeded
His father. Claudius, in adopting Nero,
Confounded by that choice the former rights
Of his son and yours. Rome might have chosen him.
Thus, without being unjust, she chose Tiberius,
Adopted by Augustus; and young Agrippa,
Descended from his blood, saw himself barred
From the rank to which he aspired. His power established
On such foundations cannot now be weakened
By you, madam; and if he listens to me,
His indulgence towards you soon will be exhausted.
I have begun, I mean to persevere
In the work I am about.   [*Exit* Burrhus.

(III.4)

   Albine.   In what a passion
Sorrow involves you, madam. Let the Emperor
Not know of it!
   Agrippina.   Ah! let him show himself
Before my eyes!
   Albine.   Madam, in the name of the gods,
Conceal your anger. Must you for the sake
Of sister or of brother sacrifice
The quiet of your days? Would you constrain
Great Caesar in his loves?
   Agrippina.   Do you not see
How far I am abused, Albine? Myself
Am given a rival. If I do not break
This fatal tie, my place will soon be taken,
And I no longer will be anything.
Octavia bore till now an empty title,
And she was powerless and ignored at court.
The favors and the titles were poured forth
By me alone, which drew to me the prayers
Of covetous mortals; and now another
Has kindled Caesar's love. She'll have the power
Of wife and mistress. The fruit of so much care,
The pomp of the Caesars, will become the price

Of a single glance of hers. What do I say?
I am avoided, already am deserted.
I cannot bear the thought of it, Albine!
When I must expedite the fatal sentence
Of heaven, Nero, ungrateful Nero . . . But here
His rival comes.

Enter BRITANNICUS *and* NARCISSUS.   (III.5)

Britannicus.   Our common enemies
Are not invincible, madam; our misfortunes
Find sympathetic hearts. Your friends and mine,
Till now so secret while we wasted time
In vain regrets, aroused by anger which
Injustice kindles, have just confessed their grief
Unto Narcissus. Nero is not yet
The calm possessor of the ungrateful woman
He loves to my sister's scorn. If you are still
Sensible of my wrongs, the perjurer
Can be recalled to duty. Half of the Senate
Is on our side—Sulla, Piso, Plautus.
    Agrippina. What do you say, Prince? Sulla, Piso, Plautus,
The leaders of the nobles!
    Britannicus.   I see too well,
Madam, this discourse wounds you; that your wrath
Irresolute and trembling fears already
To obtain all that it asked. No, you have too well
Established my disgrace. You need not fear
The boldness for me of another friend.
No more of them remain. Your careful prudence
Has scattered or seduced them long ago.
    Agrippina. Give less belief, my lord, to your suspicions.
Our safety hangs upon our understanding.
I have given my word. That is enough. In spite
Of all your enemies I will not retract
What I have promised. In vain the guilty Nero
Flies from my anger. He will have to listen
Sooner or later to his mother. I
Will try both force and kindness. Or I myself,
Taking your sister with me, will sow abroad
My fear and her alarms, and range all hearts
Upon the side of her tears. Farewell, my lord.

Nero I will besiege from every side.
But you, if I may advise, avoid his sight.

[*Exeunt* AGRIPPINA *and* ALBINE.

(III.6)

Britannicus. Have you not flattered a false hope? Can I
Put any trust, Narcissus, in your story?
Narcissus. Yes, my lord, but not within these walls
Must I expound this mystery to your eyes.
Let's go. Why are you waiting?
Britannicus.   Why am I waiting,
Narcissus? Alas!
Narcissus.   Explain.
Britannicus.   If by your cunning
I could see again . . .
Narcissus.   Who?
Britannicus.   I am blushing.
But with a heart less troubled I would await
My destiny.
Narcissus. Do you believe her faithful
After all I have said?
Britannicus.   No, I believe her
Ungrateful, criminal, worthy of my wrath;
But I feel, despite myself, I don't believe it
As much as I ought. In its bewilderment
My stubborn heart attributes reasons to her,
Excuses her, and worships. I would conquer
My incredulity at last, would wish
To hate her calmly. Who would believe a heart
Apparently so noble, the foe since youth
Of the false court, would yet renounce so much
Of glory, and, the first day, plot a treason
Unheard of even at court?
Narcissus.   Who knows if the ingrate
In her seclusion did not meditate
The conquest of the Emperor? Too sure
Her eyes could not be hidden, perhaps she fled
In order to be sought, to arouse Nero
By the hard glory of subduing pride
Till then invincible.
Britannicus.   Then I cannot see her?

Narcissus. My lord, at this moment she receives the vows
Of her new lover.

Britannicus.   Well, let us go, Narcissus.
But what do I see? It is Junia.

Narcissus [*aside*].   Let's carry
This news to the Emperor.   [*Exit* NARCISSUS.

Enter JUNIA.   (III.7)

Junia.   Retire, my lord,
And fly an anger that my perseverance
Kindles against you. Nero is incensed.
I have escaped—his mother's occupied
In stopping him. Farewell. Keep for yourself
The joy of seeing me vindicated one day,
And do not harm my love. Your image always
Is present to my soul. Nothing from thence
Can banish it.

Britannicus. I understand you, madam.
You wish my flight to assure your happiness,
That I should quit the field to your new love.
Doubtless, in seeing me, a secret shame
Lets you taste now but a troubled joy.
Well, I must leave you.

Junia.   My lord, without imputing . . .

Britannicus. At least you should discuss the matter more.
I don't complain now that a vulgar love
Is ranged upon the side that fortune flatters;
That an empire's splendor should have dazzled you;
That you should wish to enjoy it at the expense
Of Octavia, my sister; but that, concerned
Like any other with the thought of greatness,
You have deceived me all this while. No, madam,
I still confess that my disconsolate heart
Was not prepared against this one misfortune.
I've seen injustice raised upon my ruin,
And heaven the accomplice of my persecutors;
So many horrors had not drained its wrath:
There still remained that I should be forgotten
By you.

Junia. In a happier time my just impatience

Would have made you to repent your sad mistrust.
But Nero threatens you: in this pressing danger
I have to afflict you but with other cares.
Go, set your mind at rest, cease to complain.
Nero was listening and told me to dissemble.
   Britannicus. What! the cruel . . .
   Junia.   Witness of all our interview,
With a stern countenance he inspected mine,
Ready to make his vengeance burst upon you
At a gesture that betrayed our understanding.
   Britannicus. Nero was listening, madam! But, alas,
Could not your eyes dissemble, and not mislead me?
Could they not tell me the author of this outrage?
Is love then dumb, or has it not a language?
From what misunderstanding could one glance
Have saved me. It was necessary. . . .
   Junia.   Necessary
For me to hold my tongue and save you. Alas!
How many times—since I must speak of it—
My heart in its confusion was about
To instruct you! How often, cutting short my sighs,
Did I avoid your glance which I sought still!
What torment to be silent while I saw
The one I loved, and while I heard him groan,
Torturing him, when by a single look
He could have been consoled! But yet what tears
That look had made to flow! Remembering this,
Anxious, confused, I felt that I had not
Enough dissimulated: I feared the pallor
Upon my frightened brow; I thought my looks
Too full of grief; I thought continually
That Nero, in wrath, was coming to reproach me
Of too much care to please you. I feared my love
Was hidden in vain; I could have wished at last
That I had never loved. Alas! my lord,
For his happiness and for ours—he is informed
Only too well about my heart and yours!
Once more, depart and hide you from his eyes.
My heart, when more at leisure, will tell you more.
I would reveal a thousand other secrets.
   Britannicus. Too much already—to make me realize

My happiness, my crime, your kindness to me.
Do you know all that you have left for me?

> [*Throwing himself at* JUNIA's *feet.*

When at your feet can I expiate my guilt?

Junia. What are you doing? Alas! your rival comes.

Enter NERO.   (III.8)

Nero. Continue, Prince, with these delightful raptures:
Madam, I gauge your kindness by his thanks—
I saw him at your knees. But he should also
Offer some thanks to me for favoring him
With such a meeting place. I kept you here
To let him have this tender meeting with you.

Britannicus. But I can lay my grief or joy before her
In any place her kindness gives consent
That I should see her; and there's nothing here,
Where you detain her, which should startle me.

Nero. Nothing to warn you that I must be respected
And be obeyed?

Britannicus.   It has not seen us both
Brought up together, myself at your command,
And you to brave me; nor did it expect,
When we were born, that Domitius one day
Would speak to me as master.

Nero.   So by fate
Our prayers are thwarted. I obeyed you then,
Now you obey. If you have not yet learnt
The art of obedience, you are still young,
And you can be instructed.

Britannicus.   Who will instruct me?

Nero. The Empire as a whole. Rome.

Britannicus.   Does Rome place
Among your rights all cruelty, injustice,
Force, poisoning, rape, divorce?

Nero.   Rome does not look
Too curiously into secrets which I hide
From prying eyes. Copy her reverence.

Britannicus. One knows what she is thinking.

Nero.   She is silent
At least. Copy her silence.

Britannicus.   So Nero starts
To throw away restraint.
Nero.   With your discourse
Nero begins to weary.
Britannicus.   Everyone
Should bless your happy reign.
Nero.   Happy or not,
It suffices that they fear me.
Britannicus.   I do not know
Junia well, or else such sentiments
Will not gain her applause.
Nero.   If I do not know
The art of pleasing her, at least I know
The art of punishing a headstrong rival.
Britannicus. For me, whatever peril overwhelms me
Only her enmity can make me tremble.
Nero. Desire it: that is all that I can say.
Britannicus. The happiness of pleasing her is all
That I aspire to.
Nero.   She has promised you
That you will always please her.
Britannicus.   I've not the art
To eavesdrop on her talk. I leave her now
To speak of everything that touches me,
And will not hide to make her shut her mouth.
Nero. I understand you. Guards!
Junia.   What are you doing?
He's your brother. Alas! he is a jealous lover.
My lord, a thousand woes torment his life:
Ah! can his happiness excite your envy?
Let me, to knit again your sundered hearts,
Hide me from your eyes, and escape from his.
My flight will stop your fatal strife. My lord,
I'll go to join the Vestals. Dispute no more
For my ill-fated vows; let the gods alone
Be troubled by them.
Nero.   Madam, the enterprise
Is strange and sudden. Guards, take her away
To her apartment. Guard Britannicus
In that of his sister.

Britannicus.   It is thus that Nero
Would win a woman's heart!
     Junia.   Do not incense him,
Prince. Let us bow to the storm.
     Nero.   Guards, obey,
Delay no longer.

                    [*Exeunt* JUNIA, BRITANNICUS, *and* GUARDS.

                    Enter BURRHUS.   (III.9)

Burrhus.   What do I see? O heavens!
     Nero [*without seeing* BURRHUS]. And so their fires are
          redoubled now;
I recognize the hand responsible
For bringing them together. Agrippina
Came in my sight and talked with me so long
Only to work this odious assignation.   [*Seeing* BURRHUS.
Find if my mother is still within the palace,
Burrhus. Make her stay here. Replace her guard
With mine.
     Burrhus. Without hearing her, my lord? Your mother!
     Nero. Stay a while! I do not know what project
You're meditating, Burrhus; but for some days
All I desire has found in you a censor,
Ready to contradict me. I tell you now:
Answer my wishes; or, on your refusal,
Others will answer me for her and you.

ACT FOUR

AGRIPPINA *and* BURRHUS.

BURRHUS. Yes, madam, you can defend yourself at leisure:
Caesar consents to listen to you here.
If to the palace you have been confined,
Perhaps he ordered it to arrange this meeting.
In any case, if I dare tell my thought,
Do not remember now that he has wronged you;
Rather prepare to offer him your arms.
Defend yourself: do not accuse him, madam.
You see, it's him alone the court considers.

Though he's your son and even your handiwork,
He is your Emperor. You are, as we, subject
To the power you gave him. According as he threatens
Or else caresses you, the court around you
Shuns you or throngs about you. It's his support
They seek in seeking yours. But here's the Emperor.
   Agrippina. Pray leave me with him.   [*Exit* Burrhus.

Enter Nero.   (IV.2)

   Agrippina [*sitting*].   Come hither, Nero: take
Your place. I am desired to satisfy you
On your suspicions. I know not with what crime
I can be stained. Of those I have committed
I will enlighten you. You reign. You know
How by your birth a gulf was set between
You and the throne. The rights of my ancestors,
Which Rome had consecrated, were in themselves—
Without me—useless steps in your advancement.
When the mother of Britannicus was condemned,
No more disputing Claudius's marriage,
Among so many beauties who intrigued
For the honor of his choice and begged his freedmen
To back their causes, I desired his bed,
With the sole thought that I would leave to you
The throne on which I sat. I stooped my pride;
I went to Pallas, to implore his aid.
His master, each day in my arms caressed,
Caught in his niece's eyes, insensibly,
The love to which I wished to bring his fondness.
But the blood tie which joined us kept him off
A bed of incest; and he dared not marry
His brother's daughter. The Senate was seduced.
A milder law put Claudius in my bed,
Rome at my knees. Though this was much for me,
For you it was nothing. I made you, in my footsteps,
Enter his family. I named you then
His son-in-law by giving you his daughter.
Silanus, who loved her, saw himself abandoned,
And marked that fatal day with his own blood.
This was still nothing. Could you have presumed

To hope that Claudius would one day prefer
His son-in-law to his son? I again implored
The help of Pallas. By his eloquence
Claudius was conquered: he adopted you;
He called you Nero, wished you to take part,
Before the time, in his imperial power.
Then everybody, remembering the past,
Revealed my plan, already well advanced;
That Britannicus' disgrace—still in the future—
Aroused the murmuring of his father's friends.
My promises dazzled the eyes of some:
Banishment freed me from the most seditious;
Claudius himself, tired of my endless pleading,
Dismissed from his son those followers whose zeal,
Long pledged to his fortunes, could reopen for him
The road to the throne. I did still more. I chose
From my own suite the men to whom I wished
To entrust his upbringing. But I named for you,
Preceptors whom Rome honored. I was deaf
To intrigue, and I increased their fame. I called
From exile, took from the army, this same Seneca,
And this same Burrhus, who since that time . . . Rome
        then
Valued their virtues. At the same time consuming
The wealth of Claudius, in your name my hand
Scattered largesse. The spectacles, the gifts,
Invincible attractions, drew to you
The people's and the soldiers' hearts, who also,
Reawakening their first affection,
Favored in you Germanicus, my father.
Claudius, meanwhile, was sinking to decline.
His eyes, long shut, were opened at the end.
He knew his error. Busied with his fear,
He let some lamentation for his son
Escape his lips, and wished, too late, to assemble
His friends together. But his guards, his palace,
His bed were in my power. I let his love
Fruitlessly waste away. I made myself
Mistress of his last sighs. Sparing his grief,
As it appeared, I took good care to hide
His son's tears from him as he died. He died.

A thousand rumors of it circulated,
All to my shame. I stopped the news of his death
From being published; and while Burrhus went
Secretly to the army to exact
Their oath of fidelity to you, and while
You went to the camp under my auspices,
In Rome the altars smoked with sacrifices;
And all the people, roused by my false orders,
Prayed for the health of a prince already dead.
At last the complete obedience of the legions
Having made firm the power of your rule,
Claudius was seen; astonished at his fate
The people were informed at the same time,
Of your accession and his death. This is
The frank confession which I wished to make you:
Those are my crimes. And these my wages for them:
Scarcely enjoying the fruit of all my cares,
For six months only did you show your thanks,
Till wearied with respect which you disliked,
You do not recognize me any more.
I have seen Burrhus, Seneca, augmenting
All your suspicions and outlining for you
The lessons of disloyalty. They rejoice
That you outdo them in their knowledge now.
I have seen favored by your confidence
Otho, Senecion, youthful libertines,
And flatterers of your pleasures; and when, your scorn
Arousing my resentment, I have asked
The reason of so many injuries,
You have replied to me with new affronts—
The sole recourse of an ungrateful man
Who sees himself confounded. Today I promise
Junia to your brother. They both are pleased
With your mother's choice. What, therefore, do you do?
Junia, seized and taken to the court,
Becomes in a night the object of your love.
I see Octavia blotted from your heart,
Ready to leave the bed where I had placed her;
Pallas is banished; your brother is arrested;
You proceed at last against my liberty:
Burrhus upon me lays presumptuous hands.

And when, convicted of these perfidies,
You ought to see me but to expiate them,
You order me to justify myself.

    Nero. I always bear in mind it is to you
I owe the Empire; I would not tire you, madam,
By making you repeat it. Your goodness could
Rely in peace on my fidelity.
But these suspicions and complaints of yours
Have made all those who heard you utter them
Believe—I dare to tell you here between ourselves—
That you, under cover of my name, have worked
For yourself alone. "So many honors," they said,
"And so much deference, of her benefits
Are they such feeble recompense? What crime
Has then this son, so much condemned, committed?
Was it but to obey that she has crowned him?
And is he merely the depositary
Of his mother's power?" Not that, if I could please you
By going so far, I'd not have taken pleasure
In yielding to you, madam, the power your cries
Seem to ask back again. But Rome requires
A master, not a mistress. You have heard
The rumors which my weakness has aroused.
Each day the Senate and the people, vexed
To hear themselves, by me, dictate your will,
Have whispered that, in dying, Claudius left me
Not merely his power but his obedience.
You have seen our wrathful troops a hundred times
Grumble when they before you bear their eagles,
Ashamed by this unworthy use to lower
The heroes there portrayed. Everyone else
Would have given way. But if you do not reign,
You still complain. Joined with Britannicus
Against me, you strengthen him with Junia's party;
And the hand of Pallas hatches all these plots.
And when, despite myself, I guarantee
My peace of mind, you burn with hate and anger,
And wish to show my rival to the army:
Already the rumor of it has spread abroad
Even to the camp.

Agrippina.   I make him Emperor?
Ungrateful man, have you believed it? What
Would be my plan? What could I have claimed?
What honors in his court, what rank indeed
Could I expect? Ah! if beneath your rule
I am not spared, if my accusers watch
Each step I take, if they pursue me now,
The mother of their Emperor, what would I do
Amidst an alien court? They would reproach me
Not with a powerless outcry or with plots
Stifled at birth, but rather with crimes committed
For you, and in your sight—for which I'd be
Only too soon convicted. You don't deceive me;
I see all your devices. You're an ingrate:
You always were one. From your youngest years
My tender care has drawn you to respond
Only with feigned caresses. There was nothing
Could win you; and your hardness should have stopped
The course of my kindness. How unfortunate
I am! And by what ill luck must my cares
Make me importunate! I have but one son.
O heaven, who hear'st me now, have I addressed
To thee prayers not for him? Remorse, fear, perils,
Nothing has stopped me. I have overcome
Even his scorns. I've turned away my eyes
From evils from that time predicted for me.
I've done what I could. You reign. That is enough.
And with the freedom you have reft from me,
Take my life also, if you wish it—provided
That all the people, enraged, do not snatch from you
What has cost me so much.
   Nero.   Well, then, declare
What you would have me do?
   Agrippina.   That the insolence
Of my accusers should be punished; that
The wrath of Britannicus should be appeased;
That Junia should be allowed to take
The husband that she chooses; that both of them
Should be set free; that Pallas should remain;
That you should let me see you any hour;

[Perceiving BURRHUS *at the back of the stage.*
That this same Burrhus, who comes to listen now,
Shall never dare to bar me from your door.

Nero. Yes, madam, I wish my gratitude henceforth
To engrave your power upon the hearts of all;
And I already bless that happy coldness
Which will relight the warmth of our affection.
Whatever Pallas did—it is no matter,
I will forget it. I am reconciled
To Britannicus; and for this love which has
Divided us, I make you arbiter,
And you shall judge between us. Go, therefore,
And to my brother bear this joy. Guards!
Let my mother's orders be obeyed.   *[Exit* AGRIPPINA.

Enter BURRHUS.   (IV.3)

Burrhus.   This peace,
My lord, and these embraces to my eyes
Present a pleasant sight! You know if ever
My voice was contrary to hers, if I
Have ever wished to break your friendship with her,
And if I have deserved this unjust wrath.

Nero. I do not flatter you, I have complained
About you, Burrhus. I believed you had
An understanding with her. This enmity
Restores my confidence in you. She hastens
Too much to triumph. I embrace
My rival, but it is to stifle him.

Burrhus. What, my lord!

Nero.   It is too much! His ruin
Must deliver me forever from the frenzies
Of Agrippina. As long as he still breathes
I'm only half alive. She has wearied me
With my foe's name; and I do not intend
That his guilty rashness for a second time
Should promise him my place.

Burrhus.   Then she will soon
Weep for Britannicus.

Nero.   Before night falls,
I shall fear him no more.

Burrhus.   And who inspires you
With a longing for this scheme?
    Nero.   My reputation,
My love, my safety, and my life.
    Burrhus.   No, Sire,
Whatever you say, this horrible design
Was never formed within your breast.
    Nero.   Burrhus!
    Burrhus. O heaven, can I learn it from your mouth?
Could you yourself have heard it without trembling?
Do you consider in what blood you're going
To imbrue yourself? Is Nero tired of reigning
In every heart? What will be said of you?
What are you thinking of?
    Nero.   What! always chained
To my past glory, shall I keep before me
A love that's given us by chance, and then
Snatched from us in a day? To all their prayers
Submissive, contrary to my desires,
Am I their Emperor only to please them?
    Burrhus. And does it not suffice your wishes, Sire,
That public happiness should be indeed
One of your benefits? It is for you
To choose: you are still master. Until now
You have been virtuous; you can still be so.
The route is charted; nothing holds you back;
You've but to go from virtue unto virtue;
But if you followed flatterers' advice
You'd have to run from crime to crime, maintain
The harshness of your rule by cruelty,
And bathe your bloodstained arms in yet more blood.
The death of Britannicus would excite the zeal
Of friends all ready to take up his cause;
And those avengers would find new defenders
Who, when they died, would have successors still.
You light a fire now which will not be able
To be extinguished. Feared by all, you're bound
To be afraid of all; forever punishing,
Forever trembling in your plans; and all
Your subjects counted as your enemies.

Is it the experience of your happy youth,
My lord, which makes you hate your innocence?
Do you recall its happiness? How calmly
The days flowed by? What joy to think and say
Within yourself: "Everywhere, at this moment,
The people bless me, love me; no one is seen
To fear my name; heaven, in all their tears,
Hears me not named; no secret enmity
Hides from my face; but everywhere I see
Hearts uplifted as I pass." My lord,
These were your pleasures. What a change, O Gods!
The meanest blood was precious to you then.
One day, I remember, the just-dealing Senate
Urged you to sign a death warrant. You resisted
Their sternness which your milder heart accused
Of too much cruelty; and lamenting then
The miseries of rule, "I wish," you said,
"I knew not how to write." No, either you
Will lend me credence, or my death will spare me
The grief of this misfortune. I shall not
Survive your glory, should you perpetrate
So black a deed.   [*Throwing himself at Nero's feet.*
              Here I am ready, Sire:
Before you go, pierce through this heart of mine
Which cannot acquiesce in it. Call now
Upon those cruel men who have inspired you
And let them try now their uncertain hands. . . .
My tears, I see, have touched my Emperor.
I see his virtue trembles at their fury.
Lose no time; tell me the villains' names
Who dare to give you murderous advice;
Send for your brother, in his arms forget. . . .
    Nero. What do you ask of me?
    Burrhus.   He does not hate you;
He is betrayed; I know his innocence;
I'll answer, my lord, for his obedience.
I'll run to him. I'm going to expedite
So sweet a meeting.
    Nero.   In my chamber, then,
Let him await for me with you.   [*Exit* BURRHUS.

Enter NARCISSUS.   (IV.4)

Narcissus.   My lord,
I have provided for so just a death.
The poison is all ready. The famed Locusta
For me has doubled her obliging pains:
She made a slave expire before my eyes;
And the new poison she has let me have
Is swifter than the sword to end a life.

  Nero. Enough, Narcissus. I recognize your pains,
And wish you to proceed no further.

  Narcissus.   What!
Your hatred for Britannicus is lessened,
And this forbids me . . .

  Nero.   Yes, Narcissus. We
Are being reconciled.

  Narcissus.   I shall take care
Not to dissuade you from it. But only today
He has seen himself imprisoned; this offense
Will, for a long time, in his heart be fresh.
There are no secrets time will not reveal.
He'll know my hand would have presented him
With poison which your orders had made ready.
O may the gods conceal from him that scheme!
But he may do the thing you dared not do.

  Nero. His heart is answered for: I'll conquer mine.

  Narcissus. Is Junia's wedding, then, to seal this pact?
Are you to make this sacrifice as well
To him, my lord?

  Nero.   You want to know too much.
But be that as it may, I count him, Narcissus,
No more among my enemies.

  Narcissus.   Agrippina
Was well resolved. She has recovered now
Her sovereign rule upon you.

  Nero.   What then? What has she said?
What do you mean?

  Narcissus.   She has openly bragged of it.

  Nero. Of what?

  Narcissus.   That she had but to see you a moment;

That to this uproar and this fatal wrath
A modest silence would be seen succeed;
That you would be the first one to subscribe
To such a peace, relieved that of her goodness
She deigned to overlook all you had done.

   Nero. But, tell me, what do you wish that I should do?
I'm much inclined to avenge her insolence,
And, if I obeyed my instinct, this rash triumph
Would soon be followed by a lasting sorrow.
But what will all men say? Do you wish that I
Should follow tyrants' footprints and that Rome,
Effacing so many honorable titles,
Should leave me but the name of poisoner?
They'd rank my vengeance among parricides.

   Narcissus. And do you take their whims to be your
    guides?
Did you expect them to be always silent,
My lord? Is it for you to lend an ear
To their discourse? Will you lose the memory
Of your own desires? And will you fear to believe
Yourself alone? But, Sire, you do not know
The Romans. No, in their speech they're more restrained.
Too much precaution weakens now your reign:
They'll think, indeed, that they deserve to be feared.
For long they have been fashioned to the yoke;
And they adore the hand that holds them chained.
You'll see them always burning to do you pleasure:
Their ready servitude fatigued Tiberius.
Myself invested in a borrowed power,
Which I received from Claudius with my freedom,
In the course of my past glory, I have tried,
A hundred times, their patience, and never yet
Exhausted it. You fear the heinousness
Of poisoning? Have the brother killed, abandon
The sister—Rome, all prodigal with victims
Upon her altars, were they innocent
Would find them crimes: you'll see put in the list
Of unlucky days the birthday of the sister
And of the brother.

   Nero.   Narcissus, I say again,
I cannot undertake it. I've given my word

To Burrhus—I had to do so. I don't wish,
In breaking faith with him, to give his virtue
A weapon against me. To oppose his reasons
I have but useless courage. I do not hear him
With a tranquil heart.

    Narcissus.   Sire, Burrhus does not think
All that he says. His cunning virtue saves
His credit; nay they've all the selfsame thought:
They'll see by this one blow their power diminished;
You will be free, then, Sire; and these proud masters
Will bow, like us, before you. What! don't you know
All that they dare to say? "Nero, if what
They say is true, was never born to rule;
He says and does only what is prescribed:
For Burrhus guides his heart, and Seneca
His mind. For all ambition, for signal virtue,
He excels at driving a chariot in the races,
Competing for prizes unworthy of his hands,
At giving himself a spectacle to the Romans,
Coming to lavish his voice on a theatre,
Reciting poems he wishes to be adored,
While soldiers, every moment, extort for him
Appropriate applause." Do you not wish
To force them to be silent?

    Nero.   Come, Narcissus:
Let's see what we should do.

ACT FIVE

Britannicus *and* Junia.

Britannicus. Yes, madam, Nero—who would have sup-
    posed it?—
Awaits me in his chamber to embrace me.
He has invited all the youth of the court:
He wants the pomp and gaiety of a feast
To ratify the pledges that we make
In the sight of all, and kindle once again
The warmth of our embraces. He stamps out
This love, the source of so much hate; he makes you

The sovereign arbitress of my fate. For me,
Though banished from the rank which I derived
From ancestors, in whose spoils in my sight
He is adorned, since he has ceased to oppose
My love, and seems to yield to me the pride
Of pleasing you, my heart (I will confess it)
Secretly pardons him, and lets him have
The rest with less regret. To think that we
Shall not be separated any more!
Why! even now, without fear, I can see
Those eyes which neither sighs nor threats have moved,
Which sacrificed for me the Emperor
And the Empire! Ah, madam . . . But what new fear
Amid my raptures holds your joy in check?
And why, as you listen to me, do your eyes,
Your mournful eyes, look upwards to the heavens?
What is it that you fear?

　　Junia.　　　　　　　　　I do not know;
But yet I fear.

　　Britannicus. You love me?

　　Junia.　　　　　　　　Alas! I love you.

　　Britannicus. Nero no more disturbs our happiness.

　　Junia. But can you answer me for his good faith?

　　Britannicus. Do you suspect him of a covered hate?

　　Junia. Just now he loved me and he vowed your ruin;
But now he flees from me and seeks for you;
And could so great an alteration be
The work of a moment?

　　Britannicus.　　　　　　Madam, it is the work
Of Agrippina: she believed my fall
Involved her ruin too. Thanks to the warnings
Her jealous spirit gave, our greatest foes
Have fought for us. I trust the rage she showed me;
I put my trust in Burrhus and even rely
Upon his master. I believe that he,
By my example, powerless to betray,
Hates openly, or ceases to hate.

　　Junia.　　　　　　　　My lord,
Judge not his heart by yours—you're out of step
With him. I have known Nero and the court

For a day only; but, if I dare to say it,
How in this court, alas, all that one says
Is far from what one thinks! How heart and lips
Seldom agree together! With what joy
Is faith betrayed! What an alien abode
For you and me!

Britannicus. But whether his friendship is
Genuine or false, if you fear Nero,
Is he himself without fear? No, he will not
By a vile outrage raise against him now
The people and the Senate. What do I say?
He admits his last injustice; his remorse
Is evident, even in Narcissus' eyes.
Ah! if he'd told you, my Princess, how far . . .

Junia. But does Narcissus not deceive you?

Brittanicus.   Why
Do you wish me to mistrust him?

Junia.   How should I know?
Your life is at stake, my lord. All are suspect to me.
I fear lest all should be seduced. I fear
Nero; I fear misfortune which pursues me.
Warned by a dark presentiment, I grieve
To let you leave my sight. O! if this peace
On which you feast conceals some hidden snares
Against your life; if Nero angered by
Our mutual understanding, this very night
Has chosen for his secret vengeance; if,
While I see you, he prepares his blows;
And if I speak to you for the last time!
Ah, Prince!

Britannicus. You are weeping! Ah! my dear Princess!
And is your heart concerned for me so much?
What, madam, in a day, when filled with grandeur
Nero thought to dazzle you with his splendor,
Here, where all flee from me and honor him,
To prefer my poverty to all the pomps
Of Nero's court! In the same day and place
To refuse an empire and to weep before me!
But, madam, stay those precious tears; for soon
My safe return will dissipate your fears.

I've stayed too long, and I shall be suspect.
Farewell. I'm going, my heart filled full of love,
Amid the violent feelings of blind youth,
To see and converse but with my princess.
Farewell.
   Junia.   Prince . . .
   Britannicus.   I am expected, madam.
I must go.
   Junia.   But wait at least until they come
To inform you.

Enter AGRIPPINA.   (V.2)

   Agrippina.   Why do you tarry, Prince. Depart
In haste. For Nero now impatiently
Complains of your absence. The joy and pleasure
Of all the guests is waiting to burst out
When you embrace. Do not allow to flag
Their just desires. Go. And let us, madam,
Go to Octavia's.
   Britannicus.   Go, my lovely Junia;
And hasten with a tranquil mind to embrace
My sister who awaits you. As soon as I can
I'll seek you out, madam, and give you thanks
For all your pains.   [*Exit* BRITANNICUS.

(V.3)

   Agrippina.   Either I am mistaken,
Or else some tears you shed in your farewells
Have dimmed your eyes. Can you let me know what
   trouble
Has formed this cloud? Do you mistrust a peace
Which I have brought about?
   Junia.   After the grief
This day has cost me, could I have recomposed
My agitated spirits? Hardly yet
Do I conceive this miracle. I fear
Some obstacle to your kindness; and, besides,
Change, madam, is common at court, and fear is ever
The accompaniment of love.
   Agrippina.   But all is well.

I've spoken. All has changed. What I have done
Has left no room for your suspicions.
I guarantee a peace that has been vowed,
Myself as witness. Nero has given me
Sure pledges of his faith. If you had seen
With how many caresses he renewed
His plighted word, by what embraces he
Stopped me from going! His arms, in our farewells,
Could not release me. His kindness, unrestrained,
Showed in his face and then poured out to me
His inmost secrets; he talked to me as a son
Who freely to his mother's bosom comes
To forget his pride; but reassuming soon
A countenance severe, as of an emperor
Who comes to consult his mother, his confidence
Put secrets in my hands on which depend
The fate of men. No, it must be confessed
His heart is far from harboring any malice;
And only our foes, who falsify his goodness,
Against us take advantage of his mildness.
But now in turn their power declines; once more
Rome will know Agrippina: already
The rumor of my favor is adored.
Yet in these precincts let us not await
The night; but pass to Octavia's house and give her
The remainder of a day which proves as happy
As I believed it fatal. But what do I hear?
What confused tumult! What can it be?
    Junia. O heaven! Save Britannicus!

Enter BURRHUS.   (V.4)

    Agrippina.   Burrhus,
Where are you running? Stop! What do you mean? . . .
    Burrhus. Madam, it is all over. Britannicus
Is dying.
    Junia. Ah! my prince!
    Agrippina.   He's dying.
    Burrhus.   Or rather
He is dead.
    Junia.   Forgive the violence of my grief.

I go to help him if I can, or else
To follow him.   [*Exit* JUNIA.

(V.5)

  Agrippina.   What an outrage, Burrhus!
  Burrhus.   I
Shall not be able to survive it, madam.
I must leave the court and leave the Emperor.
  Agrippina. Had he no horror of his brother's blood?
  Burrhus. This plot had greater subtlety. The Emperor
Had scarcely seen his brother entering
Than he rose up and took him in his arms.
There was a silence. Suddenly Caesar took
A goblet in his hand. "To consummate
This day under happiest auspices, my hand
Sprinkles libations"; he said, "O Gods I call
To this effusion, come to give your blessing
To our reunion." Britannicus was bound
By the same vows. The goblet in his hands
Was filled up by Narcissus; but his lips
Had hardly touched the rim of it, when—the sword
Is not so potent, madam—the light of his eyes
Was snatched away. Without or warmth or life
He fell upon his couch. Judge how this blow
Smote on the minds of all of us. Half took fright,
And rushed out, crying. But those who were more used
To the ways of the court, composed their countenance
By watching Caesar's eyes. Still on his couch
He lolled, appearing not to be surprised.
"This sickness of which you fear the violence,"
Said he, "has often, without danger, attacked
His infancy." Narcissus wished in vain
To affect concern; and his perfidious joy
Shone out despite himself. And as for me,
Although the Emperor is bound to punish
My rashness, I pushed through the hateful press
Of courtiers, and I went quite overcome
By this assassination to lament
Britannicus, Caesar, and the State itself.
  Agrippina. Here he is. You will see if it is I

Who have inspired him.

Enter NERO and NARCISSUS. (V.6)

Nero [*seeing* AGRIPPINA]. O Gods!
  Agrippina.   Stay, Nero.
I have two words to say. Britannicus
Is dead. I recognize the stroke. I know
The murderer.
  Nero.   Who is it, madam?
  Agrippina.   You.
  Nero. I! You are capable of such suspicions!
There is no evil of which I am not guilty,
And if your talk were listened to, my hand,
Madam, would even have cut short the days
Of Claudius. His son was dear to you.
His death may well confound you, but I cannot
Answer for blows of destiny.
  Agrippina.   No, no.
Britannicus was poisoned. Narcissus did it.
You ordered it.
  Nero.   Madam! who can say such things?
  Narcissus. O! my lord, does this suspicion so outrage
  you?
Britannicus had secret plans, madam,
Which would have cost you grief more justified:
He had a loftier aim than wedding Junia;
He would have punished you for your own kindness.
He deceived you yourself: his injured heart
Intended, soon or late, to recall the past.
Be glad that fate, despite yourself, has served you,
That Caesar, informed of plots that threatened him,
Relied on my fidelity. Leave weeping,
Madam, only to your enemies; let them
Put this misfortune among their worst disasters;
But you . . .
  Agrippina. Continue Nero; with such ministers
You will be famous for your glorious deeds.
Go on. You did not take this step to retire.
Your hand has started with your brother's blood:
And I foresee your blows will reach your mother.

I know that in your inmost heart you hate me;
You would free yourself from the yoke of my benefits.
But yet I wish that even my death should prove
Useless to you: do not believe that I,
Dying, would leave you tranquil. Rome, this sky,
The daylight you received from me, each moment,
Everywhere, would present my shape to you.
Your remorse, like furies, would pursue you still.
You'd think to calm it by fresh outrages;
Your fury, self-inflamed in its career,
Will mark each day with blood that's ever fresh.
But I hope that heaven, at last, tired of your crimes,
Will add your ruin to so many others;
That after wallowing in their blood and mine,
You'll see yourself compelled to shed your own;
And then your name will appear in time to come
A cruel insult to the cruelest tyrants.
Thus does my heart presage of you. Farewell.
You can depart.
    Nero.   Narcissus, follow me.
                     [*Exeunt* NERO *and* NARCISSUS.

                                  (V.7)

    Agrippina. O! heaven! How false were my suspicions!
Condemning Burrhus, to hearken to Narcissus!
Burrhus, did you behold what furious glances
Nero, in leaving, left me for farewells?
It is all over: nothing will stop him now.
The stroke, of which I was warned, is going to fall
Upon my head. He'll crush you in your turn.
    Burrhus. Ah, madam! I have lived a day too many.
Would to heaven his hand, happily cruel,
Had made on me the essay of his new rage!
That he'd not given me by this grim outrage
Too sure a token of the State's misfortunes!
It is not his crime alone makes me despair;
His jealousy could have made him arm himself
Against his brother; but if I must explain
My grief, madam, Nero beheld him die
Without a change of color. Unconcerned,
His eyes already have the constancy

Of a tyrant hardened since his infancy
In crime. Let him succeed and make to perish
A troublesome minister who is not able
To tolerate him. I am far from wishing
To avoid his wrath. The soonest death will be
To me the dearest.

Enter ALBINE.   (V.8)

  Albine.   Ah, madam! Ah, my lord!
Run to the Emperor; come to save Caesar
From his own madness. He sees himself forever
Separated from Junia.
  Agrippina.   What! has Junia
Ended her life?
  Albine.   To overwhelm Caesar, madam,
With an everlasting grief, she, without dying,
Is dead to him. You know how she escaped
Out of this palace: she made pretense of going
To sad Octavia's house; but soon she took
To unfrequented roads, down which my eyes
Followed her hurried steps. From the palace gates
She emerged distraught and wild. At first she perceived
The statue of Augustus; and with her tears
Moistening the marble of his feet, which she
All earnestly embraced: "Prince, by these knees
That I embrace," she said, "protect the remnant
Of thy great race. Rome in thy palace has seen
The one descendant who might have been like thee
Murdered. After his death they wish me to be
False to him; but to preserve for him a faith
Forever pure, Prince, I devote myself
To those immortal gods, whose blessed altars
Thy virtue makes thee share." Meanwhile the people,
Astonished by this sight, rushed from all sides,
Surrounding her, affected by her tears;
And, pitying her grief, by common consent,
They took her under their protection;
They bore her to the temple, where for ages
Our virgins destined to the altars' cult
Guard faithfully the precious depositary
Of fire which burns forever for our gods.

Caesar beheld them go and did not dare
To intercept them. Then, more rash, Narcissus
Hastened to please him. He stole towards Junia,
And, without dismay, with hand profane
Began to stop her. His audacity
Was punished by a thousand mortal blows.
His faithless blood spurted on Junia.
Caesar then left him there among the hands
Which had enveloped him. He returned to the palace,
Everyone shunning his ferocious silence.
The one word "Junia" escaped his lips.
He walked without an aim; his eyes dared not
Lift their bewildered glances to the heavens;
And it is feared, if night to solitude
Is joined to exasperate the disquietude
Of his despair, if you abandon him
Longer without your aid, that his keen anguish
Will make him kill himself. Time presses. Run.
The slightest thing will make him kill himself.

    Agrippina. He would do justice on himself. But, Burrhus,
Let's go and see how far his violence goes.
Let's see what alteration his remorse
May yet produce; if he will wish henceforth
To follow other maxims.

    Burrhus.   Would to heaven
This were the last of his crimes!

BERENICE

PREFACE

*Titus, reginam Berenicen . . . cui etiam nuptias pol-
licitus ferebatur statim ab Urre dimisit invitus invitam.*
(Suetonius in *Tito,* cap. vii.)

That is to say, "Titus, who passionately loved Berenice,
and who even, it was believed, had promised to marry her,
sent her away from Rome, against both his will and hers,
in the first days of his rule." This action is very famous in
history; and I found it very suitable for the theatre by
reason of the violence of the passions which it could excite.
There is, indeed, nothing more touching in any poets,
except the separation of Dido and Æneas in Virgil. And
who doubts that what could furnish enough matter for a
whole book of an epic, where the action lasts several days,
cannot suffice for the action of a tragedy of which the
duration should not be more than a few hours? It is true
that I have not driven Berenice to kill herself, like Dido,
because Berenice not having here the complete union with
Titus which Dido had with Æneas, she is not obliged, like
her, to renounce her life. Except for that, the last farewell
she says to Titus, and the effort which she makes to part
from him, is not the least tragic of the play; and I venture
to say that it renews in the hearts of the audience the emo-
tion which the rest of the play was able to arouse in them.
It is not necessary that there should be blood or deaths in
a tragedy: it suffices that its action should be great, that
the actors should be heroic, that the passions should be
excited, and that all should experience that majestic sadness which constitutes the whole pleasure of tragedy.

I thought that I could find all these characteristics in
my subject; but what pleased me more with it is that I
found it extremely simple. For a long while I had wanted
to try if I could make a tragedy with that simplicity of

action which was so strongly to the taste of the ancients: for it is one of the major precepts which they have left us: "Whatever you do," said Horace, "let it be simple and single." They admired the *Ajax* of Sophocles, which is concerned only with Ajax killing himself for grief, because of the rage into which he had fallen after he had been refused the arms of Achilles. They admired the *Philoctetes,* of which the whole subject is Ulysses who comes to obtain by artifice the arrows of Hercules. *Œdipus* itself, although full of recognitions, is less full of matter than the simplest tragedy of our days. We see too that the partisans of Terence, who is rightly elevated above all comic poets for the elegance of his diction and for the verisimilitude of his manners, do not scruple to admit that Plautus has a great advantage over him by the simplicity of most of his subjects. And it is doubtless this marvelous simplicity which attracted to the latter all the praises that the ancients gave him. How much more simple was Menander, since Terence is obliged to take two comedies of that poet to make one of his own!

And one need not believe that this rule is based only on the fancy of those who made it: only the credible touches us in tragedy. And what credibility is there when a multitude of things happen in a single day which could scarcely happen in several weeks? There are some who think that this simplicity is a mark of barrenness of invention. They do not realize that on the contrary all invention consists of making something of nothing, and that a large number of incidents has always been the refuge of poets who do not feel that they possess either enough abundance or enough power to hold their audience during five acts by a simple action, upheld by the violence of the passions, the beauty of the sentiments, and the elegance of the expression. I am very far from believing that all these things are to be found in my work; but nor do I believe that the public is ungrateful to me for having given them a tragedy which has been honored by so many tears, and of which the thirtieth performance was as much attended as the first.

It is not merely that some people have reproached me with this same simplicity which I have sought so carefully:

they have thought that a tragedy which was so little charged with intrigues could not be according to the rules of the theatre. I inquired if they complained that they had been bored. I was told that they all admitted that it had not bored them at all, that it had even moved them in several places, and that they would see it again with pleasure. What else do they want? I beseech them to have a good enough opinion of themselves not to believe that a play which moves them, and which gives them pleasure, can be absolutely against the rules. The principal rule is to please and to move: all the others are made only to bring about the first; but all these rules are details which I would advise them not to bother about: they have more important tasks. Let them leave to us the fatigue of interpreting the difficulties of the *Poetics* of Aristotle; let them keep for themselves the pleasure of weeping and being moved to pity; and let them permit me to tell them what a musician said to Philip, King of Macedon, who asserted that a song was not according to the rules: "God forbid, my lord, that you should ever be so unfortunate as to know these things better than I!"

That is all I have to say to those persons whom I shall always glory in pleasing; as for the libel [1] which has been made against me, I believe that readers will willingly dispense me from replying to it. And what would I reply to a man who thinks nothing and who does not even know how to express what he thinks? He speaks of *protasis* as if he understood the word, and wants this first of the four parts of a tragedy to be always nearest the last, which is the catastrophe. He laments that too great a knowledge of the rules prevents him from enjoying comedy. Certainly, to judge by his dissertation, there was never a complaint less well founded. It appears plainly that he has never read Sophocles, whom he praises very unjustly for *a great multiplicity of incidents;* and that he has not even read any of the *Poetics*, except in the prefaces to tragedies. But I forgive him for not knowing the rules of the theatre, since, happily for the public, he does not apply himself to this

[1] This refers to a criticism of the play by the Abbé de Villars. Racine, however, made a few alterations as a result of this attack.

kind of writing. What I cannot forgive him is to know so little of the rules of jesting when he does not wish to say a word without jesting. Does he think to delight sensible people by these *pocket-sighs,* these *My Ladies the Rules,* and many other wretched affectations which he will find condemned in all good authors, if he ever bothers to read them?

All these criticisms are the work of four or five unfortunate little authors, who have never been able by themselves to excite the curiosity of the public. They always await the chance of some work which has succeeded to attack it—not out of jealousy, for on what grounds could they be jealous?—but in the hope that one will be given the labor of replying to them, and that one will draw them from the obscurity in which their own works would have left them all their life.

DRAMATIS PERSONÆ

TITUS, *Emperor of Rome*
BERENICE, *Queen of Palestine*
ANTIOCHUS, *King of Comagena*
PAULINUS, *confidant of Titus*
ARSACES, *confidant of Antiochus*
PHENICE, *confidante of Berenice*
RUTILIUS, *a Roman*
TITUS' ATTENDANTS

SCENE—ROME, in a chamber between the rooms of Titus and Berenice

BERENICE

ACT ONE

ANTIOCHUS *and* ARSACES.

ANTIOCHUS. Let us stop a moment. The grandeur of this
    place
Is new to you, Arsaces, as I see.
Often this chamber, splendid and secluded,
Is the depositary of Titus' secrets.
It's here he often hides him from his court,
When to the Queen he comes to speak of love.
This door is next his chamber; and this other
Leads to that of the Queen. Go to her now;
Say that, regrettably importunate,
I dare to beg a secret interview.

    Arsaces. You importunate, my lord? The faithful friend,
Ever solicitous for her interests? You,
Antiochus, her former lover? You
Whom the Orient counts among her greatest kings?
What! does the rank of Titus' destined bride
Put so much distance between her and you?

    Antiochus. Go, I say; and without concerning yourself
With other cares, see if I can, in private
Soon speak with her.   [*Exit* ARSACES.

                                    (I.2)

    Antiochus.   Well, Antiochus,
Are you still the same? Will I, without trembling,
Be able to say to her "I love you"? Why!
I tremble already and my beating heart
Now fears the moment that I had desired.
Berenice once took from me every hope,
Imposing on me an eternal silence.
So, for five years I have held my peace,
And, till this day, I've veiled my love with friendship.
Should I believe that in the higher rank

Which Titus destines for her, she'll listen better
Than once in Palestine? He marries her.
Have I waited for this moment then
To come again to declare myself her lover?
What fruit shall I pluck now from a rash avowal?
Ah! since I must depart, let me depart
Without displeasing her. Let me withdraw,
And go, without uncovering my heart,
Far from her eyes, forget her, or else die.
But yet, to suffer still an endless torment
Of which she's ignorant, still to pour out tears
I must consume! What! even in losing her
To fear her anger! Lovely Queen, why should you
Be angry with me? Do I come to ask you
To renounce the Empire? or that you should love me?
Alas! I only come to let you know—
After I've been deluded all this while,
Thinking my rival in the end would find
Some fatal hindrance to his love, and now,
Today, all things are possible to him,
And your marriage is at last in preparation—
That I, sad model of long constancy,
After five years of love and fruitless hope,
Am now departing when I hope no more,
Though faithful still. Instead of being angry,
She may feel pity for me. In any case
I'll speak. I've had enough concealment.
And what can I, a hopeless lover, fear,
Who can resolve never to see her more?

Enter ARSACES.   (I.3)

Antiochus. Shall I go in, Arsaces?
    Arsaces.   My lord, I've seen
The Queen; although I had some difficulty
In breaking through the ever-changing waves
Of worshippers, drawn by her imminent greatness.
After a week's austere retirement, Titus
Has ceased to mourn Vespasian, his father.
That lover gives himself to love again;
And if I can believe the talk of the court,

Before nightfall the happy Berenice
May change the name of Queen for Empress.
    Antiochus.   Alas!
    Arsaces. How! can these words disturb you?
    Antiochus.   So, I cannot
Speak to her privately?
    Arsaces.   My lord, you'll see her.
Berenice knows that you would see her here,
Alone and unattended. With a glance
The Queen was pleased to inform me she consented
To your request; and doubtless she awaits
A favorable moment to elude
The throng which crowds about her now.
    Antiochus.   Enough.
But have you not neglected anything
Of the important orders which I gave you?
    Arsaces. My lord, you know my prompt obedience.
Vessels in Ostia are well prepared,
Ready to sail from port at any moment.
They only wait your orders to depart.
But whom are you sending home to Comagena?
    Antiochus. When I have seen the Queen, they must
        depart.
    Arsaces. Who must depart?
    Antiochus.   Myself.
    Arsaces.   You?
    Antiochus.   When I leave
The palace, I leave Rome; and leave forever.
    Arsaces. I am, indeed, surprised, not without cause.
It is a long time since Queen Berenice
Tore you, my lord, from the bosom of your country.
Three years ago she stayed your steps in Rome,
And when her conquest is assured, and she
Expects you as a witness of the marriage,
When loving Titus, wedding her, prepares
A glory for her which will shine on you. . . .
    Antiochus. Let her enjoy her fortune; and drop a subject
Which I find troublesome.
    Arsaces.   I understand you,
My lord. These dignities have made the Queen

Ungrateful for your kindness. Enmity
Succeeds to friendship which she has betrayed.

Antiochus. No, Arsaces, never have I hated her
Less than I do.

Arsaces.   Has the new Emperor then,
Anticipating greatness, slighted you?
Does some presentiment of his coldness make you
Avoid his presence, far from Rome?

Antiochus.   No. Titus
Has not appeared to change. I should be wrong
To make complaint.

Arsaces.   Why leave then? What caprice
Makes you an enemy of yourself? The heavens
Have set upon the throne a prince who loves you,
A prince who, witness of your former battles,
Saw you seek death or glory in his steps,
Whose valor, seconded by you, at last
Brought underneath the yoke the rebel Jews.
And he recalls that famous, grievous day
Which finally decided a long siege.
The confident foe upon their triple ramparts
Looked, without peril, on our vain assaults:
The battering-ram was but an empty threat;
You only, with a ladder in your hand,
Brought death upon their walls. That day, my lord,
Nearly beheld your funeral. Titus kissed you,
As you lay dying in my arms. Your death
Was mourned by all the camp. Now is the time,
My lord, when you should wait for the reward
Of all the blood which they have seen you shed;
If, urged by the desire to see your country,
You're tired of living where you do not reign,
Must the Euphrates see you once again
Unhonored? Wait for your departure now
Till Caesar sends you home in triumph, laden
With sovereign titles which the Roman friendship
Adds to the name of King. Can nothing change
Your mind, my lord? You do not answer?

Antiochus.   What
Would you have me say? I await a moment's speech
With Berenice.

Arsaces.   Well, my lord?
Antiochus.   Her fate
Will decide mine.
    Arsaces.   How?
    Antiochus.   I am waiting
For her to tell me of her marriage. If
Her mouth confirms the general voice, and if
She is indeed being raised to Caesars' throne,
If Titus has spoken to her, if he weds her,
Then I depart.
    Arsaces.   Why should this marriage be
So fatal in your sight?
    Antiochus.   When we have gone,
I'll tell you all.
    Arsaces.   My lord, my mind is troubled
By what you have said.
    Antiochus.   The Queen is coming. Farewell.
Do all as I commanded.   [*Exit* ARSACES.

            Enter BERENICE *and* PHENICE.   (I.4)

    Berenice.   At last, my lord,
I've stolen from the too officious joy
Of all the new friends made me by my fortune:
I flee their tedious courtesies, to seek
A friend who speaks his heart. To tell the truth,
I was impatient with you, with some cause,
And I accused you of some negligence.
"What!" I said, "this Antiochus, whose friendship
Has had the East and Rome for witnesses,
He whom I've always seen with constant heart
Follow my steps in good and evil fortune,
Today when heaven seems to promise me
An honor I intend to share with you,
This same Antiochus, hiding from my sight
Leaves me at mercy of an unknown crowd."
    Antiochus. It's true, then, madam, as your words imply?
Marriage is going to follow your long courtship?
    Berenice. I'd like, my lord, to confide to you my fears.
Some tears I've shed during these last few days.
The long mourning which Titus had imposed
Upon his court had made him put aside

His love, yes, even in secret. He showed no longer
That ardor for me which made him pass the days
Within my sight. Silent, laden with cares,
And his eyes filled with tears, he had for me
Nothing but sad farewells. Judge then my grief:
For as I've told you many times, I love him
For himself alone, and would have rather chosen,
Far from the greatness he's invested with,
His heart and virtue.

  Antiochus.   Has he now resumed
His first affection for you?

  Berenice.   You were witness
Of this last night, when his religious cares
Had the Senate's backing and they set his father
Among the gods. His piety, content
With this act of duty, has given place, my lord,
To caring for his love; and at this moment,
Without informing me, he is in the Senate,
Met by his order. There he extends the frontier
Of Palestine: he joins Arabia to it,
And all of Syria; and if I should believe
What his friends tell me, if I trust his vows,
A thousand times redoubled, he is going
To make me queen of all those states, and join
To many titles that of Empress. He
Is coming here himself to assure me of it.

  Antiochus. And I have therefore come to bid you now
Farewell for ever.

  Berenice. What do you say? Ah, heaven!
What a farewell! What words are these you speak!
Prince, you are troubled and change countenance!

  Antiochus. Madam, I must depart.

  Berenice.   May I not know
What cause . . . ?

  Antiochus [*aside*]. I should have gone without seeing
  her.

  Berenice. What do you fear? Speak now. You have been
  silent
Too long, my lord. What is the mystery
Of your departure?

Antiochus.   Remember then, at least,
I yield at your command, and that you hear me
For the last time. If in your high degree
Of power and glory you remember where
You took your birth, you will remember too
That there my heart received, shot from your eyes,
The first of many darts. I loved. I gained
The favor of your brother, King Agrippa.
He spoke to you for me. Perhaps indeed
You were about to accept without demur
The tribute of my heart. But Titus came—
To my misfortune—saw you, won your heart:
For he appeared before you in the glory
Of one who brought Rome's vengeance in his hands.
Judaea went pale; and sad Antiochus
Was numbered first among the vanquished. Soon
That stern interpreter of my misfortune,
Your mouth, commanded mine to silence. Then
For a long time I argued; my eyes spoke;
My tears and sighs pursued you everywhere.
At last your rigor tipped the scales, imposing
Exile or silence on me. I had to promise,
And even swear it. But, since at this moment
I dare speak openly, when you exacted
That unfair promise, my heart made a vow
To love you without end.

Berenice.   What are you saying?

Antiochus. Five years I have been silent, and I shall
    soon
Be silent longer. I accompanied
The forces of my rival. I hoped to pour
My blood after my tears, or that at least
By a thousand exploits carried to your ears,
My name would speak for me, since I could not.
Heaven seemed to promise me an end of pain.
You wept my death, which proved, alas, to be
A false alarm. Vain perils! How great my error!
For Titus' valor overpassed my fury.
I had to esteem his virtue. Although expecting
The empire of the world, cherished by all,

Loved, above all, by you, he seemed to invite
All strokes to himself, while hopeless, hated, tired
Of life, his unhappy rival only seemed
To follow him. I see your heart in secret
Applauds me; that you hear with less regret;
And that, attentive to my fatal story,
For Titus' sake you pardon me the rest.
At last, after a siege prolonged and cruel,
He crushed the rebels, a pale and bleeding remnant
Of flames, of famine, and of civil war,
And left their ramparts hidden beneath their ruins.
Rome saw you arrive with him. In the desolate East
How huge was then my grief! For a long time
I wandered aimlessly in Caesarea,
A country sweet to me because my heart
Had once adored you there. I asked for you
In your sad realm. Weeping I sought your footprints.
At last succumbing to my melancholy
I was driven to Italy by my despair.
Fate there reserved for me a final blow.
Titus, embracing me, brought me before you.
You both were hoodwinked by a veil of friendship—
My love became the confidant of yours.
But still my griefs were flattered by some hope:
Rome and Vespasian went through your sighs.
After so many struggles Titus, perhaps,
Would yield. Vespasian is dead and Titus
Is master now. Why, then, should I not flee?
I wished some days in which I could examine
The course of his new rule. My fate is settled.
Your glory is prepared. There'll be enough,
Without me, to be witness of this day,
And add their joy to yours. But as for me,
Who could but mingle tears with them—a victim,
Too constant, of a fruitless love, but glad
To have been able, without crime, to tell,
In my misfortunes, to the eyes that caused them
All my sad tale—I leave you, more in love
Than I have ever been.
   Berenice.   I did not think,
My lord, that on the day that should unite

My fate with Caesar, a man could, with impunity,
Come in my sight to declare himself my lover.
My silence is a proof of friendship now,
And for its sake I overlook a speech
Which is an insult. I did not interrupt
While you were speaking: and I will do more—
Receive your farewells with regret. Heaven knows
That in the midst of honors which it sends,
I hoped you'd be a witness of my joy.
With all the world I held your worth in honor.
You admired Titus: Titus cherished you.
A hundred times it has been sweet to me
To encounter Titus in his other self.

   Antiochus. And that is why I flee. I shun, too late,
Those cruel meetings where I have no part.
I flee from Titus—flee from the very name
Which troubles me, that name which, every moment,
Is uttered by your lips. What more shall I say?
I flee from eyes which, always seeing me,
Never see me. Farewell. I go, my heart
Too full of your image, to await, still loving,
The death which is my lot. But do not fear
That my blind grief will fill the universe
With talk of my misfortune: for the news
Of a death, for which I pray, will alone remind you
That I had lived till then. Farewell.   [*Exit* ANTIOCHUS.

(I.5)

   Phenice. Oh, how I pity him! Such faithfulness
Deserved a happier fate. Do you not, madam,
Pity him too?
   Berenice.   His prompt departure leaves me,
I must confess, a secret sorrow.
   Phenice.   I
Would have made him stay.
   Berenice.   I make him stay?
I'd rather lose all memory of him.
Should I encourage an insensate love?
   Phenice. Titus has not yet told you of his thought.
Rome looks upon you, madam, with jealous eyes:
The rigor of her laws makes me afraid

On your account: marriage among the Romans
Is but with Roman women; Rome hates all kings;
And Berenice is Queen.

   Berenice.   The time is past,
Phenice, when I could tremble. Titus loves me;
He is all-powerful; he has but to speak,
And he will see the Senate bring me homage,
And the people crown his images with flowers.
Have you seen, Phenice, the splendor of this night?
Have not your eyes been feasted with its grandeur?
The torches, the bonfire, the whole night ablaze,
The eagles, the fasces, the people and the army,
The crowd of kings, the consuls, and the Senate
All borrowing luster from my lover, the gold,
The purple, which enhanced his glory, and
The laurel, witnessing his victory;
The eyes which came from all parts of the world,
Fixing on him their eager looks; and then
His splendid bearing and his gentle presence. . . .
O heavens! with what respect and what compliance
All hearts assure him of their inward faith!
Tell me: can one behold him without thinking,
As I do, that if by chance he had been born
In some obscurity, the world would still,
In seeing him, have recognized its master?
But, Phenice, where are my pleasant memories
Leading me now? While at this very moment
The whole of Rome is offering prayers for Titus,
And consecrating the beginning of his reign
By sacrifices, why do we delay?
Let us go also to offer up our prayers
To heaven, which protects him, for his rule.
Soon without waiting for him, unawaited,
I will return to seek him, and at this meeting
Tell all that feelings held in check so long
Inspire in hearts contented with each other.

ACT TWO

TITUS, PAULINUS, *and* ATTENDANTS.

TITUS. Have you informed the King of Comagena
That I await him?
   Paulinus.   I ran to the Queen's apartment
Where he was said to be: but he had gone
When I arrived. I have commanded one
To tell him of your orders.
   Titus.   It is well.
What is the Queen doing?
   Paulinus.   At this moment
Queen Berenice, appreciative of your bounties,
Prays heaven for your prosperity, my lord.
She has gone out.
   Titus.   Too lovable princess!
Alas!
   Paulinus. Whence comes this sadness for her sake?
Almost the whole East now is going to bow
Beneath her law, and yet you pity her!
   Titus. Paulinus, let them leave you now with me.

                       [*Exeunt* ATTENDANTS.

                             (II.2)

   Titus. Rome now is still uncertain ᶠ my plans
And waits to learn the future destiny
Of the Queen, Paulinus. The secrets of her heart
And mine are made a topic of debate
For all the world. The time has therefore come
When I must speak. What does the public voice
Say of the Queen and me? Speak. What do you hear?
   Paulinus. On every hand, my lord, I hear them praise
Your virtues and her beauties.
   Titus.   What do they say
Of the sighs I breathe for her? What do they think
Will come of love so faithful?
   Paulinus.   Do what you will:
Love, cease to love, the court will always be
A party to your wishes.

Titus.   And I have seen
This court of flatterers, always too anxious
To please its masters, even approve the horrors
Of Nero's crimes; I've seen it on its knees,
Sanctifying his fury. I do not take
Idolatrous courtiers for my judge, Paulinus.
I set myself a nobler stage, and deaf
To the voice of flattery, I wish to hear,
Through your mouth, every heart. Such was your promise.
Respect and fear around me shut the way
To all complaint; the better to see and hear,
I've asked you, dear Paulinus, for your eyes
And ears; my intimate friendship I have put
Even at this price: I've wanted you to be
The interpreter of hearts; that your sincerity
Should always through the ring of flatterers
Bring me the truth. Speak therefore. What ought now
Queen Berenice to hope? Will Rome be indulgent
Or cruel to her? Ought I to believe
So beautiful a queen on Caesars' throne
Offends their sight?

Paulinus.   Be sure of it, my lord.
Through reason or caprice, Rome does not want her
To be their Empress. They know she is delightful;
And that her beauty seems to ask of you
The world's dominion; they even say she has
The heart of a Roman; she has a thousand virtues,
But she is Queen, my lord. Rome, by a law
Which cannot be repealed, does not allow
The mingling of a foreign blood with hers,
And does not recognize the unlawful fruits
Born of a marriage made against her rules.
Besides, you know, in banishing her kings,
Rome to this name, sacred and noble once,
Attached a strong and everlasting hatred;
And though she is obedient and loyal
To Caesars, yet this remnant of her pride,
This hatred, has survived in every heart
The loss of liberty. Julius, the first
To subdue her, who in the midst of loud alarms
Silenced the laws, for Cleopatra burned;

And then, without proposing, left her there
Alone in the Orient to sigh in vain.
Mark Antony, who loved her beyond reason,
Forgot indeed his glory and his country
Upon her breast, but dared not call himself
Her husband: till Rome went to seek him there
Even at her feet, refusing to unarm
Her avenging fury till she had destroyed
The lover and the mistress. Since that time,
My lord, Caligula and Nero, monsters
Whose names I mention only with regret,
Who, keeping the appearance of a man,
Trod underneath their feet the laws of Rome,
Feared that one law, and did not dare to kindle
The torch of a marriage odious in our eyes.
You've ordered me, above all, to be frank.
You've seen the brother of the freedman Pallas,
Felix, still branded by the irons of Claudius,
Become the husband of two queens, my lord;
And, if I must obey you to the end,
Those queens were of the blood of Berenice.
And you believe you could without offense
Into the bed of Caesars introduce
A queen, while the Orient beholds a slave
Pass straight from our chains to its own queens' bed?
That is what Romans think about your love;
And it may be the Senate, before nightfall,
Bearing the wishes of the Roman world
Will here repeat to you what I have said;
And say that Rome itself falls at your feet
And asks that you should make another choice
Worthy of her and you. You might, my lord,
Prepare your answer.
    Titus.   Alas! What love
They wish me to renounce!
    Paulinus.   Your love is strong,
I must confess.
    Titus.   Stronger a thousand times
Than you can think, Paulinus. It has come
To be for me a necessary pleasure
To see her every day, to love and please her.

I have done more—I've nothing secret from you—
For her I've thanked the gods a thousand times,
For having chosen my father from the depths
Of Idumea, for having placed the East
And the army under him, and stirring up
The rest of the world, for having entrusted Rome
Into his peaceful hands. I've even wished
For my father's place; I who a hundred times,
If fate had been less harsh and wished to extend
His span of life, had gladly given my days
To prolong his: all this (how ill a lover
Knows that which he desires!) in the fond hope
Of setting Berenice upon the throne,
Of giving recognition to her love
And loyalty, and seeing at her feet
The world as well as me. But now, Paulinus,
In spite of all my love, and all her charms,
After a thousand vows backed up by tears,
Now I can crown her loveliness, and now
I love her more than ever, when a marriage,
Joining our fates, can pay in a single day
Five years of promises, I'm going, Paulinus . . .
O heavens! can I declare it?
    Paulinus.   What, my lord?
    Titus. I'm going to part for ever. At this moment
I have not come to yield my heart, Paulinus.
If I have made you speak, if I have wished
To listen to you, it was because I hoped
Your zeal in secret would at last confound
A love I crush reluctantly. For long
Berenice held the victory in the balance,
And if at last I lean towards the scale
In which my honor's poised, you must believe
That it has cost to conquer so much love
Battles from which my heart will surely bleed
For longer than a day. I loved, I sighed
In a deep peace—another then was charged
With the world's rule—then master of my fate,
Free in my love, and only to myself
Accountable for my desires. But heaven

Had scarcely called my father to his rest,
As soon as my sad hand had closed his eyes,
I was disabused of my romantic error.
I felt the burden which was placed on me;
Far from belonging to the one I loved,
I knew that soon I must, my dear Paulinus,
Renounce my very self; that the will of the gods
Contrary to my loves, delivered me,
For the rest of my days, to all the world. Today
Rome watches my new conduct. What disgrace
To me, how ominous to her, if I
Should, from my first step, overturn her rights,
And found my happiness upon the ruins
Of ancient laws! Resolved now to accomplish
This cruel sacrifice, I wished to prepare
Sad Berenice; but how can I begin?
For twenty times, during this week, I've wished
To speak of it to her; but from the first
My halting tongue seemed frozen in my mouth.
I hoped at least my trouble and my grief
Would make her guess our common misery;
But she, quite unsuspecting, though aware
Of my distress, offered me then her hand
To wipe away my tears, and in her blindness
Does not foresee the ending of a love
She has too much deserved. At last this morning
I have recalled my constancy. I must see her
And break my silence. Meanwhile I await
Antiochus to recommend to him
This prize I cannot keep. I wish him now
To take her back to the Orient. Tomorrow
Rome shall behold the Queen depart with him.
She'll soon be informed of it by me. I go
To speak with her for the last time.
    Paulinus.   I expected
No less from the love of honor which everywhere
Has brought you victory. Judaea enslaved,
Its smoking walls the eternal monuments
Of your noble spirit, gave me enough assurance
That your great heart would not destroy its work;

And that a hero, conqueror of many nations,
Would sooner or later find the way to conquer
His passions too.
  Titus.   Ah! under its fine names
How cruel is this glory! How my sad eyes
Would find her now more beautiful if I had
Only to outface death! What do I say?
This passionate love of glory Berenice
Once kindled in my breast. As you well know,
I did not always have the same renown.
My youth was nourished in the court of Nero,
And there by bad example was misled,
To follow the too easy slope of pleasure.
I fell in love with Berenice, Paulinus.
What will a heart not do to please the one
It loves, and win its conqueror? I poured out
My blood; and all submitted to my arms.
Triumphant I returned. But blood and tears
Were not sufficient to deserve her love.
And so I undertook the happiness
Of a thousand of unfortunates. My bounties
Were spread on every side. Happy!—and happier
Than you can comprehend—when I could come
Before her approving eyes, and bring with me
A thousand hearts vanquished by benefits!
I owe her all, Paulinus. Cruel reward!
All that I owe to her will fall and crush her.
To pay for all my glory, all my virtues,
I shall say to her: "Go, and never see me more."
  Paulinus. How now, my lord! Does this magnificence
Which will extend her power to the Euphrates,
And all those honors which surprised the Senate
By their excess, still let you fear the name
Of ingrate? Berenice is made to rule
A hundred peoples.
  Titus.   Weak distractions for
A grief so great! I know the Queen, Paulinus,
And know too well her heart has never asked
For anything save mine. I fell in love
With her, and she with me. And since that day
(Should I say fatal day, or fortunate?)

She had, in loving, only love for goal;
A foreigner at Rome, unknown at court,
She passed her days without a single claim
Except some time to see me, and the rest
To wait for me. Yet if sometimes, remiss,
I fail to come at the appointed hour,
I find her drenched in tears, and spend a while
In drying them. In short, the strongest bonds
That love possesses—sweet reproaches, joy
Ever reborn, an artless care to please,
Fear always fresh, loveliness, honor, virtue—
I find them all in her. For five whole years
I've seen her every day, and always thought
I saw her for the first time. But enough!
Let's go, Paulinus, for the more I think
The more I feel my cruel constancy
Begin to waver. What news I bring to her!
Once more, let's go! I must no further think.
I know my duty. I must follow it,
And not consider if I can survive it.

Enter RUTILIUS. (II.3)

Rutilius. My lord, Queen Berenice would speak with
you.
Titus. Ah, Paulinus!
Paulinus. You seem already to recoil!
May you remember all your noble plans!
Now is the time.
Titus. Well, let us see her then.
Let her come in.

Enter BERENICE *and* PHENICE. (II.4)

Berenice. Do not be vexed, my lord,
If my rash zeal breaks in upon the secret
Of this your solitude. For while around me
The assembled court rings with the benefits
With which you've loaded me, is it right, my lord,
That I alone, this moment, should remain
Silent and without gratitude? But, my lord,
(For I know this friend acquainted with the secrets
Of both our hearts)· your mourning now is ended,

Nothing can stay your steps, you are alone,
And yet you do not seek me. I have heard
You'll offer me another crown, but yet
I cannot hear you. Give me peace of mind
And less of glory. Can your love appear
But to the Senate? Ah! Titus! (for love at last
Shuns the constraint of all the formal names
Respect and fear must use) say with what care
Your love is troubled. Has it only kingdoms
Which it can give me? Since when have you thought
That greatness touches me. A sigh, a glance,
One word from your lips: this is the whole ambition
Of a heart like mine. See me more often, Titus,
And give me nothing. Are all your moments now
Devoted to the Empire? Has your heart,
After a whole week, nothing to say to me?
Only a word would reassure my spirits!
But did you speak of me when I surprised you?
Was I the subject of your secret talk?
Was I at least then present to your thought?

   Titus. Doubt it not, madam; and I attest the gods
That always you are present to my eyes.
And neither time nor absence—this I swear—
Can snatch you from this heart which still adores you.

   Berenice. You swear to me an everlasting love,
But with such coldness! Why even do you attest
The power of heaven? And do you need such vows
To conquer my mistrust? This heart, my lord,
Intends not to belie you. I'll believe
A simple sigh of yours.

   Titus.   Madam . . .

   Berenice.   Well, my lord?
Without replying you avert your eyes
And seem to be confounded! Will you now
Offer me only a grief-stricken face?
Does a father's death still occupy your mind?
Can nothing charm now this devouring grief?

   Titus. O would to heaven that my father lived!
How happy I lived then!

   Berenice.   All these regrets
Are true effects of filial piety.

But now your tears have honored him enough:
You owe to Rome and glory other duties.
I do not dare to speak of my own interest.
Berenice once was able to console you
And you have listened with greater pleasure to me.
How many evils I have borne for you.
But for a word from you have sacrificed
Even my tears! You mourn a father. Alas!
Poor griefs! And I—the memory makes me tremble—
Would have been torn from all that I adore,
I, whose grief and torment you well know,
When you have left me only for a moment;
Who on the day when you refused to see me
Would die. . . .

    Titus.   Alas, what have you said to me?
What time have you chosen, madam? Stop, I pray you.
To throw away your bounties on a man
Who is unworthy of them . . .

    Berenice.   Unworthy, my lord?
Can you be that? Perhaps my kindness then
Now wearies you?

    Titus.   No, never was my heart,
Since I must speak, more desperately in love.
But . . .

    Berenice. Continue.

    Titus.   Alas!

    Berenice.   Speak.

    Titus.   Rome . . . the Empire . . .

    Berenice. Well?

    Titus.   Let us go, Paulinus. I cannot speak
Another word to her.   [*Exeunt* TITUS *and* PAULINUS.

                                      (II.5)

    Berenice.   To leave so soon?
And to say nothing to me? Dear Phenice,
How dreadful was this meeting! What have I done?
What does he want? What does his silence mean?

    Phenice. Like you, madam, the more I think of it
The more I'm lost. But can you not recall
Something that might have biased him against you?
Consider now.

Berenice.   Alas! you can believe me:
The more I summon up past memories,
From the day I saw him until this sad day,
The more I see that I can be reproached
For loving him too well. But you have heard.
I need keep nothing back. Speak. Did I say
Anything to displease him? But who knows?
Perhaps with too much warmth I have belittled
His gifts, or blamed his sorrow. Does he fear
The hate of Rome? Alas! if that were true . . .
But no, a hundred times he's reassured
My love against their laws; a hundred times . . .
Let him explain to me his hurtful silence:
I cannot breathe in this uncertainty.
How would I live, Phenice, if I believed
That he neglected me, or else, still worse,
That I'd offended him? Let us return
Upon his steps. But when I think of it,
I do believe I've found the origin
Of this disturbance. He'll have known what's happened:
The love of Antiochus is what offends him.
They told me he awaited now the King.
Let us not seek elsewhere, Phenice, the cause
Of my distress. And doubtless this affliction
Which made me fear is but a light suspicion
That's easy to disarm. I do not boast
Of such a trivial victory. Ah! Titus,
Would to heaven that, without a stain
Upon your honor, a more powerful rival
Would test my faith by putting at my feet
More empires than you bring, that he could offer
Numberless scepters for my love, while you
Could give me nothing but your soul! Ah! then,
Dear Titus, loved, victorious, you would see
The value that I place upon your heart.
Let's go, Phenice, a word will satisfy him.
Take heart again, for I can please him still.
Too soon I ranked me with the unfortunate:
If Titus is jealous, Titus is in love.

ACT THREE

TITUS, ANTIOCHUS, *and* ARSACES.

TITUS. What! Prince, you're leaving Rome? What sudden
   cause
Now hurries your departure, nay, your flight?
Did you wish to hide even your farewell from me?
Is it as enemy you leave the city?
What will the court, and Rome, and the Empire say?
But what can I not say who am your friend?
Of what do you accuse me? Have I ranked you
Among the common crowd of kings? My heart
Was open to you: while my father lived
That was the only present I could make you;
And when my hand is ready as my heart
You flee the benefits that I propose!
Do you imagine that I will forget
My former fortune, and only fix my thoughts
Upon my greatness? And that all my friends
Will seem to me but distant nobodies
Whom I no longer need? You yourself, Prince,
Who wish to steal away, out of my sight,
Are now more necessary to me than ever.
   Antiochus. I, my lord?
   Titus.   You.
   Antiochus. Alas! what can you expect
Of an unfortunate prince except his prayers?
   Titus. I've not forgotten that my victory
Owed half its glory to your deeds; that Rome
Beheld among the vanquished more than one
Wearing Antiochus' chains; and that she saw
The spoils of the Jews extorted by your hands
Displayed in the Capitol. I do not want
Such deeds of blood from you. I only wish
To borrow now your voice. For Berenice,
Indebted to your pains, believes she has
In you a genuine friend. In Rome she sees
And hears no one but you; you are one heart,

One soul with us. And therefore, in the name
Of such a fine and constant friendship, use
The power which you have over her. See her
On my behalf.
    Antiochus.   Appear before her eyes?
But I have said farewell to her forever.
    Titus. Prince, for my sake, you must speak to her again.
    Antiochus. Ah! speak to her yourself. The Queen adores
    you:
Why should you now deprive yourself, my lord,
Of the joy of making her a sweet avowal?
She waits for you impatiently, my lord.
I'll answer, as I leave, for her obedience;
She has even told me that, ready to marry her,
You'll see her only to prepare her for it.
    Titus. Ah! such sweet words should please me! And if I
Had this to do, how happy I would be!
My joy was waiting to burst out today,
And yet today, Prince, I must leave her.
    Antiochus.   Leave her!
You, my lord?
    Titus.   Such is my destiny. For her
And Titus there will be no wedding now.
I flattered me in vain with such a hope.
Prince, she must leave with you tomorrow.
    Antiochus.   O heavens!
What do I hear?
    Titus.   Pity my onerous greatness.
As master of the world I guide its fortunes;
I can make and unmake kings, but not dispose
Of my own heart. Rome was at all times hostile
To kings, and now disdains a lovely queen
Born in the purple: the brightness of her crown,
Her hundred kingly ancestors, dishonor
My love, and wound the sight of all. My heart,
Free otherwise, can without risk of murmuring,
Love one of humble birth; and Rome with pleasure
Would at my hands receive the unworthiest beauty
She hides within her bosom. Julius himself
Yielded to that same resistless torrent
Which sweeps me now away. If on the morrow

The people do not see the Queen depart,
She'll hear that people come to me enraged
To ask for her departure from their sight.
Let us, then, spare my name and her renown
This insult; and since we must yield indeed,
Let's yield to our glory. During this last week
My mouth and looks, both mute, should have prepared her
For this sad utterance; and even now,
Anxious and eager, she wished me to express
What I was thinking. Relieve the torment now
Of a frustrated lover. Spare my heart
The pain of telling her. Explain to her
My grief and silence; beg her, above all,
To let me avoid her. Be the only witness
Of her tears and of mine. Take my farewells
To her, and hers to me. Let us both flee,
Flee from a deadly sight which would destroy
The remnant of our constancy. Ah, Prince,
If the hope of reigning still within my heart
Can soften now the harshness of her fate,
Swear to her that with ever-faithful heart,
Lamenting in my court, and more in exile
Even than her, bearing the name of lover
Until the tomb, my reign will only be
An endless banishment—if heaven, indeed,
Still not content with snatching her from me,
Would doom me to a long, afflicted life.
You are attached to her by friendship, Prince:
Do not abandon her in her distress.
Let the Orient see you coming in her train,
And let it be a triumph, not a flight;
Let such close friendship have eternal ties,
And let my name be always on your lips.
To make your countries closer to each other,
Let the Euphrates be your common frontier.
I know the Senate, ringing with your name,
Will, with a common voice, confirm this gift.
I join Cilicia to your Comagena.
Farewell. Do not desert my love, the Queen;
She was the one desire of my heart,
And I will love her till I breathe my last.   [*Exit* TITUS.

(III.2)

Arsaces. So heaven learns at last to give you justice.
You will depart, my lord, but with the Queen.
She is not snatched from you; she is delivered
Into your hands.
    Antiochus.   Arsaces, give me time
To breathe. The change is great, and my surprise
Is overwhelming; Titus puts all he loves
Into my hands! Should I believe, O Gods!
What I have heard? And when I do believe it,
Should I rejoice?
    Arsaces.   What should I think of you,
My lord? What obstacle is there to your joy?
Did you deceive me when you left her presence,
When, agitated by your last good-bys,
Trembling at having spoken out at last,
You told me of your new audacity?
You fled a wedding which had made you tremble.
That wedding now is broken. What can disturb you?
Follow the joys to which love now invites you.
    Antiochus. Arsaces, I am charged to escort her home.
For long I shall enjoy her company:
Her eyes may well grow used to mine; her heart
Will see the difference between Titus' coldness
And my long constancy. Titus' greatness
Here overwhelms me; everything in Rome
Pales now beside his splendor; but though the East
Is full of his memory, yet Berenice
Will find there traces of my glory too.
    Arsaces. Be sure, my lord, that everything falls out
According to your wishes.
    Antiochus.   How we both
Love to deceive ourselves!
    Arsaces.   How so, my lord?
    Antiochus. What! could I please her? And would Bere-
        nice
No longer be indifferent to my pleas?
Would Berenice soothe my sorrows with a word?
Do you think merely that among her woes,
When all the world neglects her loveliness,

The ungrateful one would let me weep for her,
Or that she'd stoop from my hands to receive
What she would know my love was bound to give.

Arsaces. Who can console her better than yourself
In her disgrace, my lord? Her fortune now
Puts on a different face, for Titus leaves her.

Antiochus. But from this change nothing will come to
me
Save the new torment of learning from her tears
How much she loves him. I shall see her grieve;
And I myself shall pity her. For fruit
Of all my love I'll have the mournful task
Of gathering tears which are not shed for me.

Arsaces. What! will you still delight to vex yourself?
And was there ever so much weakness seen
In an heroic heart. Open your eyes,
My lord, and let us think between ourselves
By how many reasons Berenice is yours.
Since Titus now no longer seeks to please her,
Think that your marriage to her is necessary.

Antiochus. Necessary?

Arsaces.   Allow some days for tears.
Let her first storm of weeping run its course.
Everything then will speak for you: scorn, vengeance,
Titus' absence, time, and your own presence,
Three scepters that her arm cannot uphold
Without assistance; your two neighboring states
Which seek to be united. Interest, reason,
Friendship—all bind you now.

Antiochus.   Arsaces,
I breathe again: you bring me back to life.
I joyfully accept such sweet presage.
Why do we now delay? Let us perform
What is expected of us. Let us go in;
And, as we are commanded, tell the Queen
Titus abandons her. . . . But rather stay.
What am I doing? Is it for me, Arsaces,
To take upon me now this cruel task?
Whether because of virtue or of love
My heart shrinks from it. That lovely Berenice
Should hear from my lips that she is forsaken!

Ah! Queen! Who would have thought that you would hear
That word pronounced to you!

Arsaces.   Her hate will fall
On Titus only. If you speak, my lord,
It is at his request.

Antiochus.   Let us not see her.
We should respect her grief. Enough will come
To bring the evil tidings. Is she not
Unforunate enough that she must hear
To what scorn she has been condemned by Titus,
Without the addition of the fatal blow
Of learning of this scorn from his own rival?
Once more, let us depart; and not be burdened
With her eternal hatred by these tidings.

Arsaces. Here she is, my lord. Make up your mind.
Antiochus. O heavens!

              Enter BERENICE *and* PHENICE.   (III.3)

Berenice.   My lord! you have not gone!
Antiochus.   Madam,
I see you are disappointed. It was Caesar
You hoped to find. But you have him to blame,
If, after my farewells, my presence still
Distresses you. Perhaps I would have been
In Ostia, if he had not forbidden
My exit from his court.

Berenice.   For you alone
He seeks: and he avoids us all.

Antiochus.   He kept me
Only to speak of you.

Berenice.   Of me, Prince?
Antiochus.   Yes,
Madam.

Berenice. And what could he have said to you?
Antiochus. Thousands could tell you better than I can.
Berenice. What, my lord! . . .
Antiochus.   Suspend your wrath a while.
Others, at such a time, would not be silent,
But rather triumph, and with joyful boldness
Give way to your impatience. But I, still trembling,

I, to whom your quiet, as you well know,
Is dearer than my own, would rather vex you
Than cause you such distress, and fear your grief
More than your anger. Before the day is past
You will acquit me. Farewell, madam.

Berenice. O heavens!
What strange words! Stay, Prince. I cannot hide
My trouble from your sight. You see before you
A queen distressed, who at the point of death
Asks you two words. You are afraid, you say,
To trouble my repose; but your cruel silence
Spares me no pain: it rather stirs in me,
Sorrow and wrath, and hatred. If, my lord,
My peace of mind is precious to you still,
If I was ever dear unto your eyes,
Enlighten now my soul's perplexity:
What did Titus say to you?

Antiochus. Madam,
In the name of the gods . . .

Berenice. Do you so little fear
To disobey me?

Antiochus. I have but to speak
For you to hate me.

Berenice. Speak, I charge you.

Antiochus. Gods!
What violence! Madam, once again, you'll praise
My silence.

Berenice. Prince, content my wishes now,
Or be assured for ever of my hate.

Antiochus. After that, madam, I cannot remain silent
Well, since you wish it, I must satisfy you.
Be under no illusion: for the news
I have to break to you is worse, perhaps,
Than what you've dared to think. I know your heart.
And you must be prepared for me to strike it
Even in its tenderest spot. Titus has asked me . . .

Berenice. What?

Antiochus. To say that you and he must separate
For ever.

Berenice. Separate? Who? Titus and Berenice?

Antiochus. I must, before you, render justice to him.
All that a sensitive and generous heart,
Wrung by despairing love, can hold of horror,
I've seen in his. He weeps. He worships you.
But yet what use for him to love you still?
A queen is suspect to the Roman Empire.
So you must separate, and you leave tomorrow.
    Berenice. We separate! Alas, Phenice!
    Phenice.   Show now
The greatness of your soul. This blow, indeed,
Is bitter; it must shock you.
    Berenice.   To leave me now
After so many vows! Titus who swore . . .
I cannot believe it. No, he does not leave me.
His honor is at stake. They try to turn me
Against his innocence. This snare is laid
Only to disunite us. Titus loves me.
Titus does not desire that I should die.
Let's go and see him. I wish to speak with him
At once. Come.
    Antiochus.   Could you look at me and think . . . ?
    Berenice. You long too much for this that you have said
For you to persuade me. I do not believe you.
But, true or false, take care you never come
Within my sight. [*To* PHENICE.] Don't leave me now,
        Phenice,
In my sad plight. Alas! I do what I can
To delude myself.   [*Exeunt* BERENICE *and* PHENICE.

(III.4)

    Antiochus.   Am I deluded too?
Did I hear aright? That I should keep myself
Out of her sight! I'll take good care of it.
And should I not have gone by this if Titus,
Against my will, had not prevented me?
I must indeed depart. Come, Arsaces.
She thought to hurt me, but her hatred is
A blessing to me. A little while ago
You saw me leaving restless and bewildered,
Loving her, jealous, in despair—and now

I will depart, perhaps, with unconcern.
    Arsaces. Now, less than ever, should you go away.
    Antiochus. I to stay here to see myself disdained,
And held responsible for Titus' coldness?
See myself punished for my rival's guilt?
With what injustice, what unworthiness,
She doubted my sincerity to my face:
Titus, she said, still loves her; I betray her.
Ungrateful woman! To accuse me now
Of such base treachery! At the very moment
When I was spreading out before her eyes
My rival's tears; and when to comfort her
I made him appear loving and constant, more
Than he really is perhaps.
    Arsaces.   With what distress
Do you vex yourself, Prince? Give this torrent time
To flow away. In a week, in a month, perhaps,
It must have passed. Only remain.
    Antiochus.   No, Arsaces,
I'm leaving her. I feel that I could pity
Her grief: my honor and my peace of mind
Both urge me to depart. Come, let us go
So far away, Arsaces, that for long
We do not hear of her. There still remains
Enough of daylight. In my palace now
I'll wait for your return. See if her grief
Has not affected her too much. Run now;
Before we go let us at least be sure
That she is still alive.

ACT FOUR

BERENICE, *alone.*

BERENICE. Phenice does not come! O cruel time,
How dilatory you seem to my swift wishes!
I fret, rush to and fro, weak and dejected;
My strength abandons me, and waiting kills me.

She does not come! How this delay affrights
My heart with ill foreboding! She will not have
Any reply to give me: ungrateful Titus
Declined to hear her. He flees, he steals away
From my just wrath.

Enter PHENICE.   (IV.2)

Berenice.   Dear Phenice, have you seen
The Emperor? What has he said? Is he coming?
    Phenice. Yes, I have seen him, madam. I have depicted
Your soul's distress; and seen the flowing tears
He tried to restrain.
    Berenice.   Is he coming?
    Phenice.   Doubt not, madam,
He's going to come. But do you wish to appear
In this disordered state? Compose yourself,
Recover your possession. Let me fasten
These loosened veils, fix this disheveled hair
By which your eyes are hidden. Let me mend
The ravage of your tears.
    Berenice.   Let be, let be.
He'll see his own work. And what avail to me
These useless ornaments, if my faith and tears,
If my complaints . . . But what do I say? My tears!
If my sure ruin, if my death prepared,
Brings him not back, tell me then what effect
Your needless help, and all this feeble luster,
Which touches him no longer, will produce?
    Phenice. Why do you make him this unjust reproach?
I hear a noise. The Emperor approaches.
Come, madam, shun the crowd. Come in, at once.
Meet him alone, in private, in your room.
                    [*Exeunt* BERENICE *and* PHENICE.

Enter TITUS, PAULINUS, *and* ATTENDANTS.

                                    (IV.3)

    Titus. Paulinus, soothe the Queen's anxiety:
I'm going to see her. I wish a little time
In solitude. Let all depart.
    Paulinus.   O heavens!
How I dread this struggle! O great Gods,

Preserve his glory and the country's honor!
Let's see the Queen.

[*Exeunt* PAULINUS *and* ATTENDANTS.

(IV.4)

Titus.   Well, Titus, what will you do?
Berenice now awaits you. Where are you going?
Are your farewells ready? Is your mind made up?
And will your heart be cruel enough? For now
In this coming struggle it is not enough
To be but steadfast—I must be barbarous.
Shall I hold out against those dovelike eyes
Which know so well the ways into my heart?
When I shall see them, armed with all their beauty,
Fastened on mine, dismay me with their tears,
Shall I remember then my mournful duty?
Shall I be able to say then to her:
"I do not wish to see you any more"?
I come to pierce a heart which I adore,
A heart that loves me. Why should I pierce it then?
Who orders it? Myself. For has Rome yet
Expressed her wishes? Do we hear her cry
Around the palace? Do I see the State
At the edge of a precipice? And can I save it
But by this sacrifice? All tongues are silent;
And I alone, too prompt to be disturbed,
Put forward evils that I can repel.
Who knows if Rome, aware of the Queen's virtues,
Will not regard her as a Roman? Rome
Can justify my choice by hers. No, no,
Once more, let's not be hasty. For when Rome
Puts in the balance with her laws such love,
So many tears, and so much constancy
Rome will be for us. . . . Titus, open your eyes!
What air do you breathe? Are you not in a land
Where everyone sucks in with mother's milk
Hatred of kings, which cannot be effaced
By fear or love? By casting out her kings
Rome judged your queen. Have you not heard this voice
From your earliest years? Did you not hear again
Fame tell your duty even in your army?

Did you not hear, when Berenice crossed your path,
How Rome regarded her? How many times
Must it be repeated to you? Ah, coward! Choose love;
Renounce the Empire: go to the end of the world
And live alone with her. Give place to hearts
Worthier to reign. Are these the glorious plans
That were to consecrate my memory
In all men's hearts? I've reigned now for a week:
And till this day what have I done for honor?
I have done all for love. Then what account
Of time so precious can I render now?
Where are the happy days that I should bring?
What tears have I dried? In what contented eyes
Have I already feasted on the fruit
Of my beneficence? Have the destinies
Of the world been changed? Do I know how many days
Heaven has allotted me? And of those few,
So long awaited—Ah! unfortunate!
How many I have lost already! No,
Delay no longer: do what honor asks.
Break the one link. . . .

Enter BERENICE.   (IV.5)

Berenice.   No. Leave me now, I tell you.
In vain, Phenice, your counsels hold me back,
For I must see him. Ah, my lord, you're here.
Well, is it true indeed that Titus leaves me?
That we must part? That he has ordered it?

Titus. Do not crush further an unfortunate prince.
We must not here be moved to tenderness.
I am devoured by misery cruel enough
Without the addition of your precious tears
To torture me still more. Recall instead
That heart that often made me recognize
The voice of duty. It is time for it.
Compel your love to silence: with an eye
Enlightened both by honor and by reason
Look on my duty in its sternest guise.
Against yourself now fortify my heart;
Help me, if possible, to overcome
My weakness, to restrain my ceaseless tears;

Or, if we cannot thus command our tears,
Let honor help us to sustain our griefs,
That all the world may recognize the tears
Shed by an emperor and a queen. 'Tis true,
My Princess, we must separate.
    Berenice.   Ah, cruel!
Is it not late to tell me? What have you done?
Alas! I thought I was beloved. My soul,
Accustomed to the joy of seeing you,
Lived but for you. Did you not know your laws
When for the first time I confessed my love?
To what excess of love have I been brought!
Why did you not say then: "Unfortunate Queen,
Where would you pledge your love? What is your hope?
Give not your heart which cannot be received."
Did you receive it only to give it back
Now when that heart is anxious to belong
To you alone? The Empire twenty times
Conspired against us. Then was the time indeed:
Why did you not forsake me? A thousand reasons
Would then have comforted my wretchedness:
I could accuse your father of my death,
The Roman people, the Senate, all the Empire,
The world itself rather than your dear hand.
Their hatred, declared against me long ago,
Had long ago prepared me for my fate.
I should not have received this cruel blow
Now when I hope for lasting happiness,
And your blest love can have all it desires,
When Rome is silent, when your father dies,
When all the world is bowing at your feet,
And I have nothing more to dread, save you.
    Titus. And it was I alone who could destroy
Myself, also. I lived then in a state
Of self-deception: for my heart forbore
To look into the future, to discover
What might in time to come disjoin our hearts.
I wished that nought should be invincible
To my desires, I pondered nothing closely,
I hoped the impossible. Who knows? I hoped
To die within your sight before there came

This grievous parting. The very obstacles
Seemed to increase my love. The Empire spoke:
I did not hear the voice of glory then
As now it speaks within an emperor's heart.
I know the agonies to which this plan
Delivers me; I feel that without you
I shan't know how to live—my heart is ready
To leave me. But it is no more a question
Of living. I must reign.

    Berenice.   Then reign, harsh man.
Appease your glory. I dispute no longer.
Before believing you, I had to wait
That that same mouth, after a thousand vows
Of love which should unite us every moment,
That very mouth, confessing in my sight
Its infidelity, should prescribe for me
An everlasting absence. I myself
Wished, in this place, to hear you. I'll hear no more.
Farewell forever. Forever! Ah! my lord!
Do you consider how that cruel word
Is terrible when one loves? In a month, a year,
How will we suffer that so many seas
Divide me from you; that the day begins,
That the day ends, and Titus cannot see
His Berenice, nor all the livelong day
Can I see Titus! But how blind I am,
And how my pains are wasted! Will the ingrate,
Consoled for my departure in advance,
Deign to count up the days of absence? Days
So long for me will seem too short for him.

    Titus. I shall not have to count so many days.
I hope that soon you'll hear the mournful tidings
That force you to admit that you were loved.
You'll see that Titus could not, without dying . . .

    Berenice. If it is true, my lord, why sever us?
I do not speak of happy nuptials now.
Has Rome condemned me not to see you more?
Why do you grudge me even the air you breathe?

    Titus. Alas! you can prevail; stay, if you will.
I'll not forbid it. But I feel my weakness,

For I shall have to struggle, and to fear you,
Without a pause, and always watch my steps
Drawn every hour towards you by your charms.
What do I say? Even at this very moment
My heart, beside itself, remembers only
How much it loves you.

Berenice. Well, my lord, what then?
What can happen? Do you see the Romans
Ready to rise against you?

Titus. Who can tell
How they would take this wrong? If they should talk,
If cries succeed complaints, must I by bloodshed
Then justify my choice? If they are silent,
And abrogate their laws to my desires,
To what would you expose me? By what depth
Of base compliance must I in the end
Pay for their patience? What will they not dare
To ask of me? Could I maintain the laws
I cannot keep myself?

Berenice. You count for nothing
The tears of Berenice.

Titus. Count them for nothing!
Ah! heaven! How unjust!

Berenice. For unjust laws,
Which you could change, you will now plunge yourself
In everlasting grief. Rome has her rights,
My lord; have you not yours? Are hers indeed
More sacrosanct than ours? Answer me. Speak.

Titus. You torture me.

Berenice. You are Emperor, my lord,
And yet you weep!

Titus. Yes, it is true; I weep,
I sigh, I tremble. But yet when I accepted
The Empire, I was made by Rome to swear
To uphold her rights—and this I ought to do.
Rome more than once has tried the constancy
Of men like me. If you trace back her story
Even to her birth, you'll see that they were always
Obedient to her orders. There was one
Who, jealous of his word, went to her foes

To seek the punishment of death ordained;
And one proscribed his own victorious son;
Another with dry eyes, almost unmoved,
Beheld his two sons dying by his orders.*
Unfortunate man! But always with the Romans
Their country and their glory won the day.
I know that Titus, in forsaking you,
May well surpass their great austerity
Which cannot touch this great attempt of mine;
But, madam, do you think I am unworthy
To leave to future ages an example
Which, without great endeavors, none can copy?

  Berenice. No, I believe that everything is easy
To your barbarity: I think you worthy
To tear my life away. My heart's informed
Of all your sentiments. I'll speak no more
Of letting me stay here. Should I have wished,
Ashamed and scorned, to be the laughingstock
Of those who hate me? I have wished to drive you
To this rejection! It's all over now,
And soon you will not fear me any more.
Do not expect me to burst out in insults,
Or call on heaven, the foe of perjuries;
If heaven is still affected by my tears,
I pray that it forget my sorrows now,
Even as I die. If I should form a vow
Against your injustice, if before she dies
Sad Berenice should wish for an avenger,
I'll seek him only in your inmost heart.
I know such love can never be effaced:
My present sorrow and my former bounty,
My blood which in this palace I would shed
Are enemies enough to leave you with:
And, unrepentant of my perseverance,
I leave my vengeance unto them. Farewell.

                              [*Exit* BERENICE.

               Enter PAULINUS.   (IV.6)

  Paulinus. What will she do, my lord? Is she at last
Disposed to leave?

  * Regulus, Manlius Torquatus, and Brutus.

Titus.   Paulinus, I am lost.
I'll not be able to survive. The Queen
Wishes to die. Come, we must follow her.
Run to her aid.
     Paulinus.   What! have you not commanded
That they should watch her? Her women, every hour
Thronging about her, will divert her mind
From these sad thoughts. No, no, you need not fear.
The worst is over now. Go on, my lord.
The victory is yours. I know too well
You could not hear her without pity—I,
Myself, in seeing her, could not resist it.
But look beyond: think, in this misery,
What glory follows from a moment's pain,
What plaudits the whole world prepares for you,
What future rank . . .
     Titus.   No, I am barbarous.
I hate myself. Not even Nero pushed
His cruelty so far. I'll not endure
That Berenice should die. Come. Let Rome say
What she would say.
     Paulinus.   What, my lord!
     Titus.   I know not,
Paulinus, what I say. Excess of grief
Now overwhelms my spirit.
     Paulinus.   Do not check
The course of your fame. The news of your farewells
Has spread already. Rome, which had lamented,
Is now rejoicing. All the temple altars
Smoke in your honor; and the people laud
Your virtues to the skies, and everywhere
With laurels crown your statues.
     Titus.   Rome! Berenice!
Unfortunate Prince! Why am I Emperor?
Why do I love?

Enter ARSACES *and* ANTIOCHUS.   (IV.7)

     Antiochus.   What have you done, my lord?
The lovely Berenice perhaps is dying
In Phenice's arms. She listens not to tears,
Advice, or reason. She cries for sword or poison.

You alone can take this wish from her.
Your name is mentioned, and that name revives her.
Her eyes are always turned towards your room,
And seem to ask for you. I can't endure it.
The sight is killing me. Why do you tarry?
Show yourself to her. Save so many virtues,
Graces, and beauty, or renounce, my lord,
Humanity itself. Say but one word.

    Titus. What word can I say to her? Do I myself
Know if I still am living?

Enter RUTILIUS.   (IV.8)

    Rutilius.   My lord, the tribunes,
The consuls, and the Senate ask for you
In the name of the whole State. A great concourse
Is following them, who wait impatiently
For you to give them audience.

    Titus.   I hear you,
Immortal Gods! You wish to strengthen now
The heart you see prepared to go astray.

    Paulinus. Come, then, my lord; let us go in and see
The Senate.

    Antiochus. Run to see the Queen.

    Paulinus.   My lord,
Would you by this indignity tread down
The majesty of the Empire? Rome . . .

    Titus.   Enough,
Paulinus. We will go and hear them. Prince,
This is a duty which I can't refuse.
Go you to see the Queen. On my return
I hope she will no longer doubt my love.*

    * In the first edition only, Act Four concludes with a scene
in which Antiochus shamefacedly confesses to Arsaces that, on
finding Berenice in tears, he could not persist in his anger and
had begged Titus to come to her.

ACT FIVE

ARSACES, *alone.*

ARSACES. Where shall I find this ever-faithful prince?

Kind heaven, conduct my steps, and aid my zeal;
So that I can inform him, at this moment
Of happiness he dares no longer dream.

Enter ANTIOCHUS.   (V.2)

Arsaces. What happy fate has brought you to this place,
My lord?

Antiochus. If my return brings you some joy,
Then pity my despair.

Arsaces.   The Queen is leaving,
My lord.

Antiochus. She's leaving?

Arsaces.   By tonight. Her orders
Are given. She is incensed that the Emperor
So long has left her to her tears. Her wrath
Gives way to generous scorn; and Berenice
Renounces Rome and Titus. She desires
To leave before the Romans hear the news
And see her thwarted and rejoice at it.
She writes to Caesar.

Antiochus   Who would have believed it?
And Titus?

Arsaces. He has not appeared before her.
The people, in their joy surrounding him,
Applaud the titles given him by the Senate;
And these respects, these titles, this applause
Become for Titus even as obligations
Which, binding him in honorable chains,
In spite of all his sighs and the Queen's tears,
Fix in his duty his irresolute vows.
All's over now.
Perhaps he will not see her any more.

Antiochus. Causes of hope, Arsaces! I confess it.
But Fortune sports with me so cruelly,
So many times my plans have been upset,
That I have trembled as I listened to you;
Forewarned by nagging fears, my heart believes
That even hoping may vex Fortune now.
But what do I see? Titus comes here to us.
What does he want?

Enter TITUS.　　　　　(V.3)

Titus [*to* ATTENDANTS]. Stay. Do not follow me.
At last I come, Prince, to discharge my promise.
Berenice fills my thoughts, and tortures me
Without relief. I come with heart pierced through
Both by your tears and hers, to soothe your griefs
Less bitter than mine own. Come, Prince, I wish
That you yourself should see for the last time
Whether I love her.　　　　　　[*Exit* TITUS.

　　　　　　　　　　　　　　　(V.4)

Antiochus.　　　　　So much for the hopes
Which you held out to me! You see the triumph
That was awaiting me! So Berenice
Was leaving here in righteous indignation!
And Titus had forsaken her forever!
Great Gods, what have I done? What fatal course
Have you ordained for me? Each living moment
Is a continual move from fear to hope,
From hope to rage. And I still live! Berenice!
Titus! Two cruel creatures! At my tears
You will laugh no more. [*Exeunt* ANTIOCHUS *and* ARSACES.

Enter TITUS, BERENICE, *and* PHENICE.　　(V.5)

Berenice.　　　　　No— I will not hear you.
I am resolved. It is my will to go.
Why do you come into my sight? And why
Come once again to embitter my despair?
Are you not satisfied? I do not wish
To see you any more.
　　Titus.　　　　　For pity's sake,
Hear me.
　　Berenice. The time is past.
　　Titus.　　　　　Madam, one word.
　　Berenice. No.
　　Titus.　　　　Into what trouble does she cast my soul!
Princess, whence comes this sudden change?
　　Berenice.　　　　　　　　All's over.
You wanted me to leave tomorrow—now

I have resolved to leave at once. I'm going.

Titus. Stay.

Berenice.   I stay! And why? To hear the people
Shouting their insults over my misfortune?
Do you not hear their cruel joy while I
Am drowned in tears? What crime or what offense
Has roused them so? Alas! what have I done
Except to love too well?

Titus.   Why listen, madam,
To a senseless mob?

Berenice.   There is nothing that I see
By which I am not wounded. All this chamber
Prepared for me by you, and every place,
Which witnessed for so long my love for you,
Which seemed to speak to me of yours forever,
These festoons where our names are interlaced
Offered on every side to my sad eyes,
Are such impostures that I can't endure it.
Come, Phenice.

Titus.   O heaven! how unjust you are!

Berenice. Return, return to that venerable Senate
Which now applauds you for your cruelty.
Well, have you listened with a glow of pleasure?
Are you contented with your glory now?
And have you promised to forget me quite?
That's not enough to expiate your love:
Have you then promised that you'll always hate me?

Titus. No, I have promised nothing. I to hate you!
That I could ever Berenice forget!
In what a moment did her harsh injustice
Come to afflict me with this cruel thought!
Understand me. Reckon every moment,
And every day for these five years, when I
Have ever with more fervor or more sighs
Told you my heart's desires—no, no, this day
Surpasses all. Never, I do confess,
Have you been loved with so much tenderness;
And never . . .

Berenice.   You love me, you maintain; and yet
I leave at your command! What! do you find
Such charms in my despair? Are you afraid

My eyes will weep too little? What use to me
This heart you vainly offer me again?
Ah, cruel! For pity, show me less of love:
Do not remind me of a thought too dear,
And let me go from here at least persuaded
That I, exiled in secret from your soul,
Leave one who loses me without regret.

[TITUS *reads a letter.*

You've torn from me the letter I've just written.
That's all that I desire of your love now:
Read it, ungrateful man, read it at once,
And let me go.
   Titus.   You shall not go. I cannot
Give my consent: for this departure is
Only a cruel stratagem! You intend
To die! There will remain of all I love
Only a sad remembrance. Seek Antiochus.
Let him come here.

[*Exit* PHENICE. BERENICE *falls on a seat.*

(V.6)

   Titus.   Madam, I now must make you
A true confession. When I tried to imagine
The dreadful moment when, driven by the laws
Of a strict duty, I was bound for ever
To give up seeing you, when I foresaw
That sad good-by approaching, my fears, my struggles,
Your tears, and your reproaches, I prepared
My soul for all the griefs the worst misfortunes
Can make one feel. But I must tell you now,
Whatever I had feared, I'd not foreseen
The smallest part of it. I thought my virtue
Less ready to succumb, and I'm ashamed
Of this confusion into which I've fallen.
I've seen the whole of Rome before my eyes;
The Senate spoke to me, but my vexed soul
Heard without understanding, and in return
For all their joy, gave but a frozen silence.
Rome now is still uncertain of your fate:
And I myself can hardly recollect

If I am Emperor, or even Roman.
I've come to you not knowing my intent,
Brought by my love; and came perhaps to seek
Myself, and know myself. What have I found?
I see death pictured in your eyes; I see
That you are leaving Rome to seek for it.
It is too much. My grief, at this sad sight,
Has reached its final limit. I feel the worst
That can be felt, but yet I see the road
By which I can escape. Do not expect
That, tired of such disquiet, I'll stop your tears
By bridal happiness. To whatever straits
You have reduced me, my unpitying honor
Pursues me every moment. It presents
The Empire ceaselessly to my dazed soul
As incompatible with our marriage still;
Tells me that after all I have achieved,
The luster of my name, I ought to wed you
Now less than ever; and still less to tell you
That I am ready to forsake the Empire
To follow you, contented with my chains,
To sigh with you at the world's end. For you
Yourself would blush at my base conduct then:
You'd see me, madam, going in your train,
A worthless emperor without an empire,
Without a court, a spectacle to men
Of all love's failings. To escape the torments
Which prey upon my soul, as you well know
There is a nobler way; I have been shown
This road by many a hero of old times,
And many a Roman. When excessive evils
Have tired their constancy, they've all explained
The long-continued cruelty of their fate,
As secret orders to resist no more:
And if your tears should longer strike my sight,
And if I see you still resolved to die,
If I must always tremble for your life,
If you will vow not to respect its course,
Madam, you must expect new cause for weeping.
For in my state of mind I cannot tell
What I may do—that my hand, in your sight,

May not our fatal farewells, in the end,
Deluge with blood.
   Berenice.   Alas!
   Titus.   No, there is nothing
Of which I am not capable. My life
Is now within your hands. Think of it, madam,
And if I'm dear to you . . .

        Enter ANTIOCHUS.   (V.7)

   Titus.   Come, Prince, come in.
I sent for you. Be witness of my weakness.
See if I love with little tenderness.
Judge now between us.
   Antiochus.   I believe it all.
I know you both; but know you for yourself
As prince unfortunate. You've honored me
With your esteem, and I can swear to you
Without offense that with your dearest friends
I have disputed for this place—and done so
Even with expense of blood. Despite myself
You both confided in me, the Queen her love,
You yours, my lord. The Queen, who hears me now,
Cannot deny it; she has seen me always
Ardent to praise you, and by any means
Responsive to your trust. You think you owe me
Some thanks for it, but, in this fatal moment,
Would you believe a friend so faithful was
Your rival?
   Titus. My rival!
   Antiochus.   It's time that I should tell you.
Yes, my lord, I've always worshipped her.
I've struggled a hundred times to stop my love:
I've not been able to forget her. At least
I held my tongue. Then your apparent change
Gave me some feeble hope: the tears of the Queen
Put out that hope. Her eyes all bathed in tears
Begged for your presence; so I came, my lord,
To call you. You came back. You love; you're loved.
You have surrendered, as I knew you would.
For the last time I've communed with my self;
I've made a last proof of my courage now;

My senses are restored. I never felt
More in love. I shall need other efforts
To break so many knots; only by death
Can I destroy them; so I hasten to it.
That is the sum of what I wished to say.
Yes, madam. I have called him back to you.
I am successful: I do not repent.
May heaven pour upon your years together
A thousand blessings! Or if it harbors still
A remnant of its anger, may the gods
Exhaust the blows which threaten a dear life
Upon the days I sacrifice to you.

   Berenice [*rising*]. Stop, stop! Most generous Princes, **to**
    what a pass
Have I been brought by you! Whether I look
At you, or him, I everywhere encounter
The image of despair. I see but tears,
And hear you only speak of trouble, of horrors,
Of blood about to flow. [*To* Titus.] My lord, my heart
Is known to you; and I can truly say
It never sighed for the Empire. The Roman greatness,
The Caesars' purple—these, as you well know,
Never attracted me. I loved, my lord.
I loved, I wanted to be loved. Today,
I will confess, I've been afraid. I thought
Your love was ended. I know my error now,
And that you'll always love me. I have seen
Your troubled heart, your flowing tears. My lord,
Berenice is not worth so much disquiet,
Nor that the unhappy Empire by your love,
Just at the time you have the prayers of all,
And that it tastes the first fruits of your virtues,
Should be deprived in a moment of its joys.
I think for five years till today, I have
Assured you a true love. That is not all.
I wish, at this tragic time, by a last effort
To crown the rest. I shall go on living now.
I shall obey your absolute commands.
Farewell, my lord. Reign. I shall not see you more.
                          [*To* Antiochus.
Prince, after this good-by, you'll understand

I cannot leave the one I love, to go
Far from Rome, to listen to other vows.
Live also: make, my lord, a generous effort
To rule your conduct by Titus and by me.
I love him, and I flee him. Titus loves me,
And he forsakes me. Take your sighs and chains
Far from my sight. Farewell. Let us all three
Serve as example to the world of love,
The tenderest and most unfortunate,
Of which the sorrowful tale may be recorded.
All is ready. They await me now.
Follow me not. [*To* Titus.] For the last time, my lord,
Farewell.
    Antiochus. Alas!

PHAEDRA

PREFACE

Here is another tragedy of which the subject is taken from Euripides. Although I have followed a slightly different road from that author's for the conduct of the action, I have not scrupled to enrich my play with all that seemed to me most striking in his. While I owe only the single idea of the character of Phaedra to him, I could say that I owe to him that which I could reasonably show on the stage. I am not surprised that this character had so great a success in the time of Euripides, and that it has also succeeded so well in our century, since it has all the qualities which Aristotle demanded in the heroes of a tragedy, and which are proper to excite pity and terror. Indeed, Phaedra is neither entirely guilty, nor entirely innocent; she is involved, by her fate and the wrath of the gods, in an unlawful passion, of which she is the first to feel horror; she makes every effort to overcome it; she prefers to let herself die rather than to confess it to anyone; and when she is forced to discover it, she speaks of it with a confusion that makes plain that her crime is rather a punishment of the gods than a movement of her will.

I have even taken care to render her a little less odious than she is in the tragedies of the ancients, where she resolves of herself to accuse Hippolytus. I thought that the calumny was too base and evil to put into the mouth of a princess who elsewhere displays such noble and virtuous sentiments. This baseness appeared to me more suitable to a nurse, who could have more servile inclinations, and who nevertheless undertakes this false accusation only to save the life and honor of her mistress. Phaedra consents to it only because she is in such agitation that she is beside herself; and she comes a moment after in the action to justify innocence and declare the truth.

Hippolytus is accused, in Euripides and Seneca, of having actually violated his stepmother: *vim corpus tulit*. But he is here accused of only having had the intention. I wished to spare Theseus a confusion which would have rendered him less agreeable to the audience.

With regard to the character of Hippolytus, I have noticed among the ancients that Euripides is reproached for having represented him as a philosopher exempt of all imperfection: which made the death of the young prince cause much more indignation than pity. I thought I should give him some weakness which would make him a little guilty towards his father, without however taking away from him any of the greatness of soul with which he spares Phaedra's honor and lets himself be oppressed without accusing her. I call weakness the passion which he feels, against his will, for Aricia, who is the daughter and the sister of mortal enemies of his father.

This Aricia is not a character of my invention. Virgil says that Hippolytus married her, and had a son by her, after Æsculapius had brought him back to life. And I have also read in some authors that Hippolytus had wedded and brought to Italy a young Athenian of high birth, called Aricia, and who had given her name to a small Italian town.

I mention these authorities because I have very scrupulously set myself to follow the fable. I have even followed the story of Theseus as given in Plutarch.

It is in this historian that I have found that what gave occasion to believe that Theseus descended into the underworld to rescue Prosperpine was a journey that the prince had made in Epirus towards the source of the Acheron, at the home of a king whose wife Peirithous wishes to bear off, and who took Theseus prisoner after slaying Peirithous. So I have tried to keep the verisimilitude of the story, without losing anything of the ornaments of the fable, which is an abundant storehouse of poetical imagery; and the rumor of Theseus' death, based on this fabulous voyage, gives an opportunity to Phaedra to make a declaration of love which becomes one of the principal causes of her misfortune, and which she would never have dared to make so long as she believed that her husband was alive.

For the rest, I dare not yet assert that this play is indeed the best of my tragedies. I leave it to readers and to time to decide its true value. What I can assert is that I have not made one where virtue is put in a more favorable light than in this one; the least faults are severely punished; the very thought of a crime is regarded with as much horror as the crime itself; the weaknesses of love are shown as true weaknesses; the passions are displayed only to show all the disorder of which they are the cause; and vice is everywhere depicted in colors which make the deformity recognized and hated. That is properly the end which every man who works for the public should propose to himself; and it is that which the first tragic poets kept in sight above everything. Their theatre was a school where virtue was not less well taught than in the schools of the philosophers. So Aristotle was willing to give rules for the dramatic poem; and Socrates, the wisest of philosophers, did not disdain to set his hand to the tragedies of Euripides. It could be wished that our works were as solid and as full of useful instructions as those of these poets. That would perhaps be a means of reconciling tragedy with numerous people, celebrated for their piety and for their doctrine, who have condemned it in recent times, and who would doubtless judge it more favorably if the authors thought as much about instructing their audiences as about diverting them, and if they followed in this respect the true function of tragedy.

DRAMATIS PERSONÆ

THESEUS, *King of Athens*
PHAEDRA, *his wife*
HIPPOLYTUS, *son of Theseus and Antiope*
ARICIA, *Princess of the blood royal of Athens*
THERAMENES, *tutor to Hippolytus*
ŒNONE, *nurse and confidante of Phaedra*
ISMENE, *confidante of Aricia*
PANOPE, *woman of Phaedra's suite*
GUARDS

SCENE—TROEZEN

PHAEDRA

ACT ONE

HIPPOLYTUS *and* THERAMENES.

HIPPOLYTUS. It is decided, dear Theramenes.
I'm leaving now, and cutting short my stay
In pleasant Troezen. In my state of doubt
I blush at my own sloth. Six months and more
My father has been absent, yet I stay
Still ignorant of his fate, not even knowing
In what part of the world he hides his head.
   Theramenes. Where will you seek him then? I have already,
My lord, to satisfy your natural fears,
Crossed the Corinthian sea, and asked for Theseus
Upon those distant shores where Acheron
Is lost among the dead. I went to Elidos
And sailed from Tenaros upon the sea
Where Icarus once fell. By what new hope,
Or in what lucky region will you find
His footprints now? Who knows, indeed, who knows
Whether it is the King your father's will,
That we should try to probe the mystery
Of his long absence? While we are afraid,
Even for his life, that hero, unperturbed,
Screening from us his latest love exploit,
May just be waiting till a woman . . .
   Hippolytus.   Stop,
Dear Theramenes; respect the King
Who has outgrown the headstrong faults of youth.
No such unworthy obstacle detains him.
Phaedra has conquered his inconstancy,
And fears no rival now. In seeking him,
I do my duty, and thereby escape
A place I dare not stay in.

179

Theramenes.   Since when, my lord,
Have you been frightened of the peaceful place
You used to love in childhood? You once preferred it
To the noisy pomp of Athens and the court.
What danger, or rather, should I say, what grief
Drives you away?
    Hippolytus.   Alas, that happy time
Is now no more. For everything has changed
Since to these shores the gods despatched the Queen,
The daughter of Minos and of Pasiphaë.
    Theramenes. I know the cause indeed; for Phaedra here
Vexes and wounds your sight—a dangerous
Stepmother, who had scarce set eyes on you
Ere she procured your exile. But her hatred
Is either vanished, or at least relaxed.
Besides, what perils can you undergo
From a dying woman, one who seeks to die?
Phaedra, who will not speak about her illness,
Tired of herself and even of the sunshine,
Is scarcely hatching plots against you.
    Hippolytus.   No:
Her vain hostility is not my fear.
In leaving her, I flee another foe:
I flee—I will admit it—young Aricia,
Last of a fatal race that has conspired
Against us.
    Theramenes. What? Do you yourself, my lord,
Persecute her? The Pallantids' lovely sister
Was not involved in her treacherous brothers' plots.
And should you hate her innocent charms?
    Hippolytus.   If I
Did hate her, I would not be fleeing.
    Theramenes.   My lord,
May I explain your flight? Is it that you
No longer are that proud Hippolytus,
Relentless enemy of the laws of love,
And of a yoke to which your father bowed
So many times? Does Venus whom your pride
So long has slighted wish to justify
The amorous Theseus? While, like the rest of mortals,

You're forced to cense her altars? Are you in love,
My lord?
   Hippolytus. What do you dare to ask, my friend?
You have known my heart since it began to beat,
And can you ask me to repudiate
My former proud, disdainful sentiments?
I sucked the pride which so amazes you
From an Amazonian mother; and when I reached
A riper age, and knew myself, I gloried
In what I was. Then in your friendly zeal
You told me all my father's history.
My soul, attentive to your voice, was thrilled
To hear the tale of his heroic deeds—
Consoling mortals for Alcides' absence,
By slaying monsters, putting brigands down,
Procrustes, Cercyon, Sciron, and Sinis,
The scattered bones of the giant of Epidaurus,
Crete reeking with the Minotaur's foul blood.
But when you told of deeds less glorious,
The way his faith was pledged a hundred times—
Helen of Sparta stolen from her kin,
Salamis witness of Periboea's tears,
And many more, whose names he has forgotten,
Of credulous women by his love deceived:
Ariadne on her rocky isle
Telling her wrongs; and Phaedra at the last,
Kidnapped, but under better auspices;
You know how listening to the sorry tale
I begged you cut it short, and would have been
Happy to blot out from my memory
The worser half of the tale. And shall I now
Be bound so ignominiously by the gods?
My base affections, unlike those of Theseus,
Can claim no heap of honors as excuse,
And so deserve more scorn. As I have slain
No monster yet, I have not earned the right
So to transgress; and if my pride must melt,
Should I have chosen for my conqueror
Aricia? Surely my wandering senses
Should have recalled that we are kept apart

By an eternal obstacle. My father
Holds her in reprobation, and forbids her
Ever to marry: of a guilty stem
He fears a shoot, and wishes to entomb
With her the memory of her brothers' name.
Under his tutelage until she dies,
Never for her shall Hymen's fires be lit.
Should I support her rights against a father
Incensed against her, give example to
Temerity, and let my youth embark
Upon a wild sea? . . .

   Theramenes.   If your hour is come,
My lord, heaven cares not for our reasons. Theseus,
Wishing to shut your eyes, has opened them.
His hatred, rousing a rebellious flame,
Lends a new luster to his enemy.
But, after all, why fear an honest love?
If it is sweet, why should you not dare taste it?
Why will you trust a shy or sullen scruple?
Or fear to walk where Hercules once trod?
What spirits has not Venus tamed? And where
Would you be, you who fight against her, if
Antiope, always to her laws opposed,
Had not with modest ardor burned for Theseus?
But why do you affect a haughty speech?
Confess that all is changed: and for some days
You're seen less often, proud and solitary,
Racing the chariot on the shore, or skilled
In the art of Neptune, making the wild steeds
Obedient to the bit. The forest echoes
Less often to our shouts. Your eyes are heavy,
Charged with a secret passion. There is no doubt:
You love, you burn; you perish from an illness
Which you conceal. And are you now in love
With charming Aricia?

   Hippolytus.   Theramenes,
I'm setting off in quest of my lost father.

    Theramenes. Won't you see Phaedra, my lord, before you
      go?

    Hippolytus. So I intend; and you may tell her so.
I'll see her—since my duty thus ordains.

But what's the new misfortune which disturbs
Her dear Œnone?

Enter ŒNONE.   (I.2)

Œnone.   Alas! my lord, what trouble
Can equal mine? The Queen has nearly reached
Her fatal term. In vain both night and day
I've watched beside her. She's dying of a sickness
She hides from me; and in her spirit reigns
Continual disorder. Restless affliction
Now drags her from her bed to see once more
The light of day; and her deep grief demands
That all should keep away. She's coming now.
     Hippolytus. It is enough. I'll leave this place to her,
And not offend her with my hated face.

[Exeunt HIPPOLYTUS and THERAMENES.

Enter PHAEDRA.   (I.3)

     Phaedra. Let's go no further, dear Œnone, stay.
I've reached the limit of my strength; my eyes
Are blinded by the daylight, and my knees
Give way beneath me.   [*She sits.*
     Œnone.   O all-powerful Gods,
May all our tears appease you!
     Phaedra.   How these vain
Adornments, how these veils, now weigh me down.
What busy hand, in tying all these knots,
Has taken care to gather on my brow
This heavy load of hair? Now all afflicts me,
Hurts me, and conspires to hurt me.
     Œnone.   How
Her wishes seem now to destroy each other!
Madam, it was yourself, with your own hands,
Who dressed and decked your hair, wishing to show
Yourself, and see once more the light of day.
But now you see it, ready to hide yourself,
You hate the day you sought.
     Phaedra.   O shining Sun,
Author of my sad race, thou of whom my mother
Boasted herself the daughter, who blush perhaps

At these my sufferings, I see you now
For the last time.
  Œnone.   What! have you not lost
That cruel desire? And shall I see you still
Renouncing life and making of your death
The dreadful preparations?
  Phaedra.   O that I were seated
In the forest shade, where through a cloud of dust
I could behold a chariot racing by!
  Œnone. What, madam?
  Phaedra.   Fool! Where am I? What have I said?
Where have my wits been wandering? I have lost them.
The gods have robbed me of them. I blush, Œnone.
I let you see too much my shameful sorrows,
And, spite of me, my eyes are filled with tears.
  Œnone. If you must blush, blush rather at your silence
Which but augments your griefs. Deaf to our pleading,
Rebellious to our care, and without pity,
Do you wish to end your days? What madness now
Stops them in mid-career? What spell or poison
Has drained their source? Three nights have come and gone
Since sleep last entered in your eyes; three days
Have chased the darkness since you took some food.
What frightful scheme are you attempting now?
For you insult the gods who gave you life,
Betray the husband to whom your faith is given,
Betray your hapless children whom you throw
Under a rigorous yoke. Think that one day
Will snatch their mother from them, and give up
Their hopes to the stranger's son, to that proud foe
Of you, and of your blood, the Amazon's son,
Hippolytus.
  Phaedra. Ah Gods!
  Œnone.   Does this reproach—?
  Phaedra. Wretch! What name has issued from your
   mouth?
  Œnone. You are right to be angry: I like to see you
   tremble
At that ill-omened name. Then live! Both love and duty
Reanimate you. Live. Do not let the son
Of the Scythian, crushing your children with his rule,

Command the noblest blood of Greece and heaven.
But don't delay: each moment threatens life.
Repair your weakened strength, while yet life's torch
Can be rekindled.
    Phaedra.   I have too much prolonged
Its guilty span.
    Œnone.   What! are you torn apart
By some remorse? What crime could have produced
Such agony? Your hands were never stained
With innocent blood.
    Phaedra.   Thanks to the gods, my hands
Are guiltless still. But would to heaven my heart
Were innocent as they!
    Œnone.   What frightful scheme
Have you conceived to terrify your heart?
    Phaedra. I have said enough. Spare me the rest. I die
Because I cannot such confession make.
    Œnone. Die then; and keep inhuman silence still.
But seek another hand to close your eyes.
Although there but remains a feeble flame
In you, my soul will journey to the dead
Before you, since there are a thousand ways
By which we can go thither—mine the shortest.
Cruel! When have I betrayed your confidence?
Think, that my arms received you at your birth,
For you I've left my country and my children.
Is this the price of my fidelity?
    Phaedra. What fruit can come from so much violence?
You would be horror-struck if I should tell you.
    Œnone. What will you say to me more horrible
Than seeing you expire before my eyes?
    Phaedra. But when you know my crime and the dread
      fate
That crushes me, I shall die just the same,
And die more guilty.
    Œnone.   Madam, by all the tears
That I have shed for you, by your weak knees
That I embrace now, free my mind from doubt.
    Phaedra. You wish it: rise.
    Œnone.   Speak: I am listening.
    Phaedra. What shall I say? And where shall I begin?

Œnone. Cease to insult me by these needless fears.

Phaedra. O hate of Venus and her fatal wrath!
Love led my mother into desperate ways.

Œnone. Forget them, madam. Let an eternal silence
Hide their remembrance.

Phaedra.   My sister, Ariadne,
Stricken with love, upon a desolate coast
Despairing died.

Œnone.   What are you doing, madam?
What mortal spite enkindles you today
Against your nearest . . . ?

Phaedra.   Since Venus so ordains,
Last and most wretched of my tragic race,
I too shall perish.

Œnone.   Are you then in love?

Phaedra. All of love's frenzies I endure.

Œnone.   For whom?

Phaedra. You're going to hear the last extreme of horror.
I love . . . I shudder at the fatal name . . .
I love . . .

Œnone. Whom do you love?

Phaedra.   You know the son
Of the Amazon—the prince I've harshly used.

Œnone. Hippolytus! Great Gods!

Phaedra.   'Tis you have named him.
Not I.

Œnone. O righteous heaven! The blood in my veins
Is turned to ice. O crime! O hapless race!
Disastrous voyage! O unlucky coast!
Why did we travel to your perilous shores?

Phaedra. My evil comes from a more distant place.
Scarce had I wedded Theseus and established
My happiness, it seemed, I saw in Athens
My haughty foe. I saw him—blushed and blanched
To see him—and my soul was all distraught.
My eyes were blinded, and I could not speak.
I felt my body freeze and burn; I knew
The terrible fires of Venus, the tortures fated
To one whom she pursues. I hoped to avert them
By my assiduous prayers. I built for her
A temple, and took pains to adorn its walls.

Myself surrounded by the sacrifices,
I sought for my lost reason in their entrails.
Weak remedies of love incurable!
In vain upon the altars I burnt incense;
My lips implored the goddess, but I worshipped
Only Hippolytus; and seeing him
Each day even at the altar's foot
I offered all to the god I dared not name.
I shunned him everywhere. O heavy weight
Of misery! My eyes beheld the son
In the father's countenance. At length I dared
To rebel against myself. I spurred my spirit
To persecute him, striving thus to banish
The enemy I worshipped by assuming
A stepmother's proverbial cruelty.
I clamored for his exile till my cries
Tore my dear enemy from his father's arms.
I breathed again, Œnone. In his absence
My calmer days flowed by in innocence,
Compliant to my husband, while my griefs
Lay hidden. I bore him children. But in vain
Were all precautions, for Fate intervened.
Brought by my husband to Troezen, once more
I saw the enemy I had sent away.
My keen wound bled again—it is no more
A passion hidden in my veins, but now
It's Venus fastened on her helpless prey.
I have a just abhorrence of my crime;
I hate my life, abominate my lust;
Longing by death to rescue my good name
And hide my black love from the light of day.
Your tears have conquered me. I have confessed
All my dark secret; and I won't regret it
If you respect now my approaching death,
And do not wound me with unjust reproofs,
Or with vain remedies keep alive within me
The last faint spark of life.

Enter PANOPE.   (I.4)

Panope.   I would prefer
To hide these tidings from you, madam, but

I must reveal them. Death has robbed you now
Of your unconquerable husband, and
It is known to all but you.
    Œnone.   What do you say?
    Panope. That the mistaken Queen in vain demands
Theseus' return from heaven; and that from ships
Arrived in port, Hippolytus, his son,
Has just heard of his death.
    Phaedra.   Heaven!
    Panope.   For the choice
Of ruler, Athens is divided. Some
Vote for the Prince, your son, and others, madam,
Forgetting the laws of the State, dare give their voices
To the son of the stranger. It is even said
An insolent faction has designed to place
Aricia on the throne. I thought you should
Be warned about this danger. Hippolytus
Is ready to depart, and it is feared,
If he becomes involved in this new storm,
Lest he draw to him all the fickle mob.
    Œnone. No more, Panope. The Queen has heard you,
And won't neglect your warning.   [*Exit* PANOPE.

(I.5)

    Œnone.   I had ceased,
Madam, to urge that you should live. Indeed,
I thought that I should follow you to the grave;
I had no further voice to change your mind.
But this new blow imposes other laws.
Your fortune shows a different face; the King
Is now no more, and his place must be filled.
His death has left you with a son to whom
You have a duty; slave if he loses you,
A king if you live. On whom in his misfortune
Do you wish that he should lean? His tears will have
No hand but yours to wipe them; and his cries,
Borne even to the gods, would then incense
His ancestors against his mother. Live.
You have no longer reason to reproach
Yourself; your love becomes a usual love;

Theseus in dying cuts the sacred knots
Which made the crime and horror of your passion.
Hippolytus becomes less terrible to you,
And you can see him without guiltiness.
Perhaps, convinced of your aversion, he
Is going to lead the rebels. Undeceive him,
Appease his spirit. King of these happy shores,
Troezen is his portion; but he knows
That the laws give your son the lofty ramparts
Minerva builded. Both of you, indeed,
Have a true enemy. Unite together
To combat Aricia.

    Phaedra.   To your advice
I let myself be drawn. Well, let me live,
If I can be restored to life; and if
My love for a son can in this grievous moment
Reanimate the rest of my weak spirits.

ACT TWO

ARICIA *and* ISMENE.

ARICIA. Hippolytus asks to see me in this place?
Hippolytus seeks me here to say good-by?
Ismene, is it true? You're not mistaken?

    Ismene. It is the first result of Theseus' death.
Madam, prepare yourself to see the hearts
Scattered by Theseus fly from every side
Towards you. Aricia at last is mistress
Of her fate, and soon will see the whole of Greece
Submit to her.

    Aricia.   It's not a false report?
Do I cease to be a slave, and have no foe?

    Ismene. No, madam, the gods are now no more against
    you,
And Theseus has rejoined your brothers' shades.

    Aricia. Is it known what caused his death?

    Ismene. They spread
An unbelievable tale of it. It is said

That stealing a new love this faithless husband
Was swallowed by the waves. It is even said—
A widespread rumor this—that he descended
To Hades with Peirithous, and saw
Cocytus and the gloomy banks, and living
Appeared to the infernal shades, but then
Could not emerge from those sad regions,
And cross the bourn from which there's no return.

Aricia. Shall I believe a man before his hour
Can enter the dark dwelling of the dead?
What spell could draw him to those fearsome coasts?

Ismene. Theseus is dead, madam, and you alone
Have doubts of it. Athens is mourning for it,
Troezen, informed of it, acknowledges
Hippolytus as King; and Phaedra, here
In this palace, trembling for her son, now seeks
The advice of anxious friends.

Aricia.   Do you believe
Hippolytus, less cruel than his father,
Will make my chains less heavy, sympathize
With my misfortunes?

Ismene.   Madam, I do believe it.

Aricia. But do you really know that heartless man?
By what fond hope do you think he'll pity me?
In me alone respect a sex he scorns?
You've seen how he avoids me, seeks those places
Where I am not.

Ismene.   I know all that is said
About his coldness. But I've seen when near you
This proud Hippolytus; and in seeing him,
The rumor of his pride has doubly whetted
My curiosity. His actual presence
Seemed not to correspond. At your first glances
I've seen him get confused. His eyes, which wished
Vainly to shun you, could not leave your face.
The name of lover would offend his heart,
But yet he has a lover's tender eyes,
If not his words.

Aricia.   How my heart, dear Ismene,
Drinks in a speech which may have little basis.
Is it believable to you who know me

That the sad plaything of a pitiless fate,
Whose heart is fed on bitterness and tears,
Should be acquainted with the trivial griefs
Of love? The remnant of the blood of a king,
Erechtheus, the noble son of Earth,
Alone I have escaped war's ravages.
I've lost six brothers in the flower of youth—
Hope of a famous house!—all reaped by the sword.
The moistened earth regretfully drank the blood
Of the offspring of Erechtheus. You know
How since their death a cruel law was made,
Forbidding Greeks to breathe a lover's sighs
For me. It is feared the sister's reckless flames
May kindle once again her brothers' ashes.
But you know well with what disdainful eye
I looked upon a conqueror's suspicions;
And how, opposed to love, I often thanked
The unjust Theseus whose convenient harshness
Aided my scorn. But then my eyes had not
Beheld his son. Not that by eyes alone
Basely enchanted, I love his beauty and charm,
Gifts with which nature wishes to honor him,
And which he scorns, or seems unconscious of;
I love in him his nobler wealth, his father's virtues,
Without his faults. I love—I do confess it—
That generous pride that never yet has bowed
Beneath the amorous yoke. Phaedra took pride
In Theseus' practiced sighs. But as for me,
I am more proud, and shun the easy glory
Of gaining homage that a thousand others
Have had before me, and of penetrating
A heart completely open. But to bend
A heart inflexible, to make a soul
Insensible to love feel all its pain,
To enchain a captive by his bonds amazed,
In vain rebellion against the pleasing yoke,
That's what I wish; and that is what provokes me.
It's easier to disarm Hercules
Than Prince Hippolytus; and conquests soon
And often made will bring less glory to
The victor's eyes. But, dear Ismene, how

Unwise I am! for I shall be resisted
Only too much; and you perhaps will hear me
Lament the pride that I admire today.
If he would love! With what extreme delight
Would I make him . . .
 Ismene.   You'll hear him now, himself.
He comes to you.

     Enter HIPPOLYTUS.   (II.2)

 Hippolytus. Madam, before I leave,
I thought that I should tell you of your fate.
My father lives no more. My apprehension
Presaged the reasons of his too long absence;
And death alone, stopping his famous deeds,
Could hide him for so long within this world.
The gods have yielded to the Fates at last
The friend and the successor of Alcides.
I think your hatred, allowing him his virtues,
Will hear without regret what is his due.
One hope allays my deadly sorrow now.
From your strict tutelage I'll deliver you,
Revoke the laws whose rigor I've deplored.
Do what you will. Dispose of your own heart,
And in this Troezen, my heritage,
Which has forthwith accepted me as King,
I leave you as free, nay freer, than myself.
 Aricia. Temper your generosity, my lord,
For its excess embarrasses me. So
To honor my disgrace will put me—more
Than you think—under the harsh laws from which
You would exempt me.
 Hippolytus.   Athens, undecided
In the choice of a successor, speaks of you,
Names me and the Queen's son.
 Aricia.   Me, my lord?
 Hippolytus. I know, without self-flattery, that a law
Seems to reject me. Greece reproaches me
With an alien mother. But if my brother were
My only rival, over him I have
Some veritable claims that I would save
Out of the law's caprice. Another bridle,

More lawful, checks my boldness. I yield to you,
Or rather give you back what is your own,
A scepter which your ancestors received
From the most famous man that ever lived;
Adoption placed it in Ægeus' hands;
Athens protected and enlarged by Theseus
Joyfully recognized so good a king,
And left in oblivion your luckless brothers.
Now Athens calls you back within her walls;
With a long quarrel she has groaned enough;
Enough her fields have reeked with blood of thine.
Troezen obeys me; and the plains of Crete
Offer to Phaedra's son a rich domain.
Attica is yours, and I am going
On your behalf to reunite the suffrages
We share between us.

  Aricia.   Astonished and confused
At all I hear, I am afraid . . . afraid
A dream abuses me. Am I awake?
Can I believe in such a plan? What god,
My lord, what god has put it in your breast?
How justly is your glory spread abroad
In every place! And how the truth surpasses
Your fame! You would betray yourself for me?
Would it not be enough for you to refrain
From hating me? And to prevent your soul
So long from this hostility . . .

  Hippolytus.   I hate you,
Madam? However they depict my pride,
Do you think it bore a monster? What settled hate,
What savage manners could, in seeing you,
Not become milder? Could I have resisted
The charm that . . .

  Aricia.   What, my lord?

  Hippolytus.   I've gone too far.
I see that reason yields to violence.
Since I've begun to speak, I must continue.
I must inform you, madam, of a secret
My heart no longer can contain. You see
Before you a lamentable prince, a type
Of headstrong pride. I, rebel against love,

For long have scorned its captives. I deplored
The shipwreck of weak mortals, and proposed
To contemplate the tempests from the shore.
But now enslaved under the common law,
I see myself transported. In a moment
My mad audacity has been subdued.
My proud soul is at last enslaved. For nearly
Six months, ashamed and desperate, and wearing
The marks of torture, against you, against myself,
Vainly I strove. Present I fled from you,
Absent I sought you. In the midst of forests
Your image followed me; the light of day,
The shadows of the night, brought to my eyes
The charms I shunned, and everything conspired
To make the rebel Hippolytus your captive.
Now for all fruit of my superfluous cares,
I seek but do not find myself. My bow, my spears,
My chariot call to me in vain. No more
Do I remember Neptune's lessons; the woods
Now echo to my groans. My idle steeds
Have now forgot my voice. Perhaps the tale
Of love so wild will make you, as you listen,
Blush for your work. What an uncouth recital
Of a heart that's offered you. What a strange captive
For bonds so beautiful! But to your eyes
The offering should be the richer for it;
Remember that I speak an alien tongue,
And don't reject vows that are ill expressed,
Vows that without you I had never formed.

Enter THERAMENES.   (II.3)

Theramenes. My lord, the Queen is coming. I come
    before
To tell you that she seeks you.
    Hippolytus.   Me?
    Theramenes.   I don't know why.
But she has sent to ask for you. She wishes
To speak with you before you go.
    Hippolytus.   Phaedra!
What shall I say to her? And what can she
Expect . . .

Aricia.   My lord, you can't refuse to hear her.
Though you are sure of her hostility,
You ought to have some pity for her tears.
    Hippolytus. Yet you are going. And I depart, not knowing
Whether I have offended by my words
The charms that I adore. I do not know
Whether this heart I leave now in your hands . . .
    Aricia. Go, Prince, pursue your generous designs;
Put tributary Athens in my power.
And all those gifts that you have wished to make me,
I accept. But yet that Empire, great and glorious,
Is not to me the richest of your gifts.

                              [*Exeunt* ARICIA *and* ISMENE.

                                                    (II.4)

    Hippolytus. Friend, is all ready? But the Queen approaches.
Go, see that all's prepared for our departure.
Run, give the signal, and return at once
To free me from a vexing interview.   [*Exit* THERAMENES.

               Enter PHAEDRA *and* ŒNONE.   (II.5)

    Phaedra. He's here: my blood retreats towards my heart,
And I forget what I had meant to say.
    Œnone. Think of a son whose sole hope lies in you.
    Phaedra. It is said that your immediate departure
Is sundering us, my lord. I come to wed
My tears unto your griefs; and to explain
My anxious fears to you. My son is now
Without a father; and the day is near
Which of my death will make him witness too.
His youth is threatened by a thousand foes,
And you alone can arm against them—but
Secret remorse is fretting in my soul.
I fear you're deaf to his cries, and that you'll wreak
On him your wrath against an odious mother.
    Hippolytus. Madam, I do not harbor such base feelings.
    Phaedra. Although you hate me, I shall not complain,
My lord: for you have seen me bent to harm you.
You could not read the tables of my heart.

I've taken care to invite your enmity,
And could not bear your presence where I dwelt.
In public, and in private, your known foe,
I've wished the seas to part us, and even forbidden
The mention of your name within my hearing.
But if one measures punishment by the offense,
If only hatred can attract your hate,
Never was woman who deserved more pity,
My lord, and less deserved your enmity.

   Hippolytus. A mother jealous for her children's rights
Seldom forgives her stepson. I know it, madam.
Nagging suspicions are the commonest fruits
Of second marriage; and another wife
Would have disliked me just the same; and I
Might well have had to swallow greater wrongs.

   Phaedra. Ah, my lord! Heaven—I dare avow it now—
Has made me an exception to that rule.
And what a different care perplexes me
And eats me up.

   Hippolytus.   Madam, it is not time
To grieve. Perhaps your husband is alive.
Heaven to our tears may grant his swift return.
Neptune, his tutelary god, protects him,
To whom my father never prayed in vain.

   Phaedra. None has beheld the marches of the dead
A second time, my lord. Since he has seen
Those dismal shores, you hope in vain some god
Will send him back. The greedy Acheron
Never lets go its prey. What do I say?
He is not dead since he still lives in you.
Ever before my eyes I see my husband.
I see him, speak with him, and my heart still . . .
I'm wandering, my lord. My foolish feelings,
In spite of me, declare themselves.

   Hippolytus.   I see
Love's wonderful effects. Dead though he is,
Theseus is always present to your eyes:
Your soul is ever burning with your love.

   Phaedra. Yes, Prince, I pine and burn for Theseus.
I love him, not as when he visited
The underworld, a fickle lover, bent

To stain great Pluto's bed, but faithful, proud,
Attractive, young, and even a little shy,
Charming all hearts, an image of the gods,
Or even as you are now. He had your bearing,
Your eyes, your speech; and such a modesty
Made flush his face when over the Cretan waves
He came and turned the hearts of Minos' daughters.
What were you doing then? Why without you
Did he assemble there the flower of Greece?
And why were you too young to sail with him
Unto our shores? For then you would have slain
The Minotaur, despite the devious ways
Of his vast lair: my sister, to redeem you
From your confusion, with the fateful thread
Would have armed your hand—but no, for I myself,
Inspired by love, would have forestalled her plan.
It would have been me, Prince; by timely aid,
I would have led you through the labyrinth.
How many cares that charming head of yours
Would then have cost me! I would not have trusted
To that weak thread alone, but walked before you,
Companion in the peril which you chose:
And going down into the labyrinth,
Phaedra would have returned with you, or else
Been lost with you.
    Hippolytus.   O Gods! What do I hear?
Do you forget that Theseus is my father,
And you his wife?
    Phaedra.   By what do you judge that I
Have done so, Prince? Would I forget my honor?
    Hippolytus. Forgive me, madam. I admit, with blushing,
I misinterpreted an innocent speech.
I am ashamed to stay within your sight;
I'm going. . . .
    Phaedra.   Ah! cruel! You've understood too well.
I've said enough to save you from mistaking.
Know Phaedra, then, and all her madness. Yes,
I love; but do not think that I condone it,
Or think it innocent; nor that I ever
With base complaisance added to the poison
Of my mad passion. Hapless victim of

Celestial vengeance, I abhor myself
More than you can. The gods are witnesses—
Those gods who kindled in my breast the flame
Fatal to all my blood, whose cruel boast
Was to seduce a weak and mortal heart.
Recall what's past. I did not flee from you,
Hardhearted man, I drove you away. I wished
To seem to you both hateful and inhuman.
To resist you better I aroused your hatred.
But what have profited my useless pains?
You loathed me more: I did not love you less;
And your misfortunes lent you further charms.
I've languished, shriveled in the flames, in tears
Your eyes will tell you so—if for a moment
Your eyes could look at me. What am I saying?
Think you that this confession I have made
Was voluntary? I trembled for a son
I did not dare betray and came to beg you
No more to hate him—futile schemes devised
By a heart too full of what it loves. Alas!
I could only speak to you about yourself.
Avenge yourself; punish an odious love,
Son worthy of a noble father, free
The universe of a monster who offends you.
Theseus' widow dares to love Hippolytus!
Believe me, Prince,
This dreadful monster would not seek to flee.
There is my heart: there you should aim your blow.
I feel it now, eager to expiate
Its sin, advance towards your arm. Strike.
Or if you think it unworthy of your blows,
Your hatred envying me a death so sweet,
Or if you think your hand with blood too vile
Would be imbrued, lend me your sword instead.
Give it me.   [*She takes sword.*

   Œnone. What are you doing, madam?
O righteous Gods! But someone's coming. Leave
These hateful testimonies. Come inside,
And flee a certain shame. [*Exeunt* ŒNONE *and* PHAEDRA.

Enter THERAMENES.   (II.6)

Theramenes.   Is it Phaedra who flees,
Or rather is led away? O why, my lord,
These marks of sorrow? I see you without sword,
Speechless and pale.
    Hippolytus.   Theramenes, let's flee.
I am amazed, and cannot without horror
Behold myself. Phaedra . . . but no, great Gods!
In deep oblivion may this horrid secret
Remain entombed!
    Theramenes.   If you would now depart,
The sails are ready. But Athens has decided.
Her chiefs have taken the votes of all the tribes.
Your brother wins, and Phaedra gets her way.
    Hippolytus. Phaedra?
    Theramenes.   A herald, bearing Athens' will,
Comes to remit the reins of government
Into her hands. Her son is King, my lord.
    Hippolytus. O Gods, who know her heart, is it her virtue
That thus you recompense?
    Theramenes.   There is, however,
A muffled rumor that the King's alive.
It is said that in Epirus he's appeared.
But I, who sought him there, I know too well . . .
    Hippolytus. No matter. Let us listen to everything,
And neglect nothing. Examine this report
And trace it to its source. If it should prove
Unfounded, let's depart. Whatever the cost,
Let's put the scepter into worthy hands.

ACT THREE

PHAEDRA *and* ŒNONE.

PHAEDRA. O! that the honors which are brought to me
Were paid elsewhere! Why do you urge me so?
Can you wish me to be seen? What do you come with
To flatter my desolation? Hide me rather.
Not only have I spoken; but my frenzy
Is noised abroad. I've said those things which ought

Never to be heard. O heavens! The way he listened!
By devious means he somehow failed to grasp
What I was saying—then he recoiled. His blush
Doubled my shame. Why did you turn aside
The death I sought? Did he turn pale with fear
When with his sword I sought my breast, or seek
To snatch it from me? Since my hands had touched it
But once, it was made horrible in his eyes,
And would profane his hands.

  Œnone.   Thus in your woes
Lamenting to yourself, you feed a flame
That ought to be put out. Would it not be better,
Worthy the blood of Minos, in nobler cares
To seek your peace. To spite a heartless man
Who had recourse to flight, assume the conduct
Of affairs, and reign.

  Phaedra.   I reign? To place the State
Under my law, when reason reigns no longer
Over myself; when I have abdicated
From the empire of my senses; when beneath
A yoke of shame I scarcely breathe; when I
Am dying.

  Œnone. Fly.

  Phaedra. I cannot leave him.

  Œnone.   You dared
To banish him, and dare not shun him now?

  Phaedra. Too late. He knows of my mad passion.
I've crossed the bounds of rigid modesty,
Declared my shame before my conqueror's eyes,
And hope has slipped perforce into my heart.
It was you who rallied my declining strength,
When my departing soul was on my lips,
And by your flattering counsels knew the way
To bring me back to life. You made me glimpse
How I could love him.

  Œnone.   To save you from your ills,
Guilty or innocent, what would I not
Have done? But if an insult ever touched you,
Can you forget his haughty scorn? And how
With cruel eyes his obstinate rigor let you
Lie prostrate at his feet. How his fierce pride

Rendered him odious! If only Phaedra
Had seen him, at that moment, with my eyes!

Phaedra. Œnone, he may leave this native pride
Which wounds you. Nurtured in the pathless woods,
He has their roughness. Hardened by savage laws,
He hears love spoken of for the first time;
Perhaps it was surprise that caused his silence;
Perhaps my pleas had too much violence.

Œnone. Remember a barbarian gave him birth.

Phaedra. Although a Scythian and barbarian,
She yet has loved.

Œnone.   He has for all our sex
A deadly hatred.

Phaedra.   So I shall not see him
Prefer a rival. All your counsels now
Are out of season. Serve my passion, Œnone,
And not my reason. He opposes now
To love a heart impenetrable; let us
Discover some more vulnerable place.
The charms of ruling have appeared to touch him.
Athens attracts him; he has not been able
To hide it. His ships have turned their prows; their sails
Flap in the wind. Find this ambitious youth,
Œnone; make the royal crown to glitter
Before his eyes. Let him wear upon his brow
The sacred diadem. I only wish
The honor of his love, and yield to him
The power I cannot keep. He will instruct
My son in the art of ruling, who may perhaps
Regard him as a father. Both son and mother
I put under his power. Try every means
To bend him; he will listen to your speech
More readily than to mine. Urge, weep, and moan.
Paint Phaedra dying; do not blush to use
The tone of a suppliant. I will approve
Of all you do. You are my only hope.
I await your coming to decide my fate.   [*Exit* Œnone.

(III.2)

Phaedra. O thou who seest the shame to which I've
come,

Venus implacable, am I confounded
Enough for thee? Thou canst not further urge
Thy cruelty; thy victory is complete.
O cruel! If thou wishest another triumph
Attack an enemy who is more rebellious.
Hippolytus flees thee; and, thy wrath defying,
Has never to thy altars bowed the knee.
Thy name appears to shock his haughty ears.
Goddess, avenge thyself. Thy cause is mine.
O let him love! Œnone is returned.
I am detested then. He would not hear you?

Enter ŒNONE.   (III.3)

   Œnone. Madam, you must repress the very thought
Of your vain passion, and recall again
Your former virtue. The King that we thought dead
Will soon appear before your eyes. Theseus
Is come. The people rush to see him. I went,
At your command, to seek Hippolytus,
When I heard a thousand shouts. . . .
   Phaedra.   My husband lives,
Œnone. It is enough. I have confessed
A love which foully wrongs him. Theseus lives.
I wish to know no more.
   Œnone.   What?
   Phaedra.   I foretold it,
But you would not believe it. Your tears prevailed
Over my shame. I would have died today
Worthy of tears. I followed your advice—
I die dishonored.
   Œnone.   Die?
   Phaedra.   O righteous heaven!
What have I done today? My husband's coming,
And his son with him. I shall see the witness
Of my adulterous passion watch how boldly
I greet his father—my heart still full of sighs
To which he would not listen, and my eyes
Still moist with tears he scorned. Do you suppose
That he, so sensitive to Theseus' honor,
Will hide the fires that burn me—and betray
His father and his king? Could he contain

The horror I inspire? He would keep silence
In vain. I know my perfidies, Œnone;
I am not one of those who in their crimes
Enjoy a tranquil peace, and know the art
To keep their countenance without a blush.
I know my madness: I recall it all.
I think already that these walls, these arches,
Are going to speak; they but await my husband
Before they utter forth my crimes. Die, then.
My death will free me from a crowd of horrors.
Is it a great mischance to cease to live?
Death has no terrors for the unfortunate.
I only fear the name I leave behind me.
A dreadful heritage for my poor children!
The blood of Jupiter should puff up their courage,
With a just pride; but yet a mother's crime
Will be a heavy burden. One day, I fear,
A speech—too true!—will cast it in their teeth
They had a guilty mother; and I fear
That crushed by such a hateful load, they'll never
Dare raise their eyes.

  Œnone.   It is true. I pity them.
Never was fear more justified than yours.
But why expose them to such insults? Why
Against yourself give evidence? All would be lost.
It will be said that guilty Phaedra fled
The terrible sight of husband she betrayed.
Hippolytus will rejoice that by your death
You corroborate his tale. What could I say
To your accuser? Face to face with him
I shall be easy to confound, and see him
Rejoicing in his triumph, while he tells
Your shame to all who listen. Rather let
Fire from heaven consume me! But tell me true
Is he still dear to you? And with what eyes
Do you behold this insolent prince?

  Phaedra.   I see him
Even as a monster hideous to my eyes.

  Œnone. Why yield him then a total victory?
You fear him, madam. Dare to accuse him first
Of the crime that he will charge you with today.

Who will contradict you? Everything
Speaks against him—his sword by lucky chance
Left in your hands, your present sore distress,
Your former sorrow, his father long ago
Warned by your outcries, and his actual exile
Obtained by you yourself.

    Phaedra.   How should I dare
Oppress and slander innocence?

    Œnone.   My zeal
Only requires your silence. Like you I shrink
From such an action. You would find me readier
To face a thousand deaths; but since I'd lose you
Without this painful remedy, and your life
For me is of such value that all else
Must yield to it, I'll speak. And Theseus, angered
By what I tell him, will restrict his vengeance
To his son's exile. When he punishes,
A father is always father, satisfied
With a light penalty. But even if
His guiltless blood is spilt, your threatened honor
Is yet too valuable to be exposed.
Whatever it demands, you must submit,
Madam. And to save your threatened honor
All must be sacrificed, including virtue.
Someone is coming. I see Theseus.

    Phaedra.   Ah!
I see Hippolytus. In his haughty eyes
I see my ruin written. Do what you will,
I resign myself to you. In my disorder,
I can do nothing for myself.

                             (III.4)

    Enter THESEUS, HIPPOLYTUS, *and* THERAMENES.

    Theseus.   Now Fortune,
Madam, no longer frowns, and in your arms . . .

    Phaedra. Stay, Theseus. Do not profane the love you
        feel.
I am not worthy of your sweet caresses.
You are insulted. Fortune has not spared
Your wife during your absence. I am unworthy

To please you, or approach you; and henceforward
I ought to think only of where to hide.

[*Exeunt* PHAEDRA *and* ŒNONE.

(III.5)

Theseus. What is the reason for this strange reception?
Hippolytus. Phaedra alone the mystery can explain.
But if my ardent prayers can move your heart,
Permit me not to see her any more.
And let Hippolytus disappear forever
From places where she dwells.
 Theseus.   Leave me, my son?
 Hippolytus. I sought her not: you brought her to these
  shores,
And when you left entrusted to the banks
Of Troezen, Aricia and the Queen,
I was instructed to look after them.
But what can now delay me? In my youth
I showed enough my prowess in the forests
Against unworthy foes; and could I not,
Escaping an ignoble idleness,
In blood more glorious stain my spears? Before
You reached my present age, already
More than one tyrant, more than one grim monster
Had felt your mighty strength; already you,
Chastiser of insolence, had secured the shores
Of the two seas; the private traveler feared
Outrage no more; and Hercules could rest
From his long labors, hearing of your deeds.
But I, an unknown son of famous sire,
Am even further from my mother's deeds!
Suffer my courage to be used at last;
And if some monster has escaped your arm,
Let me then lay the honorable skin
Before your feet; or by the lasting memory
Of a fine death perpetuate the days
So nobly ended, and prove to all the world
I was your son.
 Theseus. What do I now behold?
What horror makes my frightened family

Flee from my sight? If I return so feared,
So little wanted, why, heaven, from my prison
Did you release me? I had one friend alone;
Imprudently he wished to steal the wife
Of the King of Epirus. I aided, with regret,
His amorous designs; but angry fate
Blinded us both. The King surprised me there,
Defenseless, weaponless. I saw Peirithous,
Sad object of my tears, by this barbarian
Given to cruel monsters whom he fed
With blood of luckless mortals. He shut me up
In dismal caverns underground that neighbored
The empire of the shades. After six months
The gods again looked on me. I deceived
The eyes of those who guarded me. I cleansed
The world of a perfidious enemy;
To his own monsters he became a prey.
And when with joy I approach the dearest things
Now left me by the gods—what do I say?—
When to itself my soul returns and takes its fill
Of that dear sight, for welcome I receive
A shuddering fear and horror. All flee; all shrink
From my embraces. And I feel the terror
That I inspire. I'd like to be again
In the prisons of Epirus. Speak. Phaedra complains
That I am wronged. Who has betrayed me? Why
Have I not been avenged? Has Greece, to whom
So many times my arms proved useful, now
Granted asylum to a criminal?
You do not answer! Is my son, my own son,
Leagued with my enemies? Let us go in.
I cannot stay in doubt that overwhelms me.
Let me know both the offense and the offender.
Let Phaedra tell the cause of her distress. [*Exit* THESEUS.

(III.6)

Hippolytus. Where did that speech, which petrified me,
    tend?
Does Phaedra, still a prey to her mad passion,
Wish to accuse, and so destroy, herself?
What will the King say? What destructive poison

Is scattered over all his house by love.
And I, full of a love he will detest,
How different from the man that he remembers!
What black presentiments affright me now!
But innocence has nought to fear. Let's go:
Seek by what happy art I can awaken
My father's tenderness—speak of a love
That he may wish to crush, though all his power
Will not be able to drive it from my heart.

ACT FOUR

THESEUS and ŒNONE.

THESEUS. What do I hear? A traitor, a rash traitor,
To plot this outrage to his father's honor?
How harshly, Destiny, dost thou pursue me!
I know not where I'm going, nor what I am!
O tenderness and bounty ill repaid!
Audacious projects! evil thought! To reach
The goal of his black passion he sought the aid
Of violence. I recognize the sword—
The instrument of his rage—with which I armed him
For nobler purposes. All the ties of blood
Could not restrain him! And Phaedra hesitated
To punish him! Her silence spared the villain!
    Œnone. She rather spared a pitiable father.
Being ashamed of a violent lover's scheme
And of the wicked fire caught from her eyes,
Phaedra desired to die; her murderous hand
Would have put out the pure light of her eyes.
I saw her raise her arm. I ran to stop her.
Alone I tried to save her for your love,
And, mourning for her troubles and your fears,
I have unwillingly interpreted
The tears you saw.
    Theseus.   The villain! He was not able
To stop himself from turning pale. I saw him
Tremble with fear when he encountered me.
I was astonished at his lack of joy;

His cold embraces froze my tenderness.
But was this guilty passion which devours him
Already manifest in Athens?
  Œnone.   My lord,
Recall the Queen's complaints. A criminal love
Was cause of all her hatred.
  Theseus.   And did this passion
Kindle again at Troezen?
  Œnone.   O my lord,
I have told you all that passed. Too long the Queen
Has in her mortal grief been left alone;
So let me leave, and hasten to her side. [*Exit* ŒNONE.

Enter HIPPOLYTUS.   (IV.2)

 Theseus. Ah! here he is. Great Gods! What eye, as mine,
Would not have been deceived? Why should the brow
Of a profane adulterer shine with virtue?
And should one not by certain signs perceive
The heart of villainous men?
  Hippolytus.   May I inquire,
My lord, what dismal cloud is on your face?
Dare you confide in me?
  Theseus.   Villain! Do you then dare
To show yourself before me? Monster, whom
Too long the thunder's spared, vile brigand,
Of whom I purged the earth, as I believed,
After the transport of a horrible love
Has brought your lust even to your father's bed,
You show your hostile head! You would appear
In places full of your own infamy,
And do not seek, under an unknown sky
A country which my name has not yet reached.
Flee, traitor! Do not come to brave my hatred,
Or try a rage that I can scarcely hold.
I have enough opprobrium that I caused
The birth of such a criminal, without
Your shameful death should come to soil the glory
Of all my noble deeds. Flee! If you do not wish
A sudden death to add you to the villains
This hand has punished, take good care that never
The star that lights us see you in this place

Set a rash foot. Fly, I say; and hasten
To purge my territories forever from
Your horrible aspect. And thou, O Neptune!
If formerly my courage cleansed your shores
Of infamous assassins, remember now,
That for reward of all my happy efforts,
Thou promisedst to grant one prayer of mine.
In the long rigors of a cruel prison
I did not once implore thy immortal power;
Niggardly of the help that I expected,
I saved my prayers for greater needs. Today
I do implore thee. Avenge a wretched father!
This traitor I abandon to thy wrath.
In his own blood stifle his shameless lusts.
And by thy furies I shall recognize
Thy favors.

    Hippolytus. Does Phaedra charge Hippolytus
With love incestuous? Such an excess of horror
Renders me speechless. So many sudden blows
Crush me at once, they take away my words
And choke my utterance.

    Theseus.   Traitor, you thought
Phaedra would bury in a cowardly silence
Your brutal conduct. You should not have left
The sword which in her hands has helped to damn you.
Or rather, piling up your perfidy,
You should have bought her silence with her life.

    Hippolytus. With this black falsehood righteously in-
censed,
I would now speak the truth; but I suppress
A secret that would touch you too. Approve
The respect which seals my lips; and, without wishing
To augment your griefs, I urge you to examine
My life. Remember who I am. Small crimes
Always precede the great. Whoever crosses
The bounds of law may violate at last
The holiest rights. There are degrees of crime
Just as of virtue—never innocence
Changes to utter license at one stroke.
One day alone is not enough to turn
A good man to a treacherous murderer,

Still less to incest. Suckled at the breast
Of a chaste heroine, I have not belied
The fountain of her blood. Pitheus, thought
To be the wisest of all men, did deign
To instruct me. I do not wish to give
Too favorable a picture of myself;
But if some virtue's fallen to my share,
My lord, I think that I have clearly shown
My hatred of the crimes imputed to me.
By this Hippolytus is known in Greece.
I've pushed my virtue to the edge of harshness.
My moral inflexibility is known.
The day's not purer than my inmost heart,
And people wish Hippolytus could be smitten
By some profane love. . . .

    Theseus.   Yes, it is that same pride
Which now condemns you. I see the hateful cause
Of your frigidity. Phaedra alone
Charmed your lascivious eyes; your soul, indifferent
To every other object, disdained to burn
With innocent flames.

    Hippolytus.   No, father, this my heart—
I cannot hide it longer—has not disdained
To burn with virtuous love. I do confess
My veritable offense. I love. I love
('Tis true) despite your prohibition, sir.
Aricia to her laws holds me enslaved.
The daughter of Pallas has overcome your son.
I worship her; rebellious to your orders
I can neither sigh nor burn, except for her.

    Theseus. You love her? Heavens! But no, the artifice
Is gross. You feign yourself a criminal
To justify yourself.

    Hippolytus.   For six months now,
My lord, I shunned her, but I loved. I came
Trembling to tell you. Can nothing disabuse you?
Or by what terrible oath can I convince you?
By earth, and heaven, and by the whole of nature . . .

    Theseus. Rogues always have recourse to perjury.
Cease, cease, and spare me further useless speech,
If your feigned virtue has no other aid.

Hippolytus. Although to you it may seem false and cunning,
Phaedra, within her heart, will be more just.

Theseus. Ah! how your impudence excites my wrath!

Hippolytus. How long my exile? What the place prescribed?

Theseus. Even if you should go beyond the pillars
Of Hercules, I still would be too near you.

Hippolytus. Charged with this hideous crime, I should not have
One friend to plead for me when you desert me.

Theseus. Go seek for friends who morbidly applaud
Adultery and incest, ungrateful traitors,
Dishonorable and lawless, fit protectors
Of such a villain.

Hippolytus.   You speak to me once more
Of incest and adultery. I hold
My peace. Yet Phaedra's mother . . . Phaedra springs
From a race, as you well know, my lord, more filled
With horrors than mine is.

Theseus.   What! will your rage
Lose all restraint before me? For the last time,
Out of my sight! Go, traitor. Do not wait
For a wrathful father to have you driven out
With infamy.   [*Exit* HIPPOLYTUS.

(IV.3)

Theseus.   O wretched man, you run
To inevitable destruction. Neptune, feared
Even by the gods themselves, has given his word,
And he'll perform it. An avenging god
Pursues you, and you'll not escape. I loved you,
And feel that notwithstanding your offense
My heart is yearning for you in advance.
But it was you who forced me to condemn you.
Was ever father more outraged than I?
Just gods, you see the grief that overwhelms me.
How could I father such a guilty child?

Enter PHAEDRA.   (IV.4)

Phaedra. My lord, I come to you with fearful heart.

I overheard your wrathful voice, and tremble
Lest your dire threats should have a prompt result.
If there is still time, spare your child, your blood.
I dare to implore you. Save me from the horror
Of hearing his blood cry. O do not cause me
The everlasting grief of spilling it
By a father's hand.
 Theseus.   No, madam, in my own blood
My hand has not been steeped. But none the less
He's not escaped me. An immortal hand
Is charged with his destruction. Neptune himself
Owes it to me, and you will be avenged.
 Phaedra. Neptune owes it to you! Your wrathful pray-
  ers . . .
 Theseus. What! do you fear now lest they should be
  answered?
Rather join yours unto my lawful prayers.
Recount to me his crimes in all their vileness;
Heat up my anger which is too restrained,
Too slow. For you are not acquainted yet
With all his crimes. His mad attempt against you
Has led to further wrongs. Your mouth, he says,
Is full of lies; and he maintains, his heart
And faith are given to Aricia—that he loves her.
 Phaedra. What, my lord?
 Theseus.   That's what he said, but I
Knew how to take this frivolous pretense.
Let's hope from Neptune a swift stroke of justice.
I'm going myself to pray before his altar,
To accomplish his immortal vows with speed.
           [*Exit* THESEUS.

             (IV.5)

 Phaedra. He's gone. What news has beaten on my ears!
What half-extinguished fire within my breast
Revives! What thunderbolt! What dreadful news!
I flew, with all my heart, to save his son,
Breaking away from the restraining arms
Of terrified Œnone; to my remorse
I yielded. And who knows how far it would
Have carried me? Perhaps to accuse myself;

Perhaps, if my voice had failed not, the dread truth
Might have escaped me. . . . Hippolytus feels love,
But not for me. Aricia has his heart!
Aricia has his faith! Gods! When the ingrate,
Pitiless to my pleading, armed himself
With eye so proud and brow so stern, I thought
His heart to love would be forever closed,
Invulnerable to all my sex; and yet
Another has bent his will; and in his eyes
Another has found favor. Perhaps he has
A heart that's easily touched. I am alone
The object of his scorn. And I undertook
The task of his defense!

Enter ŒNONE.   (IV.6)

Phaedra.   Do you know
Œnone, what I have just learnt?
    Œnone.   No, madam.
But trembling I have come to you, and pale,
Aware of your intentions; and I feared
A madness which might well be fatal to you.
    Phaedra. Would you believe it, Œnone? I have a rival.
    Œnone. What?
    Phaedra. Hippolytus is in love. I cannot doubt it.
That savage enemy no one could conquer
Whom pleading and respect would both annoy,
The tiger I encountered but with fear,
Has recognized a conqueror at least.
Aricia has found the way to his heart.
    Œnone. Aricia?
    Phaedra. O pain I never knew before!
To what new torment am I now reserved!
All I have suffered, all my frenzied fears,
My passion's fury and its fierce remorse,
The unbearable insult of his cruel repulse,
Shadowed but feebly what I now endure.
They love each other. By what potent spell
Have I been hoodwinked? How have they met? Since
    when?
And where? You must have known: why did you hide it?
Could you not tell me of their furtive love?

Were they not often seen to speak together,
To seek each other? Did they go to hide
Deep in the woods? But they, alas, could meet
With perfect freedom. Heaven itself approved
Their innocent desires. They could pursue
Their amorous purposes without remorse,
And every day, for them, broke clear and calm!
While I, sad castaway of Nature, hid
From day and light. Death is the only god
I dared invoke; and I waited him,
Feeding on gall and steeped in tears, but yet
I did not dare (so closely I was watched)
To weep my fill. I tasted that sour pleasure
In fear and trembling; and with brow serene
Disguising my distress, I was deprived
Too often of my tears.

    Œnone.   But their vain loves
Will bear no fruit, for they will meet no more.

    Phaedra. Forever and forever they will love.
At the moment when I speak—ah! deadly thought!—
They brave the fury of a maddened lover.
Despite the exile which will sunder them,
They vow eternal faith. I cannot bear
A joy which is an outrage to me. Œnone,
Take pity on my jealous rage. That girl
Must be destroyed; the anger of my husband
Against her hateful blood must be aroused
To no light penalty. The sister's crime
Exceeds the brothers'. In my jealous fury
I wish to urge him . . . But what am I doing?
Where has my reason fled? I jealous? I
To beg of Theseus? My husband is not dead,
And I am still aflame. For whom? Each word
Makes my hair stand on end. My crimes already
Have overflowed the measure. Both at once
I breathe the stench of incest and deceit.
My murderous hands, all apt for vengeance, burn
To plunge in innocent blood! Wretch! And I live!
And I endure the sight of sacred Phoebus
From whom I am derived. My ancestor
Is sire and master of the gods; and heaven,

Nay all the universe, is teeming now
With my forbears. Where then can I hide?
Flee to eternal night. What do I say?
For there my father holds the fatal urn,
Put by the Fates in his stern hands, 'tis said.
Minos in Hades judges the pale ghosts.
Ah, how his shade will tremble when his eyes
Behold his daughter there, confessing sins—
Crimes yet unknown in hell! What wilt thou say,
Father, to see this hideous spectacle?
Methinks I now behold the dreadful urn
Fall from thy hand! Methinks I see thee search
For some new punishment, thyself become
The torturer of thine own blood. Forgive:
A cruel god has doomed thy family.
Behold his vengeance in thy daughter's lust.
But yet, alas, never has my sad heart
Once plucked the fruit of the atrocious crime
Whose shame pursues me. Dogged by miseries
To the last gasp, in torture, I render up
A life I long to lose.

 Œnone.   Repel, madam,
An unreal terror! Behold with other eyes
A venial fault. You love. One's destiny
Cannot be overcome, and you were drawn
By a fatal spell. Is it a prodigy
Unknown before amongst us? And has love
Conquered no other hearts than yours alone?
Frailty is but too natural to us all.
You are a mortal—bow to mortals' lot.
The yoke that you bewail is nothing new:
The gods themselves—the dwellers on Olympus—
Who scare us from such crimes, have before now
Been scorched with lawless fires.

 Phaedra.   What do I hear?
What counsels do you dare to give me now?
Would you thus poison me until the end?
Wretch! Thus you ruined me; and when I fled
You brought me back. It was your pleading
Made me forget my duty. When I avoided
Hippolytus, it was you who made me see him.

What have you done? Why has your wicked mouth
Blackened his honor? Perhaps he will be slain,
The father's impious prayer to Neptune answered.
No longer will I hearken to you. Go,
Thou execrable monster, go and leave me
To my unhappy fate. May the just gods
Reward thee with a punishment to fright
Those who by servile arts feed princes' vices,
Urging them down the path they wish to take,
And smoothing it before them—base flatterers,
The most pernicious gift the angry heavens
Can give to kings.   [*Exit* PHAEDRA.
   Œnone.   Ah! Gods! to do her service
I have done all, left all. And I receive
This for reward. I get but my deserts.

ACT FIVE

HIPPOLYTUS *and* ARICIA.

ARICIA. How in this mortal danger can you still
Keep silence, and thus leave a loving father
In error? If you scorn my pleading tears,
And easily consent no more to see me,
Go, separate yourself from sad Aricia:
But yet, before you leave, preserve your life;
Defend your honor from a vile reproach,
And force your father to revoke his prayers.
There is still time. Why, by what caprice,
Do you leave the field thus free to your accuser?
Enlighten Theseus.
   Hippolytus.   What have I not said?
Should I reveal the soiling of his bed?
Should I, by telling a too truthful tale,
Make flush my father's brow? For you alone
Have pierced the hateful mystery. My heart
Can be unbosomed only to the gods
And you. I could not hide from you—by this
Judge if I love you—all I would conceal
Even from myself. But yet remember, madam,

Under what seal I have revealed it to you.
Forget, if you are able, what I've said,
And may you never open your chaste lips
To tell of this affair. Let us rely
Upon the justice of the gods, for they
Are much concerned to justify me; and Phaedra
Sooner or later punished for her crime
Cannot avoid deserved ignominy.
That's all I ask of you. I permit all else
To my unbounded anger. Leave the serfdom
To which you are reduced, and follow me.
Dare to accompany my flight, Aricia.
Dare to come with me; snatch yourself away
From this unholy place, where virtue breathes
A poisoned air. To hide your disappearance,
Profit from the confusion that is caused
By my disgrace. I can assure the means
For your departure. All your guards are mine,
Powerful upholders of our cause. Argos
Holds out its arms to us, and Sparta calls us.
Let's bear our righteous cries to mutual friends;
And suffer not that Phaedra by our ruin
Should drive us from the throne, and to her son
Promise your spoil and mine. The chance is good;
We must embrace it. . . . What fear now restrains you?
You seem uncertain. Your interest alone
Inspires me to this boldness. When I am
Ablaze, what freezes you? Are you afraid
To tread with me the paths of exile?
   Aricia.   Alas!
How dear, my lord, would such an exile be!
Tied to your fate, with what delight would I
Live, by the rest of mortals quite forgotten!
But since I'm not united by such ties,
Can I, with honor, flee with you? I know
That without blemish I can free myself
From Theseus' hands—it would not be to leave
The bosom of my family—and flight
Is lawful if we flee from tyrants. But,
My lord, you love me, and my startled honor . . .
   Hippolytus. No, no, I've too much care of your renown.

A nobler plan has brought me in your presence:
Flee from your enemies, and follow me,
Your husband. Free in our misfortunes, since
Heaven has ordained it so, our troth depends
Upon ourselves alone. Hymen need not
Be ringed with torches. At the gates of Troezen,
Among the tombs, the ancient sepulchers
Of the princes of my line, is a holy temple
Dreadful to perjurers. 'Tis there that mortals
Dare not make empty vows, lest they receive
Swift punishment; and, fearing there to meet
Inevitable death, the lie has not
A sterner bridle. There, if you will trust me,
We will confirm the solemn oath, and take
To witness it the god who's worshipped there,
Praying that he will act as father to us.
I'll call to witness the most sacred gods,
The chaste Diana, Juno the august,
And all the gods who, witnessing my love,
Will guarantee my holy promises.

    Aricia. The King is coming. Fly, Prince; leave at once.
I will remain a moment, to conceal
My own departure. Go, but leave with me
Some faithful guide to lead my timid steps
To where you wait for me.   [*Exit* HIPPOLYTUS.

        Enter THESEUS *and* ISMENE.   (V.2)

    Theseus [*aside*].   O Gods! enlighten
My troubled heart, and deign to show the truth
That I am seeking here.
    Aricia [*to* ISMENE].   Remember all,
My dear Ismene, and prepare for flight.   [*Exit* ISMENE.

                                      (V.3)

    Theseus. You change your color, and seem speechless,
    madam.
What was Hippolytus doing here?
    Aricia.   My lord,
To bid me an eternal farewell.
    Theseus.   Your eyes

Have learnt to conquer that rebellious spirit,
And his first sighs were your accomplishment.

Aricia. My lord, I cannot hide the truth from you.
He's not inherited your unjust hate;
He does not treat me as a criminal.

Theseus. I see. He vows you an eternal love.
Do not rely on his inconstant heart,
For he would swear as much to others.

Aricia.   He,
My lord?

Theseus. You ought to have made him less inconstant.
How can you bear this horrible division
Of his affections?

Aricia.   And how do you endure
That a horrible tale should smirch a blameless life?
Have you so little knowledge of his heart?
Do you discriminate so ill, my lord,
'Twixt crime and innocence? Must a hateful cloud
Conceal his virtue from your eyes alone,
Which brightly shines for others? It is wrong
To give him up to lying tongues. Cease now:
Repent your murderous prayers. Fear lest the heavens
Should bear you so much hatred as to grant
What you implored. For often in their wrath
They take our proferred victims; and their gifts
Are but the punishments of our own crimes.

Theseus. No. You wish in vain to hide his outrage.
You're blinded by your love. I put my trust
In sure and irreproachable witnesses:
I've seen, I've seen a stream of genuine tears.

Aricia. Take care, my lord. Your hands invincible
Have freed mankind of monsters without number,
But all are not destroyed, and you have left
One still alive. . . .   Your son, my lord, forbids me
To tell you more. And knowing the respect
He wishes to retain for you, I would
Afflict him sorely if I dared to speak.
I imitate his modesty, and flee
Out of your presence, lest I should be forced
To break my silence.   [*Exit* ARICIA.

(V.4)

Theseus.   What is in her mind?
What does it hide, this speech of hers, begun
So many times, and always interrupted?
Would they distract me with an empty feint?
Have they agreed together to torture me?
But I myself, in spite of my stern rigor,
What plaintive voice within my heart cried out?
I am afflicted by a secret pity,
And stand amazed. Let me a second time
Interrogate Œnone. I want to have
A clearer picture of the crime. Guards,
Send for Œnone. Let her come alone.

Enter PANOPE.   (V.5)

Panope. My lord, I know not what the Queen is plan-
    ning,
But yet I fear her violent distress.
Mortal despair is painted on her face,
Marked with Death's pallor. Œnone, from her presence
Driven away with shame, has thrown herself
Into the deep sea: it is not known why
She took her desperate action; and the waves
Have hidden her forever.
    Theseus.   What do I hear?
    Panope. The Queen has not been calmed by this dread
    deed.
Distress still grows within her doubtful soul.
Sometimes, to ease her secret griefs, she takes
Her children, bathing them with tears,
And then, renouncing her maternal love,
She suddenly repels them with her hand.
Then here and there she walks irresolute,
Her wandering eyes no longer knowing us.
Thrice she has written; then, with change of mind,
Thrice she has torn the letter she began.
Deign to see her, my lord, and try to help her.
    Theseus. O heavens! Œnone dead! and Phaedra now
Desires to die. Recall my son. Let him
Defend himself. Let him come and speak with me.

I'm ready to hear him. O Neptune, do not hasten
Thy deadly blessings. I would now prefer
That they should never be fulfilled. Perhaps
I have believed unfaithful witnesses
And raised too soon towards thee my cruel hands.
By what despair now will my prayers be followed!

[*Exit* PANOPE.

Enter THERAMENES.   (V.6)

Theseus. Theramenes, is it you? What have you done
With Hippolytus? I entrusted him to you
From a tender age. But what has caused these tears
I see you shedding. What is my son doing?
Theramenes. O tardy and superfluous cares, vain love!
Hippolytus is no more.
Theseus.   O Gods!
Theramenes.   I have seen
The most lovable of mortals die, and I must add,
My lord, the least guilty.
Theseus.   My son is dead?
When I hold out my arms to him, the gods
Have hastened his destruction. What dread blow
Has snatched him from me? What sudden thunderclap?
Theramenes. Scarce had we passed the gates of Troezen,
He rode upon his chariot; his sad guards,
Around him ranged, were silent as their lord.
Brooding, he followed the Mycenæ road,
And loosely held the reins. His splendid steeds,
Which once with noble zeal obeyed his voice,
Now with dejected eye and lowered head
Seemed to adapt themselves to his sad thoughts.
Then suddenly from out the waves there came
A dreadful cry which broke the silent air
And from the bosom of the earth a voice
With dreadful groans replied. Our blood was frozen,
Even to our hearts. The manes of the listening steeds
Stood up. Then on the liquid plain arose
A watery mountain which appeared to boil.
The wave approached, then broke, and vomited
Among the foamy seas a raging monster:
His huge head armed with menacing horns, his body

Covered with yellow scales, half-bull, half-dragon,
With his croup curved in involuted folds.
The seashore trembled with his bellowing;
The sky with horror saw that savage monster;
The earth was moved, the air infected with it;
The sea which brought it started back amazed.
Everyone fled; seeing all courage vain,
They sought asylum in a neighboring temple.
Hippolytus alone, a worthy son
Of a heroic father, stopped his horses,
Seized his javelins, approached the monster,
And, with a dart, thrown with unerring aim,
Wounded it in the flank. With rage and pain,
The monster leapt, and at the horses' feet
Fell roaring, rolled itself, and offered them
Its flaming mouth, which covered them with fire,
And blood and smoke. Then terror seized them; deaf,
This time, nor voice nor bridle did they know.
Their master spent himself in useless efforts;
Their bits were reddened with a bloody foam.
'Tis said, that in this terrible confusion
A god was seen who spurred their dusty flanks.
Fear hurtled them across the rocks. The axle
Screeched and snapped. The bold Hippolytus
Saw all his chariot shiver into splinters;
And tangled in the reins, he fell. Excuse
My grief. That cruel sight will be for me
An everlasting source of tears. I've seen,
My lord, I've seen your most unlucky son
Dragged by the horses which his hands had fed.
He tried to check them; but, frightened by his voice,
They ran; and soon his body was a single wound.
The plain resounded with our grievous cries.
At last they slackened speed; they stopped not far
From those old tombs where his royal ancestors
Are the cold relics. There I ran, in tears,
And his guard followed me. A trail of blood
Showed us the way. The rocks were stained with it.
The loathsome brambles carried bloodstained scraps
Of hair torn from his head. I reached him, called
To him; he stretched his hand to me, and opened

His dying eyes, then closed them suddenly.
"The heavens," said he, "now snatch my guiltless life.
Look after Aricia when I am dead.
Dear friend, if my father one day learns the truth,
And weeps the tragic ending of a son
Falsely accused, in order to appease
My blood and plaintive ghost, tell him to treat
His captive kindly, to give her . . ." At this word
The hero died and left within my arms
Only a corpse, disfigured, where the wrath
Of the gods had triumphed, one which his father's eyes
Would fail to recognize.

    Theseus.   My son! dear hope
Now taken from me! Inexorable gods,
Too well indeed you have fulfilled your word!
To what remorse my life is now reserved!

    Theramenes. Then gentle Aricia arrived; she came,
My lord, escaping from your wrath, to take him
Before the gods as husband. She approached.
She saw the red and reeking grass; she saw
(What an object for a lover's eyes!)
Hippolytus lying there a shapeless mass.
A while she wished to doubt of her disaster
And failed to recognize the man she loved.
She saw Hippolytus—and asked for him still.
At last too sure that he was lying there,
She with a mournful look reproached the gods;
Cold, moaning, almost lifeless, she fell down
At her lover's feet. Ismene was beside her;
Ismene, weeping, brought her back to life,
Or rather, back to grief. And I have come,
Hating the light, to tell you the last wish
Of a dead hero; and discharge, my lord,
The unhappy task his dying heart reposed
Upon me. But I see his mortal foe
Approaching.

    Enter PHAEDRA, PANOPE, *and* GUARDS.   (V.7)

    Theseus.   Well, you triumph, and my son
Is lifeless. Ah! how I have cause to fear!
A cruel suspicion, excusing him, alarms me.

But, madam, he is dead. Receive your victim,
Joy in his death, whether unjust or lawful.
I'll let my eyes forever be abused,
Believe him criminal, since you accuse him.
His death alone gives matter for my tears
Without my seeking harsh enlightenment,
Which could not bring him back, and might increase
The sum of my misfortunes. Let me, far from you,
Far from this coast flee from the bloody image
Of my rent son. Perplexed and persecuted
By deadly memories, I would banish me
From the whole world. Everything seems to rise
Against my injustice. Even my very fame
Augments my punishment. Less known of men,
I could the better hide. I hate the honors
The gods bestow upon me; and I'm going
To mourn their murderous favors, and no more
Tire them with useless prayers. Whate'er they granted,
Would never compensate me for the loss
Of what they've taken away.
    Phaedra.   No, Theseus.
I must break an unjust silence; to your son
Restore his innocence. He was not guilty.
    Theseus. Unhappy father! It was by your word
That I condemned him. Cruel! do you think
That you can be excused . . . ?
    Phaedra.   My time is precious.
Hear me, Theseus. It was I myself
Who cast upon your chaste and modest son
Unholy and incestuous eyes. The heavens
Put in my breast that fatal spark—the rest
Was undertaken by the vile Œnone.
She trembled lest Hippolytus should disclose
A passion he abhorred. The traitress then,
Relying on my utter weakness, hastened
To accuse him to your face. She's punished for it.
Fleeing my wrath she sought amidst the waves
Too soft a punishment. The sword by now
Would have cut short my life, had I not left
Virtue suspected. Baring my remorse
Before you, I wished to take a slower road

To the house of Death. I have taken—I have made
Course through my burning veins a deadly poison
Medea brought to Athens. Already the venom
Has reached my dying heart, and thrown upon it
An unimagined cold. Already I see,
As through a mist, the sky above, the husband
My presence outrages; and Death, that robs
My eyes of clearness, to the day they soil
Restores its purity.

    Panope.   She is dying, my lord.

    Theseus. Oh! that the memory of her black deed
Could perish with her! Of my error now
Only too well enlightened, let us go
To mix the blood of my unhappy son
With tears; to embrace the little that remains
Of that dear son, and expiate the madness
Of my detested prayer; to render him
The honors that he has too much deserved;
And, the better to appease his angry spirit,
Despite her family's plotting, from today
I'll hold Aricia as my own true child.

ATHALIAH

PREFACE

Everyone knows that the kingdom of Judah was composed of the two tribes of Judah and Benjamin, and that the other ten tribes who rebelled against Rehoboam composed the kingdom of Israel. As the kings of Judah were of the house of David, and as they had in their territory the town and Temple of Jerusalem, all the priests and Levites settled near them and remained attached to them: for, since the building of Solomon's Temple, it was not permitted to sacrifice elsewhere; and all those other altars which were erected to God on the mountains, called in the Scriptures for that reason the high places, were not agreeable to Him. So the legitimate cult existed no longer except in Judah. The ten tribes, except for a very few people, were either idolaters or schismatics.

Yet these priests and Levites were themselves a very numerous tribe. They were divided into different classes to serve in turn in the Temple, from one sabbath to another. The priests were of the family of Aaron; and only those of this family could perform the office of sacrificer. The Levites were subordinate to them, and had the task, among other things, of singing, of the preparation of the victims, and of guarding the Temple. This name of Levite is sometimes given indifferently to all those of the tribe. Those who were on their weekly turn of duty had, together with the High Priest, their lodging in the porches or galleries with which the Temple was surrounded, and which were a part of the Temple itself. All the building was called in general the holy place; but that part of the inner temple where the golden candlestick, the altar of the incense, and the tables of the shewbread were, was called more particularly by that name; and that part was again distinguished from the Holy of Holies, where the Ark was, and where the

High Priest alone had the right to enter once a year. There was a tradition, almost without a break, that the mountain on which the Temple was built was the same mountain where Abraham had once offered his son Isaac in sacrifice.

I thought I should explain these details, so that those to whom the story of the Old Testament is not familiar will not be held up in reading this tragedy. Its subject is Joas recognized and placed on the throne; and according to the rules I should have entitled it *Joas;* but most people having heard of it only under the name of *Athaliah,* I have not thought it proper to offer it to them under another title, since in addition Athaliah plays so considerable a part in it, and since it is her death which concludes the play. She is a party to the principal events which precede this great action.

Joram,[1] King of Judah, son of Jehoshaphat, and the seventh king of the race of David, married Athaliah, daughter of Ahab and Jezebel, who reigned in Israel, both famous, but especially Jezebel, for their bloody persecutions of the prophets. Athaliah, not less impious than her mother, soon drew the King, her husband, into idolatry, and even had a temple built in Jerusalem to Baal, who was the god of the country of Tyre and Sidon, where Jezebel was born. Joram, after having seen perish by the hands of Arabs and Philistines all the princes, his children, except Ahaziah, died himself of a long malady which burnt up his entrails. His dreadful death did not prevent Ahaziah from imitating his impiety and that of Athaliah, his mother. But this prince, after reigning for only a year, while on a visit to the King of Israel, brother of Athaliah, was enveloped in the ruin of the house of Ahab, and killed by the orders of Jehu, whom God had anointed to reign over Israel and to be the minister of his vengeance. Jehu exterminated all the posterity of Ahab and caused Jezebel to be thrown from the window, who, according to the prophecy of Elijah, was eaten by the dogs in the vineyard of the same Naboth who had been slain formerly so as to deprive him of his inheritance. Athaliah, having learned of all these massacres at Jerusalem, undertook on her part to extin-

---

[1] Jehoram in the King James Bible.

guish completely the royal race of David, by causing to be slain all the children of Ahaziah, her own grandsons. But luckily Josabeth, sister of Ahaziah and daughter of Joram, but a different sort of mother from Athaliah, arriving during the massacres of the princes, her nephews, found means to snatch from the midst of the dead the infant Joas, still at the breast, and entrusted him with his nurse to the care of the High Priest, her husband, who hid them both in the Temple, where the child was brought up secretly till the day he was proclaimed King of Judah. The *Book of Kings* says that this was seven years afterwards. But the Greek text of *Chronicles,* which Severus Sulpicius has followed, says it was eight. It is this which authorizes me to make the prince nine or ten, to make him old enough to reply to the questions put to him.

I believe I have made him say nothing beyond the capacity of a child of this age with a good intelligence and memory. But even if I have, it must be considered that this is a quite exceptional child, brought up in the Temple by a High Priest who, looking on him as the unique hope of his nation, has instructed him from an early age in all the duties of religion and royalty. It was not the same with the children of the Jews as with most of ours: they were taught the sacred writings, not merely before they had attained the use of reason, but, to use Saint Paul's expression, from the breast. Every Jew was obliged to write once in his life, with his own hand, the whole book of the Law. The kings were even obliged to write it twice, and enjoined to have it continually before their eyes. I can say here that France sees in the person of a prince of eight and a half years, who delights us even now, an illustrious example of what a child, of natural ability aided by an excellent education, can do; and that if I had given to the child Joas the same vivacity and the same discernment which shines in the repartees of this young prince, I should have been accused with reason of having transgressed the rules of verisimilitude.

The age of Zachariah, son of the High Priest, not having been mentioned, one can suppose him, if one likes, to be two or three years older than Joas.

I have followed the explanation of several skillful commentators, who prove by the actual text of Scripture, that all the soldiers whom Jehoiada (or Joad, as he is called in Josephus) armed with the weapons consecrated to God by David, were as much priests and Levites as the five centurions who commanded them. Indeed, say the interpreters, everyone had to be holy in so holy an action, and no profane person should be employed. What was at stake was not merely keeping the scepter in the house of David, but also keeping for that great king the line of descendants of whom the Messiah should be born. "For this Messiah promised so many times as the son of Abraham, should also be the son of David and of all the kings of Judah." From this it follows that the illustrious and learned prelate from whom I have borrowed these words calls Joas the precious remnant of the house of David. Josephus speaks of him in the same terms; and Scripture states expressly that God did not exterminate all the family of Joram, wishing to conserve for David the lamp which he had promised him. For what else was this lamp but the light which should one day be revealed to the gentiles?

History does not specify at all the day on which Joas was proclaimed. Some interpreters claim that it was a feast day. I have chosen that of Pentecost, which was one of the three great feasts of the Jews. In it was celebrated the memory of the publication of the Law on Mount Sinai, and in it was also offered to God the first loaves of the new harvest: which made it called still the feast of the first fruits. I thought that these circumstances would furnish me with some variety for the songs of the chorus.

This chorus is composed of maidens of the tribe of Levi, and I have put at their head a girl whom I have given as sister to Zachariah. It is she who introduces the chorus into her mother's house. She sings with them, speaks for them, and performs the functions of the person of the ancient choruses who was called the coryphaeus. I have also tried to imitate from the ancients that continuity of action which makes their stage never left empty, the intervals between the acts being marked by the hymns and moralizing of the chorus, who are in touch with all that passes.

I shall perhaps be found a little audacious in having dared to put on the stage a prophet inspired by God, who predicts the future. But I have taken the precaution to put into his mouth only expressions taken from the prophets themselves. Although the Scriptures do not state expressly that Jehoiada had had a spirit of prophecy, as they do of his son, they represent him as a man full of the spirit of God. And besides, would it not appear by the gospel that he would have been able to prophecy in the capacity of sovereign pontiff? I suppose, therefore, that he sees the fatal change of Joas who, after twenty years of a reign of great piety, abandoned himself to the evil counsels of flatterers, and stained himself with the blood of Zachariah, son and successor of the High Priest. This murder, committed in the Temple, was one of the principal causes of the wrath of God against the Jews and of all the misfortunes which happened to them afterwards. It is even maintained that since that day the responses of God ceased entirely in the sanctuary. That has given me the opportunity to make Joad depict the destruction of the Temple and the ruin of Jerusalem. But as the prophets ordinarily joined consolations to their threats, and as also the action was concerned with putting on the throne one of the ancestors of the Messiah, I have taken occasion to give a glimpse of the coming of this comforter, for whom all the righteous men of ancient times sighed. This scene, which is a kind of episode, brings in music very naturally, by the custom which several prophets had of entering into their holy trances to the sound of instruments: witness that troop of prophets who came before Saul with the harps and lyres which were borne before them; and witness Elisha himself, who being consulted on the future by the King of Judah and the King of Israel, said, as Joad does here: *Adducite mihi psaltem*. Add to that, that this prophecy serves greatly to augment the tension of the drama, by the consternation it causes and by the different reactions of the chorus and the principal actors.

DRAMATIS PERSONÆ

ABNER, *one of Athaliah's principal officers*
JOAD, *High Priest*
JOSABETH, *his wife, aunt to Joas*
ZACHARIAH }
SALOMITH } *their children*
AGAR, *woman of Athaliah's suite*
MATHAN, *priest of Baal*
ATHALIAH, *widow of Joram*
JOAS, *her grandson, the rightful King, called Eliacin*
NABAL, *confidant of Mathan*
AZARIAS, ISMAEL, *and other* LEVITES
NURSE *of Joas*
ATHALIAH'S GUARDS
CHORUS *of girls of the Tribe of Levi*

SCENE—The temple of JERUSALEM, in a vestibule of the
apartment of the High Priest

ATHALIAH

ACT ONE

ABNER and JOAD discovered.

ABNER. Yes, I have come into this Temple now
To adore the Everlasting; I have come,
According to our old and solemn custom,
To celebrate with you the famous day
When on Mount Sinai the Law was given us.
How times have changed! As soon as the trumpet blast
Proclaimed the day's return, the chosen people
Poured into the sacred porticos in crowds,
And in the Temple, garlanded with flowers,
They stood before the altar rank by rank,
And to the God of the universe they offered
The first fruits of their fields. The sacrifices
By priests alone was not sufficient then.
A woman's presumption now has put a stop
To that great concourse; and to days of darkness
Has changed those happy days. Only a handful
Of zealous worshippers enable us
To trace a shadow of those former times;
While for their God the rest of them display
Fatal forgetfulness. They even flock
To Baal's altars, there to be initiated
Into his shameful mysteries, and blaspheme
The name their sires invoked. I tremble now
That Athaliah—I will hide nothing from you—
Has not yet perfected her dire revenge.
She plans to snatch you from the altar, and . . .
    Joad. Whence comes this black presentiment of yours?
    Abner. Do you imagine that you can be just
And holy with impunity? For long
She has detested that rare constancy
Which gives a double glory to your crown;
For long she's looked on your religious zeal

As rank sedition; and this jealous queen
Hates above all the faithful Josabeth,
Your wife, even for her virtues. If you are
Aaron's successor, Josabeth's the sister
Of our last king. Mathan, moreover, Mathan,
That sacrilegious priest, who is more vile
Than Athaliah herself, at every hour
Besieges her—Mathan, the foul deserter
From the Lord's altars, ever the zealous foe
Of every virtue. 'Tis little that this Levite,
His brows encircled with an alien miter,
Now ministers to Baal: to him this Temple
Is a reproach, and his impiety
Would bring to nought the God that he has left.
There are no means to which he'll not resort
To ruin you; at times he'll pity you
And often he will even sing your praises;
Affecting for you a false tenderness,
And screening so the blackness of his rancor,
He paints you to the Queen as terrible;
Or else, insatiable for gold, he feigns
That in some place that's known to you alone
You hide King David's treasure. But Athaliah
Has seemed for two days to be plunged in gloom
I watched her yesterday, and saw her eyes
Dart furious glances on the holy place,
As if within this mighty edifice
God hid an avenger, armed for her destruction.
Believe me, Joad, the more I think of it,
The more I am convinced her wrath is ready
To burst upon you, that the bloody daughter
Of Jezebel will soon attack our God,
Even in His sanctuary.

Joad.   He who can bridle
The fury of the waves knows how to foil
The plots of the wicked. Submissive to His will,
I fear the Lord, and have no other fear.
Yet, Abner, I am grateful for the zeal
Which has awakened you to all my perils.
I see injustice vexes you in secret;
That you are still an Israelite at heart.

Heaven be praised! But can you be content
With secret wrath and with an idle virtue?
And can the faith that acts not be sincere?
Eight years ago an impious foreigner
Usurped all the rights of David's scepter,
And with impunity imbrued herself
In the blood of our true kings—foul murderess
Of the children of her son, and even against God
Her treacherous arm is raised:
While you a pillar of this tottering State,
Brought up within the camps of Jehoshaphat,
That holy king, and under his son, Joram,
Commander of his hosts, who reassured
Our fearful towns when Ahaziah was slain,
And all his army at the sight of Jehu
Scattered in panic—"I fear the Lord," you say;
"His truth concerns me." By me that God replies:
"For what use is the zeal that you profess?
Think'st thou to honor me with barren vows?
What do I get from all your sacrifices?
Do I require the blood of goats and heifers?
The blood of your kings cries out and is not heard.
Break off all compact with impiety!
Root out the evil from among my people
And then approach me with your burnt offerings."

   Abner. What can I do among this beaten people?
Judah and Benjamin are powerless now:
The day that saw their race of kings extinguished
Extinguished too their ancient bravery.
God, they say, has withdrawn Himself from us:
He, who was jealous of the Hebrews' honor,
Now, careless, sees their greatness overthrown,
And in the end His mercy is exhausted.
The countless miracles He worked for us
To terrify mankind are seen no more.
The holy Ark is dumb, and renders now
Its oracles no longer.

   Joad.   And what time
Was e'er so fertile in its miracles?
When has God shown His power to such effect?
Will you forever, O ungrateful people,

Have eyes which see not? Will great miracles
Forever strike your ears, but leave your heart
Untouched? Abner, must I recall the course
Of prodigies accomplished in our days?
The woes that fell on Israel's tyrants—God
Found faithful in his threats! The impious Ahab
Destroyed, and that field sprinkled with his blood,
Which he usurped by murder; and nearby
Jezebel slain and trampled by the horses,
So that the dogs lapped up her savage blood
And tore her frightful body limb from limb;
The troop of lying prophets all confounded,
And fire from heaven descended on the altar;
Elijah speaking to the elements
As sovereign master; the skies by him locked up
And turned to brass, so that the earth three years
Had neither rain nor dew; at Elisha's voice
The dead reanimated? Recognize,
Abner, in these deeds that still resound,
A God who is indeed the same today
As in the days of old. He manifests
His glory when He wills; His chosen people
Is always present to His memory.

    Abner. But where are those honors oft to David prom-
      ised,
And prophecied for Solomon, his son?
Alas! we hoped that of their happy race
There would descend a line of kings, of whom
One would at last establish his dominion
Over all tribes and nations, who would make
Discord and war to cease, and at his feet
Behold all kings of the earth.

    Joad.   Wherefore renounce
The promises of heaven?

    Abner.   Where shall we find
The royal son of David? Can heaven itself
Repair the ruins of this tree that's withered
Even to the very roots? For Athaliah
Stifled the child in his cradle. Can the dead,
Now eight years have gone by, come from the grave?
If in her rage she had mistook her aim,

If of our royal blood there had escaped
One drop to . . .
 Joad.   Well, what would you do?
 Abner. O joyous day for me! How ardently
I'd recognize my king. You need not doubt
The tribes would hasten at his feet to lay
Their tribute. But why delude myself
With such vain thoughts? The lamentable heir
Of those triumphant monarchs, Ahaziah
Alone remained—he and his children only.
I saw the father stabbed by Jehu; you
Beheld the sons all butchered by the mother.
 Joad. I'll not explain; but when the star of day
Has traced a third of its course across the sky,
And when the third hour summons us to prayer,
Return to the Temple with the selfsame zeal,
And God may show, by signal benefits,
His word is firm, and never can deceive.
Go now, I must prepare for this great day,
And even now the pinnacle of the Temple
Is whitened by the dawn.
 Abner.   What will this be—
This blessing that I cannot comprehend?
The noble Josabeth is coming towards you.
I'll join the faithful flock the solemn rite
Of this day has attracted.   [*Exit* ABNER.

Enter JOSABETH.   (I.2)

 Joad.   The time is ripe,
Princess, and we must speak. Your happy theft
No longer can be hidden. The insolence
Of the Lord's foes who take His name in vain
From this deep silence has accused too long
His promises of error. What do I say?
Success has fanned their fury; and on our altar
Your evil stepmother would offer Baal
Idolatrous incense. Let us show this king—
The boy your hands have saved, to be brought up
Beneath the Lord's protecting wing. He'll have
Our Hebrew princes' courage, and already
His mind's outstripped his age. Before I speak

Of his high destiny, I'll offer him
To the God by whom kings reign, and soon before
The assembled priests and Levites, I'll declare
Their master's heir.

Josabeth.   Has he himself been told
Of his real name and noble destiny?

Joad. Not yet. He answers only to the name
Of Eliacin, and thinks he is a child
Abandoned by his mother, to whom I deigned
To act as father.

Josabeth.   Alas! from what dire peril
I rescued him, and into what more peril
Is he about to enter!

Joad.   Is your faith
Already wavering?

Josabeth.   To your wise advice,
My lord, I do submit. For from the day
I snatched this child from death, into your hands
His life and fate were placed. I even feared
The violence of my love; and therefore tried
To shun his presence, lest in seeing him,
My tears for some grief not to be suppressed
Would let my secret out. To tears and prayers
I've consecrated three whole days and nights,
As duty bid; but may I ask today
What friends you have prepared to give you aid?
Will Abner, the brave Abner, fight for us?
And has he sworn that he'll be near his king?

Joad. Although his faith is sure, he does not yet
Know that we have a king.

Josabeth.   To whom will you
Entrust the guard of Joas? Obed or Amnon?
My father showered his benefits upon them. . . .

Joad. They're sold to Athaliah.

Josabeth.   Whom have you then
To oppose her satellites?

Joad.   Have I not told you?
Our priests, our Levites.

Josabeth.   I know indeed
That by your foresight secretly assembled
Their number is redoubled; that, full of love

For you, and full of hate for Athaliah,
A solemn oath has bound them in advance
To this son of David who will be revealed.
But though a noble ardor burns in them,
Can they alone their king's cause vindicate?
Can zeal alone for such a work suffice?
Do you doubt that Athaliah—when first 'tis bruited
That Ahaziah's son is cloistered here—
Will mass her foreign cohorts, to surround
The Temple and break in the doors. 'Gainst them
Will these your holy ministers suffice,
Who lifting innocent hands unto the Lord
Can only weep and pray for all our sins,
And ne'er shed blood, save of the sacrifice?
Joas, perhaps, pierced through with hostile spears,
Will in their arms . . .

Joad.   Is God who fights for us
By you accounted nothing? God who protects
The orphan's innocence, and makes his power
Displayed in weakness; God who hates the tyrant;
Who in Jezreel did vow to extirpate
Ahab and Jezebel; God, who striking Joram,
Their son-in-law, pursued the family,
Even to his son; God, whose avenging arm,
Suspended for a time, is still outstretched
Over this impious race?

Josabeth.   And His stern justice
Meted to all these kings is cause for me
To fear for my unlucky brother's son,
For who can tell, if by their crime enmeshed,
This child from birth was not condemned with them?
If God, for David's sake, dividing him
From all that odious race would grant him favor?
Alas! the horrible scene when heaven offered
The child to me again and again returns
To terrify my soul. The room was filled
With murdered princes. Relentless Athaliah,
A dagger in her hand, urged to the kill
Her barbarous soldiers, and pursued the course
Of all her murders. Joas, left for dead,
Suddenly struck my eyes; and even now

I see his frightened nurse throwing herself
In vain before his butchers, holding him
Head downwards on her breast. I took him, steeped
In blood. I bathed his face in tears. And then
I felt his innocent arms go round my neck,
In fear, or to caress me. O great God!
Let not my love be fatal to him now—
This precious relic of the faithful David
Here in thy house nourished upon the love
Of thy great Law. He knows as yet no father
Save Thee alone. Though in the face of peril,
When we're about to attack a murderous queen,
My faith begins to waver, though flesh and blood,
Faltering today, have some part in the tears
I shed for him, preserve the heritage
Of Thy sacred promises, and do not punish
Any save me for all my weaknesses.

    Joad. Your tears are guiltless, Josabeth; but God
Wills us to hope in his paternal care.
He is not wont to visit in his rage
The impiety of the father on the son
Who fears him. The faithful remnant of the Jews
Come to renew their vows to him today.
Even as David's race is still respected,
So is the daughter of Jezebel detested.
Joas will touch them with his innocence
In which the splendor of his blood reshines;
And God by His voice upholding our example
Will speak unto their hearts. Two faithless kings
Successively have braved Him. To the throne
A king must now be raised who'll not forget
God, by his priests, has placed him in the rank
Of his great ancestors, by their hand snatched him
From the tomb's oblivion, and lit again
The torch of David. Great God, if Thou foreseest
He'll be unworthy of his race, and leave
The ways of David, let him be as the fruit
Torn from the branch, or withered in its flower
By a hostile wind! But if this child should prove
Docile to Thy commands, an instrument

Useful to Thy designs, then hand the scepter
To the rightful heir; deliver into my hands
His powerful enemies; frustrate the counsels
Of this cruel queen; and grant, O grant, my God,
That upon her and Mathan shall be poured
Error and rashness, of the fall of kings
Fatal vaunt-courier! The time is short.
Farewell! Your son and daughter bring you now
The damsels of the holiest families.   [*Exit* JOAD.

Enter ZACHARIAH, SALOMITH, *and* CHORUS.   (I.3)

Josabeth. Dear Zachariah, go now. Do not stop.
Accompany your noble father's steps.   [*Exit* ZACHARIAH.
Daughters of Levi, young and faithful flock,
Kindled already by the zeal of the Lord,
Who come so often all my sighs to share,
Children, my only joy in my long sorrows,
These garlands and these flowers upon your heads
Once suited with our solemn festivals;
But now, alas, in times of shame and sorrow,
What offering suits better than our tears?
I hear already, I hear the sacred trumpet;
The Temple soon will open. While I prepare,
Sing, praise the Lord whom you have come to seek.
                    [*Exeunt* JOSABETH *and* SALOMITH.

                                                (I.4)

All the chorus. All the universe is full of His glory!
Let us adore this God, and call upon Him!
His Empire was before the birth of Time!
O let us sing, his benefits to praise!
    A Voice. In vain unrighteous violence
Upon his worshippers imposeth silence:
His name will live always.
Day telleth day of His magnificence.
        All the universe is full of His glory:
            O let us sing, His benefits to praise.
    All. All the universe is full of His glory:
O let us sing, His benefits to praise.
    A Voice. He gives unto the flowers their lovely hues,

He slowly ripens fruits upon the tree,
And gives them warmth by day and nightly dews;
The field repays his gifts with usury.

Another. The sun all nature doth reanimate
At His command; He gives the blessed light;
But His best gift to those He did create
Is still His holy Law, our pure delight.

Another. O Sinai, preserve the memory
Renowned forevermore of that great day
When from a thick cloud on thy flaming peak
The Lord made shine to mortal eyes a ray
Of His eternal glory! Why those flames,
The lightning flash, the eddying clouds of smoke,
Trumpets and thunder in the resounding air?
Came He to overturn the elemental order,
And shake the earth upon its ancient base?

Another. No, no, He came to reveal the eternal light
Of His holy laws to the children of the Jews;
He came to that happy people, to command them
To love Him with an everlasting love.

All. Divine and lovely Law,
O bounteous and just!
How right, how sweet to pledge
To God our love and trust!

A Voice. He freed our fathers from the tyrant's yoke;
Fed them on manna in the wilderness;
He gives His laws, He gives Himself to us:
And for these blessings asks for love alone.

All. O bounteous and just!

A Voice. For them He cleft the waters of the sea;
He made streams gush out from the arid rock.
He gives His laws, He gives Himself to us,
And for these blessings asks for love alone.

Chorus. Divine and lovely Law!
How right, how sweet to pledge
To God our love and trust!

A Voice. Ingrates, who only know a servile fear,
Cannot a God so gracious touch your heart?
Is love so stony and so hard a path?
It is the slave who fears the tyrant's wrath,
But filial love remains the children's part.

You wish this God to shower His gifts on you,
And never give the love that is His due.
   Chorus. Divine and lovely Law!
O bounteous and just!
How right, how sweet to pledge
To God our love and trust.

ACT TWO

JOSABETH, SALOMITH, *and* CHORUS.

JOSABETH. Enough, my daughters. Cease your canticles.
'Tis time to join us now in public prayers.
The hour is come. Let's celebrate this day
And appear before the Lord. But what do I see?

Enter ZACHARIAH.   (II.2)

  Josabeth. My son, what brings you here? Where do you run,
All pale and out of breath?
    Zachariah.   O Mother . . .
    Josabeth.   Well?
What is it?
    Zachariah. The Temple is profaned. . . .
    Josabeth.   How?
    Zachariah. The altar of the Lord abandoned!
    Josabeth.   I tremble.
Hasten to tell me all.
    Zachariah.   Even now my father,
The High Priest, had offered, according to the Law,
The first loaves of the harvest to our God
Who feeds us all. And then he held aloft
The smoking entrails of the sacrifice
In bloodstained hands, while young Eliacin,
Like me, stood by his side and ministered,
Clad in a linen robe, and while the priests
Sprinkled the altar and the congregation
With blood of the offerings—suddenly there was
A noise which made the people turn their eyes.

A woman . . . Can I name her without blasphemy? . . .
A woman . . . It was Athaliah herself.

   Josabeth. Great heaven!

   Zachariah. Into a sanctuary reserved for men
Entered that haughty woman, head held high,
And made to pass into the holy precincts
Open to Levites only. Struck with terror
The people fled away. My father— Ah! what wrath
Shone in his countenance, more terrible
Than Moses before Pharaoh. "Queen," he said,
"Go from this holy place, from whence thy sex
And thy impiety alike are banished.
Com'st thou indeed to brave the majesty
Of the living God?" Forthwith the Queen, upon him
Turning a fierce glance, opened her mouth to speak,
And doubtless to blaspheme. I know not whether
The Angel of the Lord appeared to her
Bearing a flaming sword; but this I know—
Her tongue was frozen in her mouth, and all
Her boldness seemed to crumble; while her eyes,
Affrighted, dared not turn away. She seemed
Amazed by Eliacin.

   Josabeth.   How so? Did he
Appear before her?

   Zachariah.   Both of us beheld
This cruel queen, and with an equal dread
Our hearts were struck. But soon the priests stood round us,
And led us forth. And that is all I know
Of this ominous disorder.

   Josabeth.   Ah! from our arms
She comes to snatch him; and 'tis he her fury
Seeks even at the altar. Perhaps even now
The object of so many tears . . . O! God,
Who seest my fears, remember David now.

   Salomith. For whom do you weep?

   Zachariah.   Is Eliacin's life
In danger now?

   Salomith.   Could he have attracted
The anger of the Queen?

   Zachariah.   How could they fear
A child without defense, and fatherless?

Josabeth. She's here. Come, let us go. We must avoid
   her.   [*Exeunt.*

Enter ATHALIAH, ABNER, AGAR, *and* GUARDS. (II.3)

   Agar. Your Majesty, why do you stay within
These precincts, where all objects vex and wound you?
O leave this Temple to the priests who dwell
Within its walls. Flee all this tumult now,
And in your palace strive to give back peace
To your o'ertroubled senses.
   Athaliah.   No. I cannot.
You see my weakness and disquiet. Go,
Send Mathan hither: let him come with speed. . . .
Happy if I by his aid can obtain
The peace I seek, which still eludes my grasp.
                         [*Exit* AGAR. ATHALIAH *sits.*

                                              (II.4)

   Abner. Forgive me, madam, if I dare defend
The zeal of Joad, which should not surprise you.
Such is the eternal order of our God,
For He himself marked out for us His Temple,
To Aaron's children only did entrust
His sacrifices; both their place and functions
Appointed to the Levites; and forbad
To their posterity all intercourse
With any other God. Are you, O Queen,
The daughter and the mother of our kings,
So alien to us? Know you not our laws?
And is it necessary that today . . . ?
But here is Mathan. I will leave you with him.
   Athaliah. I need your presence, Abner. Leave at that
The reckless insolence of Joad, and all
That empty heap of superstitions
Which bars your Temple to all other peoples.
Something more urgent has aroused my fears.
I know that Abner, raised from infancy
To be a soldier, has a noble heart;
And that he renders what he owes to God,
And renders what he owes unto his kings.
Remain with us.

Enter MATHAN.   (II.5)

Mathan.   Great Queen, is here your place?
What has disquieted you? What terror now
Turned you to ice? What have you come to seek
Among your enemies? Do you dare approach
This impious Temple? Have you shed your hatred?
    Athaliah. Both of you lend me an attentive ear.
I do not wish here to recall the past,
Nor give you reasons for the blood I've shed.
What I have done I thought was necessary.
Abner, I'll not accept a headstrong people
To be my judge. Whatever their insolence
Has dared to claim, I have been justified
By heaven itself. My power that is established
On my successful deeds has made the name
Of Athaliah held in great respect
From sea to sea. By me Jerusalem
Enjoys an absolute peace. The Jordan sees
No more the wandering Arab, and no more
The haughty Philistine with endless raids
(As in your kings' days) desolate her banks.
The Syrian treats me as a queen and sister:
At last the vile oppressor of my house,
Whose savagery I myself have felt,
Jehu, proud Jehu, trembles in Samaria,
On every side hemmed in by neighboring powers
Which I have raised against that murderer.
In these domains he leaves me sovereign mistress.
I now enjoy in peace my wisdom's fruits.
But yet, for some days past, a nagging fear
Has stopped the course of my prosperity.
A dream (why should a dream disturb me so?)
Brought to my heart a gnawing pain. I tried
To escape, but everywhere it followed me:
Methought that in the dreadful deep of night
My mother Jezebel rose up before me,
All gorgeously arrayed as when she died.
Her sorrows had not quenched her pride, but still
Her face was decked and painted to repair
The irreparable ravages of time.

"Tremble, my daughter, worthy of me," she said;
"The cruel God of the Jews will soon prevail
Over you also, and I mourn that you
Are falling into His relentless hands,
My child." In uttering these frightful words,
Her ghost, it seemed, bent down towards my bed;
But when I stretched my hands out to embrace her,
I found instead a horrible heap of bones,
And mangled flesh, and tatters soaked in blood
Dragged through the mire, and limbs unspeakable
For which voracious dogs were wrangling there.
    Abner. Great God!
    Athaliah.   In this confusion there appeared
Before my eyes a child with shining robes,
Like those of the Hebrew priests. On seeing him
My spirits revived, my deadly fear subsided.
But while I wondered at his noble bearing,
His charm and modesty, then all at once
I felt a murderous dagger which the traitor
Plunged deep into my heart. Perhaps you think
This mingling of such diverse images
In my strange dream was but the work of chance.
And I myself, ashamed of my own fear,
Have thought at times they must be the effect
Of some dark vapor. But my soul, possessed
With this remembrance, saw the selfsame sights
Twice visit me in sleep. Twice did my eyes
Behold this child prepare again to stab me,
Until worn down by these pursuing terrors
I went to pray to Baal for his protection,
And seek for peace of mind before his altars.
What cannot panic do to mortal minds?
Urged by a sudden impulse to this Temple
I came instead, thus hoping to appease
The Jewish God, and calm His wrath with gifts.
I thought that God, whoever He may be,
Might become merciful. Pontiff of Baal,
Forgive this strange infirmity of purpose.
I entered; the people fled; the sacrifice ceased.
The High Priest came towards me white with fury.
While he was speaking to me, I beheld—

With terror and astonishment beheld—
The very child of whom I had been warned
By such a fearful dream. I saw him there—
His air, his linen garments, his gait, his eyes,
And all his traits the same. 'Twas he. He walked
Beside the High Priest: but, on seeing me,
They made him disappear; and it is this
That troubles me and brings me to a stop.
It was on this I wished to consult you both.
What, Mathan,
Does this incredible prodigy presage?

    Mathan. Your dream and story fill me with amazement.

    Athaliah. But, Abner, have you seen this fatal child?
What is he? Of what blood? And of what tribe?

    Abner. Two children at the altar ministered:
One is the son of Joad and Josabeth,
The other I know not.

    Mathan.   Why hesitate?
Of both, madam, you need to be assured.
You know the moderation and respect
I have for Joad, that I do not seek
To avenge my wrongs, that equity alone
Reigns ever in my counsels. But, after all,
Would he himself permit a criminal
To live a moment, were it his own child?

    Abner. Of what crime can a child be capable?

    Mathan. Heaven made us see him brandishing a dagger;
Heaven is wise, and nothing does in vain.
What more do you seek?

    Abner.   But on the evidence
Of a mere dream, will you imbrue your hands
In a child's blood? You do not even know
His parentage, or what he is.

    Mathan.   We fear him.
That's all we need to know. For if he stems
From famous stock, the splendor of his lot
Should hasten now his ruin; and if fate
Has given him humble birth, what does it matter
If a vile blood at random should be spilt?
Should kings be slow in justice, when their safety
Often depends on speedy punishment?

Let us not hamper them with awkward caution;
For from the moment one is suspect to them,
He's innocent no longer.
 Abner.   What! Mathan!
Is this the language of a priest. 'Tis I,
Inured to slaughter in my trade of war,
Stern minister of royal vengeances,
Who lend a voice for the unfortunate child;
While you who owe him a paternal kindness,
You, minister of peace in times of wrath,
Covering resentment with a specious zeal—
Blood flows not fast enough in your opinion.
You have commanded me, O Queen, to speak
Without reserve. What then is the great cause
Of all your fear? A dream, a harmless child
Your eye, forewarned, believed to recognize,
Perhaps mistakenly.
 Athaliah.   I wish to think so.
I well may be mistaken. An empty dream
May too much have obsessed me. Ah, well! I must
See once again this child at closer view,
And at my leisure scrutinize his traits.
Let both appear before me.
 Abner.   I am afraid . . .
 Athaliah. That they will not comply? But what could be
Their reasons for refusal? That would cast me
Into some strange suspicions. Let Josabeth
Or Joad bring them. I can, when I wish,
Speak as a queen. Abner, I must avow
Your priests have every reason to extol
Athaliah's favors. I know that in their preaching
They abuse my power and conduct. Yet they live,
And still their Temple stands. But now I feel
My kindness nears its end. Let Joad bridle
His savage zeal, and not provoke my heart
By a second outrage. Go.   [*Exit* ABNER.

              (II.6)

 Mathan.   Now I can speak
Freely, and put the truth as clear as day.
Some newborn monster, Queen, is being raised

Within this Temple. Wait not for the cloud
To burst. I know that Abner before daybreak
Came to the High Priest's house. You know his love
For the blood of his kings; and who knows if Joad
Has not some plan to place upon the throne
This child with whom the heavens have menaced you,
His own son, or some other?

    Athaliah.   Yes, you open
My eyes, and clearly I begin to see
The meaning of this portent. But I wish
To clear my mind of doubt. A child's unable
To hide his thoughts, and oft a single word
Will let us guess at mighty purposes.
Let me, dear Mathan, see and question him.
And you meanwhile, without causing alarm,
Order my Tyrians to take up arms.   [*Exit* MATHAN.

    Enter JOAS, JOSABETH, ABNER, CHORUS, etc. (II.7)

    Josabeth. O servants of the Lord, upon these children,
So dear, so precious, keep your eyes.

    Abner.   Princess,
Assure yourself, I will protect them.

    Athaliah.   O Gods!
The more I scrutinize him . . . It is he!
And all my senses now are seized with horror.
Wife of Joad, is this boy your son?

    Josabeth. Who? He, madam?

    Athaliah.   He.

    Josabeth.   I am not his mother.
There is my son.

    Athaliah.   And you, who is your father?
Answer me, child.

    Josabeth.   Heaven, until this day . . .

    Athaliah. Why do you hasten to reply for him?
I speak to him.

    Josabeth.   From such a tender age
What information can you hope to get?

    Athaliah. This age is innocent; his artlessness
Will not pervert the simple truth. Leave him
To answer freely everything I ask.

Josabeth [*aside*]. O put Thy wisdom in his mouth, O
    Lord!

Athaliah. What is your name?

Joas.   Eliacin.

Athaliah.   Your father?

Joas. They tell me I'm an orphan, thrown since birth
Upon the arms of God. I never knew
My parents.

Athaliah. You have no parents?

Joas.   No:
They abandoned me.

Athaliah.   Since when?

Joas.   Since I was born.

Athaliah. Do you not know, at least, which is your
    country?

Joas. This Temple is my country. I know no other.

Athaliah. Where did they find you?

Joas.   Among the cruel wolves
Ready to eat me up.

Athaliah.   Who brought you here?

Joas. An unknown woman, who did not tell her name
And was not seen again.

Athaliah.   In your earliest years
Who looked after you?

Joas.   Has God ever left
His children in want? He feeds the tiniest birds;
His bounty stretches to the whole of nature.
I pray to him daily, and with a father's care
He feeds me with the gifts placed on his altar.

Athaliah. What new prodigy disturbs me now?
The sweetness of his voice, his childlike ways,
His grace, make to my enmity succeed . . .
Could I be moved by pity?

Abner.   Is this, madam,
Your terrible foe? Your dreams are plainly liars,
Unless your pity is the deadly stroke
Which made you tremble.

Athaliah.   You're going?

Josabeth.   You've heard his fortunes.
He need intrude no longer on your presence.

Athaliah. No. Come back. What do you do each day?

Joas. I worship the Lord and listen to His Law.
I have been taught to read His holy book,
And I am learning now to copy it.

Athaliah. What says this Law?

Joas.   That God demands our love;
That He takes vengeance, soon or late, on those
Who take His name in vain; that He defends
The timid orphan; that He resists the proud
And punishes the murderer.

Athaliah.   I see.
But all the people shut up in this place,
How do they spend their time?

Joas.   They praise and bless
The Lord.

Athaliah. Does God exact continual prayer
And worship?

Joas.   Everything profane is banished
Out of His Temple.

Athaliah.   What are your pleasures then?

Joas. Sometimes to the High Priest at the altar
I offer salt or incense. I hear songs
Of the infinite greatness of Almighty God;
I see the stately order of His rites.

Athaliah. Have you no sweeter pastime? I am sorry
That such a child should lead so sad a life.
Come to my palace! See my glory there!

Joas. And lose the memory of God's benefits?

Athaliah. Why, no. I would not force you to forget them.

Joas. You do not pray to Him.

Athaliah.   But you could pray.

Joas. I should see people pray to other gods.

Athaliah. I have my god, and serve him. You would
     serve yours.
There are two powerful gods.

Joas.   Mine must be feared:
He is God alone, madam, and yours is none.

Athaliah. Near me you'd find a host of pleasures, boy.

Joas. The happiness of the wicked passeth away
Even as a torrent.

Athaliah.   Who are these wicked?

Josabeth.   Oh, madam,
Excuse a child . . .
    Athaliah.   I like to see your teaching.
So, Eliacin, you please me. You are not
An ordinary child. I am the Queen,
And have no heir. Take off this robe, and leave
This mean employment. I would have you share
In all my riches. From this very day
Make trial of my promises. At my table,
Everywhere, seated at my side, I mean
To treat you as my son.
    Joas.   As your son?
    Athaliah.   Yes?
You're silent?
    Joas.   What a father I should leave!
And for . . .
    Athaliah. Well?
    Joas.   For what a mother!
    Athaliah. His memory is faithful; and in all
That he has said I recognize the spirit
Of you and Joad. This is how you use
(Infecting his simple youth) the peace wherein
I leave you; and you cultivate so young
Their hate and fury. You pronounce my name
Only with horror to them.
    Josabeth.   Can we conceal
From them the story of our woes? The world
Knows them; and you yourself take glory in them.
    Athaliah. Yes, my just fury—and I boast of it—
Avenged my parents' deaths upon my sons.
I saw my father and my brother butchered,
My mother cast down from her palace window,
And in one day (what a spectacle of horror!)
Saw eighty princes murdered! For what reason?
To avenge some prophets whose immoderate frenzies
My mother justly punished; and I, a queen
Without a heart, a girl without a friend,
Slave to a cowardly and futile pity,
Would not, transported by blind rage, commit
Murder for murder, outrage for outrage,
And treat all the posterity of David

As they have treated Ahab's luckless sons?
Where would I be today had I not conquered
My weakness, stifled a mother's tenderness,
Had I not shed a stream of my own blood
With my own hand, and by this dauntless stroke
Have quelled your plots? And now the vengeance
Of your implacable God has snapped forever
All bonds between our houses. David I hold
Abhorred, and that king's sons, yea even those
Born of my blood, are strangers to me.
    Josabeth.   **All**
Has prospered for you. May God see and judge us!
    Athaliah. This God, who has been long your only refuge,
What will become of his predictions?
Let Him give you this king, this child of David,
Your hope and expectation, who is promised
To all the nations. . . . But we shall see. Farewell.
I leave you, satisfied. I wished to see.
I have seen.
    Abner.   As I have promised you
I give you back what you entrusted me.
                        [*Exeunt* ATHALIAH *with her* GUARDS.
                     Enter JOAD.   (II.8)
    Josabeth. Did you o'erhear this haughty queen, my lord?
    Joad. Yes, I heard all, and shared your grief and fears.
These Levites and myself, prepared to help you,
Resolved to perish with you. [*To* JOAS.] May the Lord
Watch over you, my child, whose courage gives
A noble witness to your name. I'm grateful,
Abner, for what you've done. Do not forget
The hour when Joad expects you. As for us,
Whose looks are sullied and whose prayer's disturbed
By this impious murderess, let us go in,
And with a pure blood that my hands will shed
Cleanse even the marble where her feet have touched.
                      [*Exeunt* ALL, *except* CHORUS.
                                 (II.9)

    One of the Chorus. What star is shining on us now?
What will this wondrous child become one day?
    He braved the splendor of the proud,

And not allowed
Its perilous lures to lead his feet astray.
Another. While others are to alien altars hasting
To offer incense, this child, indomitable,
Proclaims that God alone is everlasting,
A new Elias before a Jezebel.
Another. Who will reveal to us your secret birth,
Dear child? Are you some holy prophet's son?
Another. So in the shadow of the tabernacle
Beloved Samuel grew,
Till he became our hope and oracle;
O may thou too
Console the children of Israel!
Another [*singing*]. O bless'd a thousand times
The child whom the Lord loveth,
Who hears his voice betimes,
And whom that God instructeth.
Secluded from the world, from infancy,
With all the gifts of heaven graced,
The contagion of wickedness has not defaced
His spotless innocency.
All. Happy, O happy, is the infancy
The Lord doth teach and takes beneath his wing!
The Same Voice [*alone*]. Thus in a sheltered valley
A crystal stream beside,
There grows a tender lily,
Kind Nature's love and pride.
Secluded from the world from infancy,
With all the gifts of heaven graced,
The contagion of wickedness has not defaced
His spotless innocency.
All. O bless'd a thousand times the child
Whom the Lord makes obedient to his laws!
A Voice [*alone*]. O God! that virtue humble
Down perilous paths must stumble;
That he who seeks Thee, longing to preserve
His innocence of mind,
Such obstacles should find,
Pitfalls and perils that may make him swerve.
How manifold are Thy foes!
Where can Thy saints repose?

The wicked cover all the face of the earth.

 Another. Palace of David, and his city dear!

O famous mount where God so long has dwelt,

 Why hast thou felt

The wrath of heaven? Zion, what dost thou say

 When thou beholdst an impious foreigner

Seated upon thy true kings' throne today?

 All. Zion, dear Zion, what dost thou say,

When thou beholdst an impious foreigner

Seated upon thy true kings' throne today?

 The Same Voice [*continuing*]. Instead of beauteous

  songs, expressing

The holy joys of David, blessing

 His God, his father, and his Lord,

Dear Zion, thou beholdst men hymning

The impious stranger's god, blaspheming

 The holy name thy kings adored.

 A Voice [*alone*]. How long, O Lord, how long shall we

  behold

The wicked rise up against Thee?

For in Thy Temple, impiously bold,

 They dare to come before Thee,

 Treating as mad the people who adore Thee.

How long, O Lord, how long shall we behold

 The wicked rise up against Thee?

 Another. What is the use (they say)

Of your harsh virtue? And why should you shun

Countless sweet pleasures? Since your God has done

Nothing for you, 'tis foolish to obey.

 Another. Come, let us sing (they say)

And take the flowery way,

 From pleasure unto pleasure, as they fly;

 Mad is it on the future to rely,

 For the uncertain-numbered years slip by,

  Bringing their inevitable sorrow:

Then let us hasten while we may

To enjoy this life today:

  Who knows if we shall live tomorrow?

 All. They shall weep, O God, and they shall tremble,

Those wretches who will never once behold

Thy holy city's splendor long foretold.

It is for us to sing, here in Thy Temple,
  To whom Thou hast shown Thy everlasting light,
  To sing of all Thy gifts, and praise Thy might.
  A Voice [*alone*]. Of all these vain delights in which they
    swim
What will remain? The memory of a dream
  Whose fond deceit is known.
When they awake—awakening full of horror!—
  While the poor at Thy throne
Shall taste the ineffable sweetness of Thy peace,
They'll drink in the day of Thy wrath the cup of terror
Thou shalt present to all that guilty race.
  All. Awakening full of horror!
O dream that quickly fades!
O blind and dangerous error!

ACT THREE

Enter MATHAN *and* NABAL *to* CHORUS.

MATHAN. Go, children. One of you tell Josabeth
Mathan would speak with her, in secret, here.
  One of the Chorus. Mathan! O God of heaven, may'st
    thou confound him!
  Nabal.   What! fled without response?
  Mathan. Let us approach.

                        [*Exit* CHORUS.

Enter ZACHARIAH.   (III.2)

  Zachariah. Presumptuous man, where would you pass?
    Approach
No further. This is the sacred dwelling place
Of holy ministers. The laws forbid
Any profane to enter. Whom do you seek?
Upon this solemn day my father shuns
The criminal sight of curst idolaters;
And prostrate now before the Lord, my mother
Fears to be interrupted.
  Mathan.   We will wait.
Cease to perturb yourself, my son. I wish

To speak with your noble mother. I have come here
Bearing the Queen's command.   [*Exit* ZACHARIAH.

(III.3)

   Nabal.   Even their children
Display their haughty boldness. But tell me now:
What does the Queen desire on this occasion?
And whence has sprung confusion in her counsels?
Insulted by the insolent Joad today,
And in a nightmare threatened by a child,
She would have slaughtered Joad in her wrath,
And in this Temple set both Baal and you.
You told me of your joy, and I had hoped
To have my share of the spoils. What then has changed
Her wavering will?
   Mathan.   My friend, these last two days
I have not known her. She is now no more
That bold, clear-sighted Queen, uplifted high
Above her timid sex, who crushed her foes
At once and unawares, and knew the price
Of a lost instant. Now fear of vain remorse
Troubles that lofty soul. She hesitates;
She drifts, and (in a word) she is a woman.
With bitterness and rancor I had filled
Her heart, already struck by heaven's threats;
Entrusting her revenge to me, she bade me
Muster the guard. But whether that same child—
A luckless waif, they say—when brought before her,
Appeased the terror of her dream, or whether
She found some charm in him, I've seen her wrath
Turn hesitant; and she postpones revenge
Until tomorrow. All her plans, it seems,
Destroy each other. "I have made inquiries,"
I told her, "of this child. They have begun
To boast his ancestry. From time to time,
Joad displays him to the factious mob,
Almost as though he were a second Moses,
And with false oracles supports his claims."
The blood at these words mounted to her face,
And never did a happy lie produce
Such prompt effect. "Is it for me to languish

In this uncertainty?" she said at once.
"Away with this disquietude! Go now:
Pronounce this sentence unto Josabeth:
The fires are kindled, and the sword prepared.
Nought can prevent the ravage of their Temple
Unless I have that child as hostage."

    Nabal.   Well,
For a child they do not know, whom chance perhaps
Has flung into their arms, would they permit
Their Temple to be razed? . . .

    Mathan.   But Joad is
Proudest of mortals. Rather than deliver
Into my hands a child he has dedicated
Unto his God, you will see him undergo
The worst of deaths. Besides, it is apparent
They love this child; and if I've understood
The Queen's account, Joad knows something more
About the child's birth than he's yet revealed.
Whoever he is, he will be fatal to them—
That I can well foresee. They will deny him.
The rest is mine. And now I hope at last
That sword and fire will take away the sight
Of this obnoxious Temple.

    Nabal.   What can inspire
So strong a hatred in you? Does the zeal
Of Baal transport you? As for me, you know,
I am an Ishmaelite, and do not serve
Either Baal or the God of Israel.

    Mathan. Do you suppose, my friend, that with vain
      zeal
I let myself be blinded for an idol,
A fragile wooden idol which the worms
Upon his altar—in spite of all my care—
Consume each day? I was born a minister
Of the God they worship here, and I perhaps
Would serve Him still, could but the love of greatness,
The thirst for power, be accommodated
Within His narrow yoke. There is no need
For me to remind you of the famous quarrel
Between myself and Joad, when I strove
To supersede him—my intrigues, my struggles,

My tears, and my despair. Vanquished by him,
I entered then a new career: my soul
Attached itself entirely to the court,
Till, by degrees, I gained the ear of kings,
And soon became an oracle. I studied
Their hearts and flattered their caprice. For them
I sowed the precipice's edge with flowers;
Nothing, except their passions, was sacred to me:
I changed both weight and measure at their whim:
When Joad's harsh inflexibility
Wounded their proud and delicate ear, I charmed them
With my dexterity, veiling from their eyes
The dismal truth, depicting all their passions
In favorable colors, and, above all,
Prodigal with the blood of the poor. At last
To the new god the Queen had introduced
A temple was built by her. Jerusalem wept
To see herself profaned. The children of Levi
In consternation howled towards the heavens.
Myself alone, setting a good example
To the timid Jews, deserter from their Law,
Approved the enterprise—and thereby earned
The primacy of Baal. I became
Terrible to my rival: I too wore
The tiara on my brows, and went his equal.
Yet sometimes, I confess, in all my glory,
The memory of the God whom I have left
Importunes me with terror: this it is
Feeds and augments my fury. I shall be happy
If I achieve my vengeance on His Temple,
And thus convict His hate of impotence;
And amidst ruin, ravage, and the dead,
By deeds of horror lose all my remorse.
But here is Josabeth.

Enter JOSABETH.   (III.4)

Mathan.   Sent by the Queen,
To re-establish peace and banish hatred,
Princess, whom heaven has given a gentle spirit,
Marvel not if I address you now.

A rumor I myself believe is false
Supports the warning she received in dreams,
And it has turned on Joad (who's accused
Of dangerous plots) the current of her wrath.
I will not brag here of my services.
Joad, I know, has treated me unjustly,
But one should always render good for evil.
So charged with words of peace I come to you.
Live, solemnize your feasts without reproof.
She only asks a pledge of your obedience.
It is—although I've done my best to dissuade her—
That orphan child she saw here.

    Josabeth.   Eliacin?

    Mathan. I'm somewhat ashamed for her. Of an empty
        dream
She takes too much account, but nonetheless
You would declare yourselves her mortal foes
If in the hour this child is not delivered
Into my hands. The Queen, impatiently,
Awaits your answer.

    Josabeth.   And that then is the peace
Which you announce?

    Mathan.   How can you hesitate
To accept? And is the small compliance asked
Too much to pay?

    Josabeth.   I would have been surprised
If Mathan, putting off deception, could
Have overcome the injustice of his heart,
And if the inventor of so many evils
Could now at last come forward as the author
Of even the shadow of good.

    Mathan.   Of what do you complain?
Is someone coming in rage to tear your son
Out of your arms? What is this other child
Who seems so dear to you? This great attachment
Surprises me in turn. Is he a treasure
So precious and so rare? A liberator
That heaven prepares for you? Well, think of it.
Should you refuse, it would confirm for me
A rumor that begins to circulate.

Josabeth. What rumor?
    Mathan.   That this child is nobly born,
Destined for some great project by your husband.
    Josabeth. And by this rumor which must fan her fury
Mathan . . .
    Mathan.   Princess, it is for you to draw me
Out of my error. I know that Josabeth,
The implacable foe of falsehood, would resign
Even her life, if saving it would cost
One word against the truth. Have you no trace
Of this child's origin? Does a dark night
Conceal his race? And are you ignorant
Both of this parents and from whose hands Joad
Received him to his arms? Speak. I am listening
And apt to give you credence. To the God
You serve, Princess, give glory!
    Josabeth.   Wicked man,
'Tis fitting you should name in such a way
A God your mouth instructs men to blaspheme.
Is it possible His truth can be attested
By you who sit on the plague-ridden throne
Where falsehood reigns, disseminating poison;
You, villain, fed on perfidy and treason?

Enter JOAD.   (III.5)

    Joad. Where am I? See I not the priest of Baal?
Daughter of David, speak you to this traitor?
Allow him speak with you? Do you not fear
That from the abyss which opens at his feet
Flames will rush out to set you in a blaze?
Or that the walls, in falling, crush you too?
What does he want? How dares the foe of God
Come to infect the air we breathe?
    Mathan.   This rage
Is like you, Joad. Yet you ought to show
More prudence; and you should respect a queen,
And not insult the man she deigns to use
To bear her high commands.
    Joad.   What evil tidings
Come from her now? What terrible command
That such an envoy brings?

Mathan.   I have conveyed
To Josabeth Queen Athaliah's will.
　Joad. Go from my presence then, thou impious monster:
Heap up the measure of thy monstrous crimes.
Go, pile up all thy horrors. God prepares
To join thee with the perjured race—with Doeg,
Abiron, Dathan, and Achitophel.
The dogs to whom He handed Jezebel,
Awaiting but His rage to be unleashed,
Are at the door and howling for their prey.
　Mathan. Before nightfall . . . it will be seen which one
　　of us
Will . . . But let us go, Nabal.
　Nabal.   Where are you going?
What has bewildered and amazed your senses?
There lies your way.   [*Exeunt* NABAL *and* MATHAN.

(III.6)

　Josabeth.   The storm has broken.
Now Athaliah in her fury asks
For Eliacin. Already they have started
To pierce the mystery of his birth, my lord,
And of your plan—for Mathan nearly named
His father.
　Joad.   Who could have revealed his birth
To the perfidious Mathan? Could he guess
Too much from your confusion?
　Josabeth.   I did my best
To master it. But yet, my lord, believe me,
The danger presses. Let us keep the child
For a happier time: while the wicked confer,
Before he is surrounded and they seize him,
Let me hide him for a second time.
The gates, the roads, are open still. If he
Must be transported to most fearful deserts,
I am prepared. I know a secret path
By which with him unseeing and unseen
I'll cross the falls of Kedron; I will go
Into the desert where weeping once, and seeking
Safety in flight, as we do now, King David
Escaped pursuit by his rebellious son.

I shall, because of him, fear less the bears
And lions. But why refuse King Jehu's help?
I'll offer now some salutary advice:
Let Jehu now be the depositary
Of this our treasure. We could leave today.
The journey is but short. The heart of Jehu
Is neither savage nor inexorable
And he is well disposed to David's name.
Alas! is there a king so harsh and cruel—
Or one at least without a Jezebel
For mother—who'll not pity the misfortune
Of such a suppliant? Is not his cause
Common to every king?

Joad.   What timid counsels
Do you dare offer me? How could you hope
For Jehu's succor?

Josabeth.   Does the Lord forbid
All care and forethought? Does one not offend Him
By too much confidence? In His sacred plans
Employing human means, has He not armed
The hands of Jehu?

Joad.   Jehu, whom He chose
In His deep wisdom, Jehu, on whom I see
Your hope is founded, has repaid His blessings
With an ingrate forgetfulness. He leaves
Ahab's vile daughter in peace. He follows now
The ungodly example of the kings of Israel,
Preserves the temples of the god of Egypt;
And now at last in the high places dares
To offer an incense God cannot endure.
He has not served His cause, avenged His wrongs;
His heart's not upright, and his hands not pure.
No, no, in God alone must be our trust.
Let us show Eliacin openly—the royal
Circlet upon his head. I even wish
To advance the hour we had determined on,
Ere Mathan's plot is hatched.

           Enter AZARIAS, CHORUS, *and* LEVITES.   (III.7)

Joad.   Well, Azarias,
Is the Temple closed?

Azarias. Yes, all the doors are shut.

Joad. Only your sacred cohorts now remain?

Azarias. Twice have I gone through all the sacred courts.
All, all have fled, and they will not return—
A miserable troop dispersed with fear.
The holy tribe alone remain to serve
The Lord of Hosts. I think that since this people
Escaped from Pharaoh, they have not been struck
By such a terror.

Joad. A coward race indeed,
And born for slavery—brave against God alone.
Let us pursue our task. But who has kept
These children still among us?

A Girl. Could we, my lord,
Divide us from you? Are we strangers here
In the Temple of God? You have beside you now
Our fathers and our brothers.

Another. Alas, for us!
If to avenge the shame of Israel
Our hands cannot, as Jael's in former days,
Pierce through the impious head of God's own foes,
At least for Him we could give up our lives.
When you, with arms, fight for His threatened Temple,
We can at least invoke Him with our tears.

Joad. See what avengers arm them for Thy quarrel,
O everlasting Wisdom—priests and children!
But if Thou dost uphold them, who can shake them?
Thou canst, at pleasure, call us from the tomb;
Strike us, and heal; destroy and resurrect.
They do not trust now in their own deserts,
But in Thy name, invoked so many times.
And in Thine oaths, sworn to their holiest kings,
And in this Temple, Thy holy dwelling place,
Which shall endure as long as doth the sun.
Whence comes it that my heart with holy dread
Begins to tremble? Is it the Holy Spirit
Who takes possession of me? It is He.
He kindles me, and speaks. My eyes are opened,
And the dark centuries unroll before me.
You Levites, with the concord of your sounds,
Accompany the raptures He inspires.

Chorus. May the voice of the Lord be heard, His will
    revealed,
And as in springtime the sweet morning dew
    Refreshes the grass of the field,
May His oracle divine our hearts renew.
    Joad. O heavens, hear my voice; O earth, give ear!
O Jacob, say no more the Lord doth sleep.
Sinners, begone. The Lord awakens now!

                [*Music.* JOAD *soon continues.*

How is the pure gold turned to vilest lead?
Who is this High Priest slaughtered without pity
In the holy place? Weep, Jerusalem, weep!
Slayer of holy prophets, perfidious city!
Now God has turned away His love from thee:
Thy incense in His eyes is now polluted.
Where are these women and children led?
God has destroyed the queen of cities:
Her priests are captives, and her kings are fled.
Men come no more to her solemnities.
    The Temple overturns;
    The sacred cedar burns!
O Zion, that in vain my sorrow pities,
What hand has ravished all your loveliness?
My eyes have changed now into water-springs
    To weep for thy distress.
    Azarias. O holy Temple!
    Josabeth.   O David!
    Chorus.   O God of Zion,
Remember now Thy ancient promises.

        [*Music again; after a moment* JOAD *interrupts.*

    Joad. What new Jerusalem rises now
From out the desert shining bright,
Eternity upon her brow,
Triumphing over death and night?
Sing, peoples, Zion now is more
Lovely and glorious than before.

Whence come these children manifold
She did not carry at her breast?
Lift up thy head, O Zion, behold
These princes with thy fame possessed;

The earthly kings all prostrate bow
And kiss the dust before thee now.

Peoples to walk within thy light
Shall strive; and happy those who feel
Their souls for Zion burning bright
With fervent and with holy zeal;
Rain down, O heavens, thy sacred dew!
Earth, may a savior spring from you!

 Josabeth. How may this signal favor be vouchsafed
If David's line, from which this savior springs
Shall be . . .

 Joad.   Prepare the gorgeous diadem
Which David wore upon his sacred brow.
And you, to arm yourselves, now follow me
To the secret chambers, far from eyes profane,
Where a great store is hid of swords and spears,
Once steeped in Philistinian blood, and then
By conquering David, laden with years and fame,
All consecrate to God. Could we employ them
In a nobler cause? Come, I myself desire
To share them now amongst you.

      [*Exeunt* ALL, *except* SALOMITH *and* CHORUS.

            (III.8)

 Salomith. Sisters, how many fears and mortal troubles!
Are these the first fruits, O omnipotent God,
Perfumes and sacrifices which should be
Offered upon Thy altar?

 A Voice.   What a sight
For timorous eyes! For who would have believed
That we should ever see the murderous swords
And lances gleaming in the house of peace?

 Another. Why does Jerusalem, to God indifferent,
Now hold her peace while pressing danger threatens?
Whence comes it, sisters, that to protect us all
Even brave Abner does not break his silence?

 Salomith. But in a court where justice is unknown
And all the laws are force and violence,
Where honor's bought with base obedience,
Who will speak up for luckless innocence?

Another. In this peril and extreme confusion
For whom is the sacred diadem prepared?

Salomith. The Lord has deigned to speak unto His
prophet:
But who can understand what is revealed?
Are they arming now in our defense?
Or will they bring destruction on us all?

All. O promise! O menace! O dark mystery!
According to the prophecy,
How many ills and blessings will there be?
How may the future for us prove
So much of anger with so much of love?

First Voice. Zion will be no more—a cruel flame
Will leave of all her glory but a name.

Second Voice. Founded upon His everlasting word,
Zion will be protected by the Lord.

First Voice. My eyes behold her glory disappear.

Second Voice. I see her brightness spreading everywhere.

First Voice. Zion has fallen into the abyss.

Second Voice. Aspiring Zion and the heavens kiss.

First Voice. What sad abasement!

Second Voice.   What immortal glory!

First Voice. How many cries of sorrow!

Second Voice.   What songs of triumph!

Third Voice. Peace, sisters, trouble not yourselves:
Some day the mystery will be revealed.

All Three. Let us revere His wrath, hope in His love.

Fourth Voice. Who can disturb the peace,
Of a heart that loves Thee, Lord?
In Thy will is its peace,
Its trust is in Thy word.
Can there be happiness
In earth or heaven
Except the tranquil peace
That Thou hast given?

ACT FOUR

Joas, Josabeth, Zachariah, Salomith, *a* Levite,
and Chorus.

Salomith. Beside his mother with majestic pace
Young Eliacin advances with my brother.
What do they bear between them in those cloths?
What is that sword that's borne before them?
    Josabeth.   My son,
Upon that table reverently place
The dread book of our Law. Dear Eliacin,
Put the royal fillet near the holy book.
Levite, the sword of David must be placed
Beside his crown. So Joad has ordained.
    Joas. What is the meaning, Princess, of this sight?
Wherefore the sword, the crown, the holy book?
For since the Lord received me in His Temple,
I have not seen a ceremony like it.
    Josabeth. All your doubts, my son, will soon be cleared.
    Joas. You wish to try this crown upon my brows?
Princess, take care that you do not profane
Its glory and respect the memory
Of the King who wore it. I, a luckless child,
Abandoned to the bears . . .
    Josabeth.   Let be, my son.
I know what is ordained.
    Joas.   But yet I hear
A sob escape you. You are weeping, Princess.
What pity moves you? Must I, as Jepthah's daughter,
Be sacrificed to appease the wrath of God?
Alas! a son has nothing not his father's.
    Josabeth. Here comes the one who will expound heaven's
       will.
Fear nothing. Now let all the rest depart.

                       [*Exeunt* ALL, *except* JOAS.

            Enter JOAD.   (IV.2)

Joas. Father!

Joad.   My son?

Joas.   What means this preparation?

Joad. 'Tis right, my son, that I should tell you all;
You must be first to hear God's great designs
For you and for His chosen. Arm yourself
With courage and new faith. 'Tis time to show
The ardor and the zeal which in your heart
I have implanted, and to pay to God
That which you owe him. Do you feel, my son,
That generous desire?

Joas.   I am prepared,
If he should wish, to give my life to Him.

Joad. You've often heard the story of our kings.
Do you recall, my son, what narrow laws
A king who is worthy of the diadem
Should self-impose?

Joas.   God himself has pronounced
That a wise king does not rely on wealth.
He fears the Lord his God, and walks before Him,
Keeping His precepts, laws, and His strict judgments;
And with excessive burdens does not load
His brethren.

Joad.   But if you had to take as model
One of our kings, my son, which would you choose
To resemble?

Joas.   David, full of faithful love
Of the Lord, appears to me the perfect model
Of a great king.

Joad.   And so, in their excess,
You would not imitate the faithless Joram,
The impious Ahaziah?

Joas.   Oh, father!

Joad.   Go on:
How does it seem to you?

Joas.   May all like them
Perish as them! Why do you kneel before me?

Joad. I render you the reverence that I owe
Unto my king. Make yourself worthy, Joas,
Of David, your great ancestor.

Joas   Joas?
I?

Joad. You shall know now by what signal grace
God overthrew the murderous design
Of a mad mother. Her knife was in your breast
When, choosing you, God saved you from the slaughter.
You have not yet escaped from her fierce rage:
Just as in former days she wished to kill
In you the last of her son's children, now
Her cruelty is bent to make you perish,
Pursuing you still under the name which hides you.
But now beneath your standards I have mustered
A loyal people, ready to avenge you.
Enter, you noble chiefs of sacred tribes,
Who have the honor to perform in turn
The holy ministry.

Enter AZARIAS, ISMAEL, *and three* LEVITES. (IV.3)

Joad.   King, these are
Thy champions against thy enemies.
Priests, here is the King that I have promised.
    Azarias. What? Eliacin?
    Ismael.   This beloved child?
    Joad. Is of the kings of Judah the true heir,
Last born of the unhappy Ahaziah,
Named Joas, as you know. This tender flower,
Cut down so soon, all Judah mourned as you,
Believing that he shared his brothers' fate.
He was indeed struck with the treacherous knife,
But God preserved him from a fatal blow
And kept some warmth within his beating heart,
Let Josabeth deceive the vigilant eye
Of the assassins, bear him at her breast,
All bleeding, with myself the sole accomplice,
And in the Temple hide both child and nurse.
    Joas. Father, alas! How can I ever pay
So much of love and such great benefits?
    Joad. For other times reserve your thanks. Behold
Therefore, you ministers of God, your king,
Your cherished hope. For you I have preserved him,
Until this hour, and here begins your part.
As soon as the murderous daughter of Jezebel
Learns that our Joas sees the light of day,

She will return, to plunge him once again
Into the horror of the tomb. Already,
Before she knows him, she would murder him.
Now, holy priests, it is for you today
Her fury to forestall, and end at last
The shameful slavery of the Jews; avenge
Your murdered princes, raise again your Law,
And make the two tribes recognize their king.
The enterprise is great and perilous,
For I attack a proud queen on her throne.
Under her flag there is a numerous host
Of doughty foreigners and renegades:
But yet my strength is in the living God
Whose interest is my guide. Think, in this child
All Israel resides. The God of wrath
Already vexes her. Despite her spies,
Already I have gathered you together.
She thinks we have no arms, and no defense.
Let us crown Joas, and proclaim him King;
And then, intrepid warriors of your prince,
Let us invoke the arbiter of battles,
And, waking in our hearts our dormant faith,
Even in her palace let us seek our foe.
And then what hearts though sunk in cowardly slumber
On seeing us advance in this array
But will not haste to follow our example?
A king whom God has brought up in His Temple,
Aaron's successor followed by his priests,
Leading the sons of Levi to the combat,
And in these same hands, reverenced by the people,
The arms of the Lord by David consecrated!
God will spread terror in his enemies.
Now without horror in the infidel blood
Imbrue yourselves. Strike down the Tyrians,
And even Israelites: for are you not
Descended from those Levites, famed in story,
Who when the fickle Israelites in the desert
To the god of the Nile gave unlawful worship,
Their hands they sanctified in traitors' blood—
Holy murderers of their dearest kin—
And by this noble deed acquired for you

The signal honor to be alone employed
At the Lord's altars? But I see that you
Already burn to follow me. Swear then, first,
Upon this solemn book, to live, to fight,
And perish for this king whom heaven today
Has given back to you.

    Azarias.   Yes, here we swear
For us and for our brethren to restore
King Joas to his fathers' throne. We swear
Never to sheathe the sword till we've avenged him
On all his enemies. If one of us
Should break this vow, let him, great God, be struck
With Thy avenging wrath, that he and his children,
Excluded from Thy heritage, may be
Among the dead Thou dost not know!

    Joad.   O King!
Wilt thou not swear to be forever faithful
Unto this Law, thy everlasting rule?

    Joas. Why should I not conform me to this Law?

    Joad. My son—I still dare call you by that name—
Suffer this tenderness; forgive the tears
That flow from me in thinking of your peril.
Nurtured far from the throne, you do not know
The poisonous enchantment of that honor.
You do not know yet the intoxication
Of absolute power, the bewitching voice
Of vilest flattery. Too soon they'll tell you
That sacred laws, though rulers of the rabble,
Must bow to kings; that a king's only bridle
Is his own will; that he should sacrifice
All to his greatness; that to tears and toil
The people are condemned, and must be ruled
With an iron scepter; that if they're not oppressed,
Sooner or later they oppress—and thus,
From snare to snare and from abyss to abyss,
Soiling the lovely purity of your heart,
They'll make you hate the truth, paint virtue for you
Under a hideous image. Alas! the wisest
Of all our kings was led astray by them.
Swear then upon this book, and before these
As witnesses, that God will always be

Your first of cares; that stern towards the wicked,
The refuge of the good, you'll always take
Between you and the poor the Lord for judge,
Remembering, my son, that in these garments
You once were poor and orphaned, even as they.

Joas. I swear to keep that which the Law ordains.
Punish me, Lord, if I depart from You.

Joad. Come:
We must anoint you with the holy oil.
Here, Josabeth: you now can show yourself. . . .

Enter JOSABETH, ZACHARIAH, *and* CHORUS. (IV.4)

Josabeth. O King! O son of David!
   Joas.   My only mother!
Dear Zachariah, kiss your brother, come.
   Josabeth. Kneel down, my son, before your king.

                       [ZACHARIAH *kneels.*
   Joad.   My children,
May you be always thus united.
   Josabeth.   You know
What blood has given you life?
   Joas.   I know as well
What hand, except for you, had snatched it from me.
   Josabeth. I now can call you by your name—Joas.
   Joas. Joas will never cease to love you.
   Chorus.   What!
Is he . . . ?
   Josabeth. 'Tis Joas.
   Joad.   Let us hear this Levite.

Enter LEVITE.   (IV.5)

Levite. I do not know what project against God
Is meditated; but the warning bronze
Clangs everywhere; among the standards now
They kindle fires; and doubtless Athaliah
Musters her army. We are even now
Cut off from succor; and the sacred mount
On which the Temple stands is everywhere
Hemmed in by insolent Tyrians. One of them,
Blaspheming, has informed us even now
That Abner is in irons and cannot shield us.

Josabeth. Dear child, whom heaven in vain has given me,
Alas! to save you I have done my best.
God has forgotten now your father, David.

Joad. Do you not fear to draw His wrath upon you
And on the King you love? And should God tear him
Forever from your arms, and seem to will
That David's house should be extinguished quite,
Are we not here upon the holy mount
Where Abraham above his innocent son
Lifted obedient arm without complaint,
And placed upon a pyre the precious fruit
Of his old age, leaving to God the task
Of carrying out his promise, sacrificing
All hope of issue with this son and heir
In whom it was bound up? Friends, let us share
The various posts between us. Let Ismael
Guard all the side that faces east. And you,
Take the north side; you the west; and you
The south. Let no one, whether priest or Levite,
Through hasty zeal discover my designs
Or leave before 'tis time. Let each one then,
Urged by a common ardor, guard the post
Where I have placed him, even to the death.
The foe in his blind rage regards us all
As flocks reserved for slaughter; and believes
He will meet nought but chaos and dismay.
Let Azarias accompany the King.
Come now, dear scion of a valiant race,
And fill your warriors with new bravery.
Put on the diadem before their eyes,
And die, if die you must, at least as King.
Follow him, Josabeth. Give me those arms.
Children, now offer God your innocent tears.

                [*Exeunt* ALL, *except* SALOMITH *and* CHORUS.

                                  (IV.6)

Chorus. Children of Aaron, go!
Never did nobler cause
Your fathers' zeal incite.
Children of Aaron, go!

'Tis for your rightful king
And for your God you fight.

   A Voice. Where are the darts you throw,
Great God, in Thy righteous anger?
Wilt Thou not take vengeance on Thy foe?
Art Thou a jealous God no longer?

   Another. Where, God of Jacob, are Thy ancient bless-
      ings?
In the horror which surrounds our lives
Hear'st Thou but the voice of our transgressions?
Art Thou no more the Lord God who forgives?

   All. Where, God of Jacob, are Thy ancient blessings?

   A Voice. Against Thee, Lord, O even against Thee
     The wicked bends his bow.
The feasts of God (they say) shall cease to be
Upon the earth; men from His yoke we'll free;
     His altars overthrow;
His saints we'll slay; so that there will remain
     Of His name and of His glory
     Only a fading story,
And neither God nor His Anointed reign.

   All. Where are the darts You throw,
Great God, in Thy righteous anger?
Wilt Thou not take vengeance on Thy foe?
Art Thou a jealous God no longer?

   A Voice. Sad remnant of our kings, the dear last bloom
Of a lovely stem, shall we behold you fall
Once more beneath a cruel mother's knife?
Did some bright angel then avert thy doom,
Or did the voice of the living God recall,
From the night of the tomb thy spirit back to life?

   Another. O God, dost Thou impute to him the sins
Of father and of grandfather? Has Thy pity
Abandoned him, and will it not return?

   All. Where, God of Jacob, are Thy ancient blessings?
Art Thou no more the Lord God who forgives?

   Voice. Dear sisters, hear you not the trumpet sound
Of the cruel Tyrians?

   Salomith.   Yes, I also hear
The shouts of barbarous soldiers, and I shudder.

Quick, let us flee to the protecting shade
Of the strong sanctuary.

ACT FIVE

ZACHARIAH, SALOMITH, *and* CHORUS.

SALOMITH. Dear Zachariah, what can you tell us now?
  Zachariah. Redouble your ardent prayers to the Lord.
Perhaps our last hour's come. The order's given
For the dreadful battle.
  Salomith.   What is Joas doing?
  Zachariah. Joas has just been crowned, and the High
    Priest
Has poured the consecrated oil upon him.
O heavens! What joy in every eye was painted
To see this king who from the tomb was snatched.
Sister, the scar from the knife can still be seen.
The faithful nurse is there, who had been hidden
In this vast edifice, and kept her charge,
And had no other witness of her cares
Than Mother and our God. Our Levites wept
With joy and tenderness, and mingled sobs
With cries of joyfulness. Among it all,
Friendly and without pride, he stretched a hand
To one, and blessed another with his glance;
He swore he would be ruled by their advice,
And called them all his fathers and his brethen.
  Salomith. But has the secret yet been spread abroad?
  Zachariah. No, it is kept within the Temple still.
The Levites in deep silence guard the doors,
Waiting to act together, and cry as signal
"Long live King Joas." Our father forbids
The King to risk his life, makes Azarias
Remain with him as guard. Yet Athaliah,
A dagger in her hand, now laughs to scorn
The feeble ramparts of our brazen doors;
To break them she awaits the fatal engines,
And breathes forth blood and ruin. Some of the priests

At first proposed that in a secret place,
A subterranean cell our fathers hollowed,
We should at least conceal our precious Ark.
"O fear," my father cried, "unworthy of you,
Insulting to our cause. The Ark which made
So many lofty towers to fall, and forced
Jordan to stay her course, so many times
Triumphant over alien gods, to flee
The aspect of an insolent woman!" Mother,
Beside the King in terrible distress,
Sometimes on him and sometimes on the altar
Fastened her eyes, sinking beneath the weight
Of her dumb fears. She would have made the eyes
Of even the cruelest to weep. The King at whiles
Embraced her, soothed her. Follow me, dear sisters,
And if today the King must perish, come,
Let us share his fate.

    Salomith.   What insolent hand is this
Redoubling knocks, which makes these Levites run
In apprehension? What precaution makes them
To hide their arms? O is the Temple forced?

    Zachariah. Banish your needless fears. God sends us
    Abner.

Enter ABNER, JOAD, JOSABETH, ISMAEL,
and LEVITES.   (V.2)

    Joad. Can I believe my eyes, dear Abner? By what path
Have you, despite the host that hems us in,
Gained access to this place? For it was said
That Ahab's sacrilegious daughter had,
To make assurance of her cruel purpose,
Laden with shameful irons your generous hands.

    Abner. Yes, my lord. She feared my zeal and courage;
This was the least reward she kept for me;
Shut in a horrid dungeon by her order,
I waited—when the Temple had been burnt
And streams of blood poured forth—for her to come
And free me from a weary life, to cut short
My days, and thus to end the pain I suffered,
That I'd outlived my kings.

Joad.   What miracle
Obtained for you your pardon?
Abner.   God only knows
What passes in that heart. She sent for me
And said distractedly: "You see this Temple
Encompassed by my host; the avenging sword
Stands poised above it, and your God's unable
Against me to defend it. But His priests
Can still—but time is short—redeem themselves.
On two conditions: that with Eliacin
Is put into my power the royal treasure—
I'm sure they know its hiding place—that treasure
Which David heaped together, and under pledge
Of secrecy, bequeathed to the High Priest:
Tell them that for this price I'll spare their lives.
   Joad. What counsel, Abner, should we follow now?
   Abner. If it is true you guard some secret hoard
Of David, give her all this gold, and all
You have been able from her greedy hands
To save of rich and rare, give it her now.
Would you that unclean murderers should break
The altar, burn the Cherubim, lay their hands
Upon the Ark, and with our proper blood
Pollute the sanctuary?
   Joad.   But does it suit
Abner, with generous hearts, thus to deliver
A luckless child to death, a child which God
Confided to my care, redeem our lives
At the expense of his?
   Abner.   God sees my heart:
And would that Athaliah, by His power,
Forgot this child, and that her cruelty,
Contented with my blood, thought thus to appease
Heaven which torments her. But what avails
Your useless care for him? When all will perish,
Will this boy perish less? Does God ordain
You should attempt the impossible? You know
That Moses, to obey a tyrant's law,
Was by his mother left beside the Nile,
Seeing himself from birth condemned to peril;
But God preserving him against all hope

Brought it to pass that he from infancy
Was nurtured by the tyrant. And who knows
What life he has reserved for Eliacin?
And if preparing for him a like fate,
He has made the implacable murderess of our kings
Already capable of pity? At least—
And Josabeth, perhaps, beheld it too—
I saw her so much moved at sight of him,
Her anger's violence declined. Princess,
You're silent in this peril. What! for a child
Who is a stranger to you, would you suffer
That Joad should allow you to be slain,
You, and your son, and all this people too,
And that the one place on the earth where God
Desires to be adored should be consumed
With fire? Were this young child a precious relic
Of the kings, your fathers, what would you do more?

    Josabeth [*aside*]. For his king's blood you see his tenderness.

Why don't you speak to him?

    Joad.   'Tis not yet time,
Princess.

    Abner.   Time is more precious than you think,
My lord. While you debate what to reply,
Mathan, near Athaliah, with flashing rage
Demands the signal, urges on the slaughter.
O must I kneel now at your sacred knees?
In the name of the holy place which you alone
May enter, where God's majesty resides,
However hard the law imposed on you
Let us consider how we may ward off
This unexpected blow. O give me but
The time to breathe! Tomorrow, even tonight,
I will take measures to assure the Temple
And to avenge its injuries. But I see
My tears and my vain words are means too weak
Your virtue to persuade. Well, find me then
Some sword, some weapon; at the Temple gates
Where the foe waits me, Abner can at least
Die fighting.

    Joad.   I surrender. You have given

Advice that I embrace. Let us avert
The threat of all these ills. 'Tis true indeed
That there remains a treasure of King David
Committed to my trust—the final hope
Of the sad Jews, and I with vigilant care
Concealed it from the light. But since it must
To your queen be disclosed, I will content her.
Our doors will open to admit the Queen,
Her bravest captains too; but let her keep
Our holy altars from the open fury
Of a gang of foreigners. Spare me the horror
Of the pillage of the Temple. Would they fear
Children and priests? Let her arrange with you
The number of her suite. As for this child,
So feared, so dreadful, Abner, I know well
The justice of your heart; I will explain
About his birth before her, and to you.
You will see if we must put him in her power,
And you shall judge between the Queen and him.

    Abner. My lord, I take him under my protection.
Fear nothing. I return to her who sent me.   [*Exit* ABNER.

                                               (V.3)

    Joad. O God! This is Thy hour. They bring to Thee
Thy prey. Listen Ismael.
    Josabeth.   Blindfold her eyes
Once more, O master of the heavens, as when
Thou rob'st her of the profit of her crime
And hid that tender victim in my breast.

    Joad. Go, Ismael, lose no time, and carry out
These orders to the letter; above all
At her entry, and when she passes through,
Show her the image of an absolute calm.
You, children, make you ready now a throne
For Joas. Accompanied by our sacred soldiers,
Let him come forth. And tell his faithful nurse
To come here also. Princess, may the source
Of these your tears, dry up. [*To a* LEVITE.] You, when
    the Queen,
Drunk with mad pride, has crossed the Temple threshold,
That she may not retreat the way she came

See that the warlike trumpet at that instant
Startles the hostile camp with sudden fear.
Call everyone to aid their king; and make
Even to his ear the miracle resound,
That Joas is preserved. Behold he comes.

Enter JOAS. (V.4)

Joad. Ye holy Levites, priests of the living God,
Surround this place on every side. Keep hidden;
And leaving me to regulate your zeal,
Show not yourselves until you hear my voice.
King, I believe this hope may be allowed
In answer to your vows: that at your feet
Your enemies will fall. She who pursued
Your infancy with fury to this place
Now strives to kill you. But be not afraid:
Think that around you, and on our side, stands
The Angel of Death. Ascend your throne and wait. . . .
The door is opening. Allow this veil
To cover you a moment. You change color,
Princess.
    Josabeth. How can I see the Temple filled
With murderers, and not turn pale. Look now,
Do you not see with what a numerous escort . . . ?
    Joad. I see the Temple doors are closed again,
All is well.

Enter ATHALIAH *and* SOLDIERS. (V.5)

    Athaliah. There thou art, seducer,
Vile author of conspiracies and plots,
Who only in sedition set'st thy hopes,
Eternal enemy of absolute power;
Thou hast reposed upon thy God's support;
Art thou yet disabused of that vain hope?
He has put thy Temple and thy life itself
Into my power. On the altar where thy hand
Is wont to sacrifice, I should . . . But I must be
Contented with the price that's offered me.
What you have promised, see you execute.
This child, this treasure, you must now deliver
Into my hands—where are they?

Joad.   Immediately
Thou shalt be satisfied. I am going to show them
Both at one time.

[*The curtain is drawn.* JOAS *is seen on his throne. His
nurse on her knees,* R. AZARIAS, *sword in hand, stands* L.
Near him, ZACHARIAH *and* SALOMITH *are kneeling on the
steps of the throne. Several* LEVITES, *sword in hand, are
ranged on both sides.*

Joad.   Appear, dear child,
Blood royal of our kings. Dost know, O Queen,
Our holiest monarch's heir? Dost know at least
These marks thy dagger made? There is thy king,
Thy grandson and the son of Ahaziah.
All people, and thou, Abner, recognize
King Joas!

    Abner. Heavens!
    Athaliah.   Traitor!
    Joad.   Dost thou see
This faithful Jewess, at whose breast he fed,
As well thou knowest. He was by Josabeth
Delivered from thy rage; and in this Temple
God has preserved him. This is what remains
To me of David's treasure.
    Athaliah.   Thy knavery,
Thou traitor, will be fatal to the child.
Deliver me, soldiers, from an odious phantom!

    Joad. Soldiers of the living God, defend your king.
[*The back of the stage opens. The inside of the Temple
is seen; and the armed* LEVITES *enter from all sides.*
    Athaliah. Where am I? Treason! O unlucky Queen!
With arms and enemies I am beset.

    Joad. Thine eyes will seek in vain. There's no escape,
And God has hemmed thee in on every side.
That God thou bravedst has now delivered thee
Into our hands. Now render an account
To Him of the blood with which thou has been drunk.

    Athaliah. What! fear has frozen my unworthy soldiers!
Into what snare, base Abner, hast thou led me?
    Abner. God is my witness, Queen . . .
    Athaliah.   Swear not by thy God,
Traitor! Avenge me.

Abner.   On whom? On Joas?
On my master?
   Athaliah.   He, Joas? He, thy king?
Know, wicked men, my arms besiege you still,
And all my camp is shouting for me now.
They are coming to my rescue. Tremble now,
You troop of rebels.

Enter ISMAEL.   (V.6)

   Ismael.   My lord, the Temple's freed
Of all its enemies. The stranger's fled;
The Jew submits. And even as the wind
Scatters the smoke, the voice of the Almighty
That army has dispersed. From the Temple gates
Our Levites have proclaimed the rightful King,
Have told how he was snatched in infancy
From the fatal sword, and how the daughter of Ahab
Is fallen in the snare. On every side
The trumpet sounded; mingled with its noise
The cries of the astounded host have spread
The sudden terror with which Gideon struck
The haughty Midian. The Tyrians,
Throwing away their swords and bucklers, fled
By diverse routes. They disappeared the first.
Some Jews, dumbfounded, also took to flight.
Wondering at God's mercy showered on Joas,
The rest, with acclamation, hailed him King.
Till all the people with the selfsame spirit
Inspired, women, old men, and children,
Embraced with joy, and blessed the Lord their God
For what He gave. All sing of David's son
Brought back to life; while in the holy city
Baal is struck with horror; and the doors
Of his sacrilegious temple are broke in.
Mathan is slain.
   Athaliah.   Thou hast conquered, O God of the Jews!
Yes, it is Joas, and I seek in vain
To deceive myself. I recognize the place
Where he was pierced. I see the mien and gesture
Of Ahaziah. Everything recalls
The blood which I detest. David has triumphed,

Ahab's alone destroyed. Remorseless God,
Thou hast brought everything to pass. 'Tis Thou,
Who flattering me with easy vengeance, made me
A score of times in a day oppose myself,
Sometimes arousing pity for a child,
And sometimes dazzling me with Thy rich treasures,
So that I've feared to give to flame and pillage
This Temple; so that this son reigns, Thy care
And the work of Thy hands; so that to signalize
His new gained empire, he will now be made
To plunge the dagger in my breast. This is
My dying wish for him. What said I? Wish?
Nay, I am confident that he will be
Repugnant to Thy yoke, tired with Thy Law,
Faithful to Ahab's blood he took from me;
That he will do what his grandfather did,
Be like his father. It shall come to pass
That this hated heir of David will abolish
Thy honors and profane Thy altar—to avenge
Ahab and Jezebel and Athaliah. [*Exit* ATHALIAH, *guarded.*

(V.7)

    Joad. Let her at once be taken from the Temple,
So that its sanctity is not profaned.
Go, you avengers of your murdered princes,
And stop their blood's cries even with her death.
If any rash men should embrace her quarrel,
Deliver him, too, to the fury of the sword.
    Joas [*descending*]. O God, who seest my trouble and
        affliction,
Turn far from me her curse. Suffer it not
To be accomplished, and let Joas die
Ere he forget You.
    Joad.   Assemble all the people;
Show them their king, who comes to renew his oath.
King, priests, and people, filled with thankfulness,
Let us confirm the covenant of Jacob
With God, and penitent for our misdeeds,
Let us now re-engage ourselves to Him
With a new oath. Abner, beside the King
Take up your place again.

Enter a LEVITE.   (V.8)

Joad.   Well? Have they punished
This rash and impious woman?
    Levite.   The sword has expiated
The horrors of her life. Jerusalem,
For long a prey to her unbridled rage,
Freed from her odious yoke at last with joy
Beheld her weltering in her blood.
    Joad.   Her end
Was terrible, but well deserved. Learn from it,
King of the Jews, and ne'er forget that kings
Have a stern judge in heaven, that innocence
Has an avenger, the fatherless a father.